Do Penance or Perish

Frontispiece:
Early nineteenth-century copy of Antonio Canova's
Penitent Magdalen (1796).
Sold at the auction of the contents of Limerick's Good
Shepherd Convent in September 1994, when it was
described in the catalogue as a "figure of a kneeling lady",
the statue is now in the possession of the author.
According to Susan Haskins, "this pervasive image of
Mary Magdalen was copied throughout the [19th] century
by artists and sculptors to whom its neo-Classical form
and combination of penitence and eroticism appealed."

Do Penance or Perish

Magdalen Asylums in Ireland

FRANCES FINNEGAN

OXFORD
UNIVERSITY PRESS

2004

Firm   Oxf   9/09   28.99

OXFORD
UNIVERSITY PRESS

Oxford   New York
Auckland   Bangkok   Buenos Aires   Cape Town   Chennai
Dar es Salaam   Delhi   Hong Kong   Istanbul   Karachi   Kolkata
Kuala Lumpur   Madrid   Melbourne   Mexico City   Mumbai   Nairobi
São Paulo   Shanghai   Taipei   Tokyo   Toronto

Copyright © 2001 by Frances Finnegan

First published by Congrave Press, 2001

First Oxford University Press edition, 2004

Published by Oxford University Press, Inc.
198 Madison Avenue, New York, New York 10016

www.oup.com

Oxford is a registered trademark of Oxford University Press

Library of Congress Cataloging-in-Publication Data
Finnegan, Frances.
Do penance or perish : Magdalen asylums in Ireland / Frances Finnegan —
1st Oxford University Press ed.
   p. cm.
Originally published: Piltown, Co. Kilkenny : Congrave Press, 2001.
Includes bibliographical references and index.
ISBN 978-0-19-517460-1
1. Women—Institutional care—Ireland—History. 2. Prostitutes—Rehabilitation—
Ireland—History. 3. Church work with prostitutes—Ireland—History. 4. Church
work with prostitutes—Catholic Church. 5. Unmarried mothers—Institutional
care—Ireland—History. 6. Reformatories for women—Ireland—History. I. Title.
HV1448.G721734 2004
365'.43'0941509034-dc22   2004044848

9 8 7 6 5

Printed in the United States of America
on acid-free paper

Contents

Illustrations

Preface

I began the research for this book twenty-three years ago, when very little was known or had been written on the subject of Magdalen Asylums. I had just completed a book on Victorian prostitution for Cambridge University Press, the final chapter of which, "Rescue and Reform", was based on the recently discovered records of the York Female Penitentiary. I was fortunate in being the first historian to have access to this archive; and realised at once the potential of the subject for a larger work.

A detailed survey of the Reformatory and Refuge Union records (housed in the Library of Barnardo's Head Office in Barkingside) revealed the scale of the Penitentiary Movement, and the vast amount of surviving contemporary material. It became clear that a general history of the topic (my original intention) would be impractical, and I decided instead, to outline the development of the system, and investigate a few selected Homes.

A temporary move to Ireland resulted in permanent residence, and in 1980 I was generously given access to the records of the Good Shepherd Magdalen Asylum in Waterford, and later to those of the Order's Houses in Limerick, New Ross and Cork. Until then I was under the mistaken impression that the Magdalen Movement – a product of the nineteenth century – had long since disappeared. I had no idea that former penitents were still housed in Refuges built for their detention and reform.

The realisation that women had been admitted to these institutions well into the nineteen seventies and that many survivors of the process were still alive, was disturbing. It became more so as, over the course of my research, the real nature of the system emerged. Equally disconcerting was what appeared to be a general indifference to the experience of these women, and to the injustice done.

As an English historian working on what soon became a controversial topic – exposing as it did, a discreditable episode in recent Irish history - I encountered various difficulties. Criticism of the system was resented as misplaced or exaggerated; and it became evident that a treatment of the subject was acceptable, only if confined to the Victorian period, to which the notion of "different standards" could be conveniently applied. None the less, I continued with the work over the next decade, lecturing on the topic and heartened by the emergence of a largely autobiographical body of literature on the related subject of Irish Industrial Schools. These personal accounts, so courageously at odds with the accepted view of Ireland's recent past, were inspiring. Rarely have the "voiceless" spoken to such effect.

Disturbed though I was by the findings of my own research - as well as by discussions with survivors of the system - I was hardly prepared for the appalling revelations that were soon to rock Irish society. Regrettably, it is significant that the most telling treatments of the closely-linked Industrial Schools and Magdalen Asylums have, to date, been those undertaken by non-historians. The courageous television documentaries, "Dear Daughter", "Sex in a Cold Climate", and "States of Fear", jolted Irish society, as did the powerful book *Suffer the Little Children*. Historians have shown themselves reluctant to be involved in such controversial matters. It is thanks to the work of others that these unsavoury aspects of the past are at last receiving the sympathetic attention they deserve.

Do Penance or Perish, though focussing largely on the Irish Magdalen system in the second half of the nineteenth century, is not confined to the Victorian period nor is it limited to Ireland. In Chapter 1, for example, I outline the history of the Female Penitentiary Movement (particularly in England) from its beginnings in the 1750s; and throughout the book, the repercussions of the system into the twentieth century are discussed. Chapter 2 examines the origins and motivations of the French Good Shepherd Sisters, whose Order dominated the Magdalen system in Ireland for well over a century; and the following chapters deal with individual Irish Homes. Other related subjects are considered in the book, particularly the Contagious

Diseases legislation and prostitution in Cork, both of which are discussed in Chapter 6. Whenever possible, comparisons are made between the short-term Protestant Homes in England and the long-term Catholic Institutions in Ireland.

By incorporating some of the literature of Rescue Work (most of which has not, until now, been examined, or even regarded as a genre) I have tried to invoke something of the passion with which that vast band of Missionaries was inspired. Conversely, by including case histories of individual penitents, I have exposed the darker side of the Penitentiary Movement.

With this book I have attempted a return to narrative history in the hope of bringing individuals and their experience to life. I have avoided intimidating theories and jargon; and statistics - though included - have been relegated to the ends of chapters.

Finally, I do not choose to be "objective" about the subject of this study, nor do I think it a necessity, or a virtue, for historians to suspend their moral judgement.

I would like to thank the following individuals and organisations for allowing me to consult their records, for assisting me in my research, and for helping to bring this book – which was completed three years ago - to publication.

E. Peter Hennock, Emeritus Professor of History, University of Liverpool, who in 1978 encouraged me to begin this work; the Staff of the Library, Barnardo's Head Office, Barkingside; the Sisters of the Good Shepherd Convents in Waterford, Limerick and Cork; and the Royal Irish Academy and Twenty-Seven Foundation, University of London, for grants in aid of the research.

Patricia McCarthy, Archivist with the Cork City Archives and Richard Fennessy, Librarian of the Waterford City Library, were particularly helpful - as were Dermot Power, Waterford local historian; and Jarlath Glynn, Local Studies Librarian, Wexford County Library. I am indebted, too, to the Staffs of the following Libraries: The National Library of Ireland, Dublin, The Public Record Office, Dublin, The Military Archives, Cathal Brugha Barracks, Dublin; The Cork County Library; The British Library; The Fawcett Library, London; The Stoke Newington Library, London; The York City Archives and the Lincolnshire County Council Archives. The two Strasbourg Good Shepherd photographs are reproduced courtesy of Roger-Viollet, Paris; and that of the Corpus Christi Procession, courtesy of Terry Fagan,

Dublin. Paddy Dwan photographed paintings and statues in my possession.

It is ironic that as a Lecturer in the Waterford Institute of Technology's School of Humanities, I now work in what was formerly a Magdalen Asylum. Dr. John P. Ennis has been a most accommodating Head of School: and I am grateful to Milo O'Raithaille for his patient work with the statistics; to Geraldine Peters, for being a computer guardian angel; to David Smyth, M.R.I.A.I., for his fine drawing of the Kildare Contagious Diseases Hospital; to Nicola Troy for her design of the dust-jacket and her valued friendship, and to Librarian Ted Lynch, for his assistance and humour. I would particularly like to thank my colleague Cyril Cawley, for his long friendship, valuable advice and for reading the final manuscript.

I am indebted to Fr. Mark Tierney, OSB, for his courage, hospitality and help with this project over many years; to Senator Michael D. Higgins for his encouragement; and to Dr. Steve Humphries, Testimony Films, for his faith in my book, and his compassionate documentary which was such an inspiration. Professor George L. Huxley, M.R.I.A., has been a valued friend and advisor; and I owe a special debt of gratitude to Dr. Peter Laslett, Trinity College, Cambridge, for his wisdom, hospitality and enthusiasm, both at the beginning and very end of this project.

Two special friends, Helen De Wynter and Geoffrey Power, have for many years been unfailing in their encouragement and kindness. I am deeply grateful to them, and to my daughter Sarah, whose wisdom and concern have helped me through difficult patches. I would also like to thank John McSweeney, for his patience and for reading aloud to me this book.

My greatest debt is to my daughter Dr. Rachel Finnegan, who has helped me in so many stages of this work.

Finally, to John O'Grady, his sister, and the many others who suffered in Irish Magdalen and Industrial Institutions, this book is dedicated.

Frances Finnegan
Piltown, Co. Kilkenny
May 2001

Introduction

The two major responses to prostitution in nineteenth-century Britain were the so called Rescue or Penitentiary Movement, which involved the detention and rehabilitation of all classes of "fallen" women; and the Contagious Diseases legislation - a series of Acts introduced in the 1860s in an attempt to reduce, through the cleansing of prostitutes, the armed forces' vulnerability to venereal disease.

The Female Penitentiary Movement - based on morbid fears of women's sexuality, and fed, approved of, and financially supported by the society from which it emerged - has been ranked, along with the Contagious Diseases Acts, as the most blatant form of class and sexual discrimination of that most hypocritical of eras - the Victorian Age. Yet the Contagious Diseases Acts survived only for two decades. They were limited in their extent to just seventeen selected districts in Britain, and in their scope only to registered prostitutes living in brothels or walking the streets. They provoked outraged popular opposition; and in response to agitation organised on an unprecedented scale, were repealed in 1886.

The Female Penitentiary System on the other hand (by no means limited to the Victorian Age) was widespread throughout Britain. It was not confined to prostitutes, and in detaining any woman against her will, the system was acting contrary to the law. In the case of Catholic Institutions it continued for a century and a half, to the 1970s at least, and in a largely irreligious climate, existed in religion's name. Blatantly anti-female, it was carried out by women - who revelled in their task. And though claiming more victims than the Contagious Diseases Acts had ever done,

1

instead of encountering opposition it enjoyed society's approval and support. Without this, it could not have endured as it did in Ireland (and to a lesser extent in Britain) until cheap washing machines destroyed its financial basis, and dwindling vocations its power to control.

Neglected for decades and little known even today, the Contagious Diseases Acts have recently received widespread attention, being loudly deplored by historians and feminists alike.[1] In contrast, the Female Penitentiary System, outliving the moral climate from which it emerged, yet overlapping with the Women's Movement itself, has been largely ignored.[2] Campaigners for women's rights were apparently unmoved, both by the history of the subject and by the fact that as late as the nineteen-seventies women and girls were still being consigned (in most cases illegally) to "Magdalen" Homes. This curious indifference to a Movement so oppressive, so outdated and so blatantly at odds with the notions of sexual equality and personal liberty, requires some explanation before the topic itself is explored.

The Contagious Diseases controversy, unlike the Female Penitentiary System, was an episode in which women performed an active and honourable role. Their moral courage and sense of outrage are irresistible, particularly since theirs was a crusade which was justified and won. The notorious legislation, devised, sanctioned and implemented by men for the protection of their own sex, left women relatively blameless. Few females were engaged in carrying out the regulations, with even "visiting" in the new Government Hospitals being confined to male Chaplains, appointed by the State. At the same time many women passionately opposed the Acts. Though initially involving only the well-educated and middle classes, the Ladies' National

---

1   Important early studies of the C.D. legislation and its effects are Judith R. Walkowitz, *Prostitution and Victorian Society* and Paul McHugh, *Prostitution and Victorian Social Reform* - both published in 1980.

2   There are a few exceptions, for example, Linda Mahood, *The Magdalenes, Prostitution in the Nineteenth Century* (1990) and Maria Luddy, "Prostitution and Rescue Work" in *Women and Philanthropy in Nineteenth-Century Ireland* (1995). Most notable, however, is the 1998 Channel Four television production *Sex in a Cold Climate*, produced by Steve Humphries, Testimony Films. This documentary, a damning indictment of the system, contains evidence from 4 former inmates of Irish Magdalen Asylums and Industrial Schools. Interviewed in 1997, their harrowing recollections are of the 1940s, 50s and 60s.

Unfortunately, I was not aware of Peter E. Hughes' unpublished doctoral thesis "Cleanliness and Godliness" (Brunel University, 1985) until after the publication of the first two impressions of this book. His excellent study examines the process of "transformation" in the Good Shepherd penitentiaries in nineteenth-century England.

Association for Repeal, led by the charismatic and revered Josephine Butler, soon encompassed women from every social class. Such organised opposition was to have important repercussions, particularly in the larger movements for women's education and political reform. Equally satisfying from a feminist viewpoint, is the fact that occasionally, even the prostitutes themselves put up a spirited resistance to the Acts. Such incidents (though limited in number and frequently instigated and exaggerated by the Abolitionists) have been seized upon as evidence of the women's independent and "unsubjected" state. They appear to counter the traditional view of the Victorian prostitute as an inarticulate outcast, a powerless victim, filled with self-loathing and remorse; lending weight, instead, to the notion that the activity was frequently a means of upward social mobility, an ironic example of Smilesian "Self-Help".

The Female Penitentiary or "Magdalen" System, on the other hand, shows women in a less attractive light. To their discredit they were, if anything, more active in the Movement than were men. In England, it was women who became "Street Missionaries", distributing tracts and inviting prostitutes to enter a Home. It was they who attended magistrates' courts, visited brothels and combed the maternity and Lock wards of workhouses and hospitals, seeking out the fallen and persuading them to undergo reform. And in the Refuges themselves, it was women who became most active - with Ladies' Committees increasingly contributing to their overall management, and female staff being responsible for the day-to-day running of the Homes. In Ireland, admittedly, women had little involvement in outside Rescue Work, which in the Catholic community was left largely to the priests. Nevertheless, they were extremely active in "recommending" women to Magdalen Asylums; and more significantly, where family members were responsible for such admissions, 72 per cent of those "brought" to the Good Shepherd Homes were consigned to the institutions by female relatives. Further, the largest, most successful and most enduring Refuges to which penitents were confined (and this was the case in Britain too) were staffed and managed exclusively by nuns.

Far from opposing a system designed to remove from society all classes of females considered sexually unsound, most educated women gave it their support - whether by direct personal involvement, by employing former penitents as cheap domestic servants, by financial contributions, or, on a much wider scale, by sending their laundry to be washed by magdalens at local Homes. Few questioned the morality of consigning "fallen" women but not men to penitentiaries; and there was no public outcry or Parliamentary debate about prostitutes, unmarried mothers and victims of incest, seduction or rape, spending years, or sometimes even lifetimes, in unregulated and supposedly "short-term" Homes.

Finally, in contrast to those much-publicised prostitutes who occasionally resisted the Contagious Diseases Acts, magdalens were lamentably lacking in spirit - their very presence in the Homes proving their demoralised condition and their acceptance of society's view of them as outcast and defiled. Those continuing in confinement were almost totally subdued; and even the more rebellious - the many thousands who departed "unsatisfactorily", were dismissed for "bad conduct", or escaped - even these registered no formal complaint about their unlawful detention or the treatment they received. They did not apply to magistrates, or instigate proceedings at court. Nor did they agitate for the release of their one-time companions whose lives continued in a still-subjected state.[3] Many, on the contrary, submitted meekly to their penance and, abandoned by their families and society, became dependent on the women who controlled their lives.

Continuing to operate even when the Women's Movement was at its height, the Magdalen System in Ireland lingered on unnoticed, its victims not, apparently, a matter of concern. Tragically, scores of penitents (or "ladies" as they were latterly called) were still in the Homes in the early nineteen-nineties, when these once thriving empires were belatedly sold. These women, who dreaded the prospect of leaving, were casualties not of the Victorian Age but of the much more recent past. Their lives were, if anything, more squandered than those of their predecessors, and to less purpose. At least earlier magdalens had been rejected by a society believing its own propaganda - that sinners must atone and that sex was a sin. Recent inmates continued their penance long past the abandonment of such

---

3   The possible exception to this in the Irish context is that referred to on pages 216-17.

views. Kept ignorant of changing attitudes, demoralised and controlled, they were excluded from the sexual revolution which, far from freeing them, made mockery of their wasted lives.

1

"Patented Villains".
Rescue Workers and the
Penitentiary System

Throughout the nineteenth century estimates regarding prostitution in Britain varied alarmingly. In 1812, for example, the fifth *Annual Report* of the London Female Penitentiary stated that no fewer than 30,000 women were engaged in prostitution in London alone. By 1850 the figure had apparently risen to 80,000[1] - a controversial and much quoted estimate, of little interest to Dr. James Miller, Professor of Surgery at the University of Edinburgh. In his opinion:

> "Let any one walk certain streets of London, Glasgow, or Edinburgh, of a night, and, without troubling his head with statistics, his eyes and ears will tell him at once what a multitudinous amazonian army the devil keeps in constant field service, for advancing his own ends. The stones seem alive with lust, and the very atmosphere is tainted."[2]

At the end of the century Arthur J. S. Maddison, Secretary of the Female Aid Society, put the total number in England at a horrifying 140,000 - in his opinion a modest estimate, since only urban prostitutes were taken into account.[3] Future prospects seemed even worse. Advancing the same figure shortly afterwards, the *Englishwoman's Year Book* described these forces as "a vast army, to which each year adds some 25,000 recruits".[4]

---

1   Quoted in William J. Taylor, *The Story of the Homes, Their Origin, Development and Work for Fifty Years*, pp. 22-23. Issued by the London Female Preventive and Reformatory Institution, 1907.
2   Quoted in William Logan, *The Great Social Evil; its Causes, Extent, Results and Remedies* (1871) p.221.
3   Arthur J. S. Maddison, *Hints on Rescue Work, A Handbook for Missionaries and Superintendents of Homes* (1898) pp.2-3.
4   *Englishwoman's Year Book*, 1900.

Whatever the extent of prostitution - and statistics vary enormously - figures for those engaged in Rescue Work are more reliable. According to Maddison, the leading authority on the subject, by 1898 there were more than 300 Magdalen Institutions in England alone, collectively housing 6,000 inmates and employing at least 1,200 full-time Rescue staff.[5] In addition there were huge numbers of part-time workers, district visitors, street and city missionaries, members of Refuge committees and chaplains appointed to workhouses, hospitals and Homes; all of whom were active in a Rescue campaign which attracted intellectuals, politicians and even Royalty to its cause. The Dukes of Kent and Sussex, for example, were Joint Patrons of the Whitechapel Guardian Society (established in 1812); and their brother King William IV was Patron of the London Female Penitentiary. He was succeeded in this office by his niece Queen Victoria, and his wife and sister-in-law were Patronesses of the same Institution.[6] Several of Queen Victoria's daughters interested themselves in the Movement too. Princess Alice for example (Grand Duchess of Hesse) had long been occupied with Rescue Work in Darmstadt, and shortly before her death in 1878 became Patroness of the Albion Home in Brighton. Her younger sister Princess Helena (Princess Christian of Schleswig-Holstein) not only took over that role but gave her name to a Rescue Home in Clapham; and during this period Princess Louise (later Duchess of Argyll) supported Josephine Butler's work with prostitutes in Liverpool, and became Patron of a Home in Wanstead.[7] Probably the most prominent "Magdalenist" of the period was William Gladstone, who as an undergraduate made a lifetime commitment to the rescue of fallen women. As well as engaging in street missionary work and contributing large sums of money to the cause, he helped found the Church Penitentiary Association for the Reclamation of Fallen Women (1848), the Clewer Home of Mercy (1854), the Newport Home of Refuge, Soho Square (1863) and the St. Mary Magdalen Home of

---

5   Maddison, *op. cit.*, p.3.
6   *Guardian Society Report*, 1815; and London Female Penitentiary *Annual Reports*, 1836-38.
7   Rev. Dr. Sell, *Alice Grand Duchess of Hesse, Biographical Sketch and Letters* (1884) pp.365-6; the 37th *Annual Report of the Albion Hill Home, Brighton* ; and Taylor, *op. cit.*, p.22. Also, Jehanne Wake, *Princess Louise, Queen Victoria's Unconventional Daughter*, pp.168-9; and *Conferences of Managers of Reformatory and Industrial Institutions* (1896).

Refuge, Paddington (1865). He was also on the Management Committee of the Millbank Penitentiary.[8]

The first Refuge in England for the reception of the penitent "fallen" was the Magdalen Hospital, opened in Whitechapel in 1758, and later transferred to Streatham. This institution admitted females aged between fifteen and twenty, and could eventually house about 140 inmates desirous of reform. Its success encouraged the establishment of a similar institution in Ireland, and in 1767, a twenty-four page pamphlet in the form of a letter, was addressed to the public on:

> "The Important Subject of Establishing a Magdalen Asylum in Dublin. Here, instead of loathsome disease these reclaimed individuals will enjoy the blessings of health. They will exchange gross ignorance for useful knowledge, the pangs of guilt for peace of mind, the base drudgery of prostitution for profitable employment in innocent recreations ... Instead of being the detested pests of society, they will be useful and well regarded members of it. In short, instead of Devils, they will become Christians."[9]

This became the Dublin Magdalen Asylum, situated in Lower Leeson Street. Its object was to rescue "first fall" Protestant cases only. By 1900 it was still a relatively small Home, containing accommodation for only between 20 and 30 inmates, preferably under twenty years of age.

In 1787, twenty years after the opening of the Dublin Home, a second English Refuge appeared. This was the London Lock Asylum, catering solely for venereal patients discharged from the Lock Hospital (established in 1746) to which the new institution was now attached. Only women aged between fourteen and twenty-six were accepted, and there was eventually accommodation for about 90 inmates undergoing reform. Finally, in 1797 the Edinburgh Royal Magdalene Asylum was founded, housing up to 90 penitents of unrestricted age.

A succession of Penitentiaries and Rescue organisations followed the establishment of these eighteenth-century Homes. The Bristol Female Penitentiary (for 40 women) was founded as a

---

8   Philip Magnus, *Gladstone, a Biography*, pp.105-7; and R. Deacon, *The Private Life of Mr. Gladstone.*

9   *A Letter to the Public on an Important Subject, Establishing a Magdalen Asylum in Dublin* (1767) p.39.

Magdalen House in 1800, for example; followed by the Bath Penitentiary (for 79 inmates) in 1805. The London Female Penitentiary Society, "for the rescue, reclamation and protection of betrayed and fallen women", opened its famous Refuge in Pentonville in 1807, later moving to Stoke Newington and providing accommodation for up to 100 women; and in 1812, the Guardian Society, "providing Temporary Asylum for [40] Prostitutes" was established in Stepney, and later transferred to Bethnal Green. Here, it continued in its preservation of public morals by providing temporary asylum, with suitable employment, for Females who had "deviated from the paths of virtue".[10]

Other early Homes include the Liverpool Female Penitentiary founded in 1810; the Hull Home of Hope, 1811; the Glasgow Magdalene Asylum, 1815; the Devon and Exeter Female Penitentiary, 1819; the Leeds Guardian and the Gloucester Magdalen Asylums, both opened in 1821; and the York Refuge, and the Manchester Asylum for Female Penitents, each established in 1822. In the following decade the Plymouth Penitentiary was opened in 1832, the influential London Female Mission (afterwards the Female Aid Society) was established in Islington in 1836, and the Cambridge Female Refuge was opened in 1838.

Meanwhile in Ireland two Homes had been opened in Cork - a Catholic Magdalen Asylum, established in 1809, and a Protestant Refuge in 1810 - both discussed in more detail in Chapter 6. A second Dublin Asylum, the Female Penitentiary in Eccles Street was opened in 1813 for "fallen females of every religious persuasion".[11] By the following year the Home's new premises on the Circular Road had two distinct wards, so that penitents "of birth and delicate education" should be separated from those of the lowest orders. Most of the women, however, were soon found to be unskilled and illiterate; confirming the Committee's view that training and the procuring of "eligible situations" were vital objectives if the reformed were to be permanently restored to society.[12]

---

10 These two Societies, placed under one management in 1888, became known as the London Female Penitentiary and Guardian Society. In 1891, "the term 'Penitentiary' now being repellent", the name was changed to the London Female Guardian Society. *Annual Report*, 1891.

11 *Report of the Committee of the Dublin Female Penitentiary to the General Meeting.* February 1814, 1st Annual Report.

12 *Ibid.*

A few years later the Westmoreland Lock Hospital, Dublin (like its London predecessor, dating from the mid-eighteenth century) opened a small penitentiary for discharged prostitutes who were willing to reform; and at about the same time (1822) a small Catholic Magdalen Asylum was founded in Galway. This was taken over in 1847 by the Sisters of Mercy, who continued to run the Institution and its large laundry for well over a century.[13]

In 1826 a similar Home was opened in Limerick, again beginning on a modest scale, but in 1848 coming under the control of nuns. This time it was a French Order, the Sisters of Our Lady of Charity of the Good Shepherd of Angers, whose quickly expanding Limerick enterprise - their first Irish Foundation - would eventually house more than 150 penitents and become the Order's Provincial House. The Good Shepherd Sisters, committed to the reform of fallen women, were to dominate the Female Penitentiary Movement in Ireland for almost a century and a half. 1858 marked the beginning of their second undertaking in the country. This was a massive operation in Waterford, the origin of which was a small Refuge opened in 1842, which they were invited to acquire. In 1860 their Mission in New Ross, Co. Wexford began; and seven years later, they opened their House in Belfast. Finally in 1870 in response to the Contagious Diseases legislation, the largest and most significant of their Irish Foundations was established. This was at Sunday's Well in Cork, and is the subject of Chapters 6 and 7.

By now hundreds of Refuges had opened in England, and Rescue Work, fired by fears of prostitution, was becoming an occupation in itself. The very language used to describe the topic indicates something of the passion it aroused. Dr. William Tait, for example, at one time Surgeon to the Edinburgh Lock Hospital and author of the influential *Magdalenism, An Inquiry into the Extent, Causes and Consequences of Prostitution in Edinburgh*, admitted to a public meeting in 1847:

---

13 For a summary of the Westmoreland Lock Hospital see Luddy, *op. cit.*, pp.103-7. The Sisters of Mercy opened a second Magdalen Asylum in Tralee in 1856. This was a much smaller institution containing only 13 inmates - "the most miserable members of the human family for whom the laws of the land have done nothing and upon whom society has ...... set its ban." *Kerry Chronicle*, 19 December 1856.

"amongst the various questions which at present agitate the public mind, there are none more momentous or of more thrilling interest than that of prostitution."[14]

and in the following year, Dr. John Campbell urged the public to confront the problem, and to shed any feelings of false delicacy and reserve:

" ... Lest fiends in human shape profit by our prudery ... homicidal poachers on the domain of virtue are allowed to walk unquestioned over the fairest cities of our globe, filling society with shame, tears, rottenness and death! Foul vampires! Patented villains ... they have fellowship with devils!"[15]

In the Rescue Movement's early years the repentant "fallen" outnumbered vacancies in the few Magdalen Asylums then in existence. Consequently the Homes could afford to be fastidious with regard to the women they admitted, often insisting on Memorials from Subscribers, or Petitions from applicants such as the following example, required by the Dublin Female Penitentiary:

"Your Petitioner is an unfortunate Female, sensible of the offence which has plunged her into guilt and misery, and deprived her of every means of getting an honest livelihood; and being desirous of quitting her vicious courses, she prays that she may be admitted into the Dublin Female Penitentiary, where she solemnly engages to behave with decency and good conduct, to submit to the orders she may receive, to endeavour to render herself useful and profitable to the Institution by her labour, and conform to all the Rules of the House."[16]

With the multiplication of Homes, however, and the dramatic rise in the number of places available, the task of filling the institutions and staffing the laundries so vital to their existence became increasingly urgent. Applicants, rather than Refuges, were now selective, and in England intense rivalry was reported

14 Quoted in Logan, *op. cit.*, p.25.
15 *Ibid.*, p.26.
16 Appendix to the Second Report of the *Dublin Female Penitentiary*, March 1815.

as institutions competed for inmates, and over-zealous Rescue Workers engaged in "unseemly scrambles" for cases at workhouses, hospitals and magistrates' courts. It was felt by the Reformatory and Refuge Union (established in 1856) as well as by the managers of many Homes, that some central organisation was needed to consolidate efforts, prevent duplication, and provide direct access to those who were "lost". Consequently, in 1858, the Social Evil sub-committee of the recently formed Union, instituted a new association - the "Female Mission to the Fallen", later described as:

> "A <u>Home Missionary Society</u>, not to those who are afar off but to those who are in our midst. It supports ... Female Missionaries, who daily and nightly undertake their missionary tours in our own crowded highways, endeavouring to reclaim those of their sex who have strayed from the paths of virtue."[17]

This organisation (later re-named the Woman's Mission to Women) took over the influential Female Aid Society in 1881 and was to dominate non-Catholic Rescue Work for most of the period. Its first Secretary, Arthur J. S. Maddison, had been a central figure in the Reclamation Movement for several years and was author of the influential handbook *Hints on Rescue Work*, published in 1898.[18]

Aware of the difficulties facing men involved in Missionary work - approaches to prostitutes, for example (especially at night) being open to misinterpretation, and visits to brothels being similarly misconstrued - the male committee members were most anxious to attract women to the activity.[19] For as Maddison was

---

17 *Annual Report of the Reformatory and Refuge Union*, 1871, p.21.

18 Maddison was appointed Secretary of the Reformatory and Refuge Union (1873), Secretary of the Reformatory and Refuge Union's Provident Benevolent Fund (1876) and Secretary of the Anchorage Mission (1889). See *Reformatory and Refuge Union Report* (1856-1906) p.54, and the *Reformatory and Refuge Union Red Book*, 1890.

19 For an indication of the reluctance with which Cork Catholic Priests undertook such duties, see the testimony of Rev. Henry Reed - from 1872-1881, Catholic Chaplain to the "Certified" Lock Hospital in the city. He stated that dying prostitutes had to be removed from brothels before a priest would visit them, so that no "odium" would be attached to his name. Canon Maguire (see below) had appointed a house next to the street where the brothels were, so that priests might attend women "not dangerously bad". Other priests, if called to a dying girl in a house of ill-fame, made it a rule to take "respectable" parishioners with them. Minutes of Evidence Taken Before the *Select Committee on the Contagious Diseases Acts*, 27 June 1881.

later to observe, though both the clergy and medical men were exceptionally well situated to initiate rescue efforts, and should, perhaps, take such responsibilities more seriously:

> " ... even they best fulfil their mission in this respect by calling in the aid of the woman worker as soon as possible in every case they wish to befriend. The services of men, too, are required in consultation, in organisation, in financing, and in giving legal advice. Still, in the main, Rescue Work is woman's work - it is a woman's mission to women."[20]

It was clearly envisaged then, that while men would control the activity, retaining responsibility for its overall management, direction and funds, women would be the grass-roots workers both in "outdoor" Rescue Work, and in the Refuges themselves.

The Society was soon employing eight full-time women Missionaries, who by day attended the police courts, visited workhouses and laboured particularly in the venereal wards of the Royal Free Hospital. Here languished hundreds of "victims of their lives of sin" - poor girls who were "peculiarly amenable to the kindly sympathy and Christian counsel" of the Missionaries who read and prayed with them. It was reported that many of these girls were "thoroughly hardened" in the life before they were twelve, and sometimes as early as eight years of age.[21]

From 8 p.m. till midnight, these bold apostles of virtue paced the London streets, remonstrating with those in danger, seeking out the lost, and offering the fallen the means of reform. Like most Outdoor Missionaries, they were required too, to visit brothels and other notorious houses, an "arduous duty", to be undertaken only with extreme caution and never by the nervously inclined. Potential crusaders may well have been sobered by Maddison's alarming advice on this topic, detailed in his Handbook for Rescue Workers:

> "1. Never let anything induce you to eat or drink the smallest thing in a bad house, and do not stand near a table, or where a person could come up behind you unawares.

---

20 Maddison, *op. cit.*, pp.3-4.
21 *9th Report of the Female Mission to the Fallen* (1876) p.12.

2. Be on you guard if the woman keeping the house, or anyone in it, offers you anything to smell.

3. Stand if possible near the door, and see that it is not shut upon you; at the same time, avoid any appearance of suspicion or fright.

4. Whatever may meet your eyes, make no observation upon it, and do not appear to see anything but the business upon which you have come.

5. Your duty does not take you in such a house to any room, but the downstairs sitting room.

6. Do not scream or appear disconcerted if attempts are made to frighten you, that you may be deterred from coming again.

7. If money is offered you in such a place, do not touch it with your hands, nor receive it, even if offered on the plea of helping with a rescue case or the Society you work for."[22]

Ideally the Outdoor Missionary was to be strong, cheerful, of suitable age (about thirty when beginning the work) quiet, quick, and devoted to her task. Total abstinence was another advantage; and though uniforms were not thought advisable it was recommended that the Missionary's dress should be dark, not easily seen at a distance, becoming and scrupulously clean.[23]

Although by the end of the period, some attempt was being made to recruit to the Mission women from the working-classes, Rescue Work continued in essence to be a middle and upper-class pursuit, centred on the reform of females drawn almost exclusively from the ranks of the poor. There is no doubt that for many educated women, the work was both exciting and a challenge, its pathos and urgency stimulating their reforming zeal. As well as voluntary work, the Movement offered scope for full-time employment, and the possibility, by the end of the century, of a rewarding career. Local and national Conferences widened horizons, as, for the first time many women attended

---

22 Maddison, *op. cit.*, pp. 21-22.
23 *Ibid.*, p.22.

meetings, spoke in public and earnestly exchanged ideas. It is likely that much experience and confidence gained in early Rescue Work (which was carried out with the full approval of men) was used to great advantage in later, less acceptable "Women's" campaigns.

In 1860 the Society extended its operations to Ireland with the establishment of the Dublin-based Mission to Friendless Females. In both capitals, Missionaries were required to approach prostitutes and distribute religious tracts, designed to be read in "sober" moments and divert the women from their vicious lives. A much favoured pamphlet, *Sins and Sorrows of London,* had been written by a founder member of the Female Mission Committee, John La Touch, of Newbridge, Co. Kildare. Other titles included the popular *Mercy for Misery, God's Invitation, If I Had Only Heeded, Picking up the Fragments* and *Come Now.*

By this time a large body of Rescue literature existed. As well as the proliferation of tracts, pamphlets and articles always in circulation, *Proceedings of Conferences* were now distributed to affiliated Homes, and most Refuges published their own Annual Reports. Popular books on Rescue Work were available, and special volumes of Prayers and Religious Stories were produced for reading aloud in Refuges, Penitentiaries and Homes.* By the 1880s, with the advent of Annual Managers' Meetings at the Society's headquarters in Charing Cross, the periodical *Notes on Work Amongst the Fallen* was widely circulated. This publication provided Homes with the latest developments in Rescue Work, and information on affiliated institutions. It also contained useful "Cautionary Lists" which were confidential descriptions of troublesome individuals "not to be entertained". And in 1890 the Reformatory and Refuge Union issued the first edition of its *Red Book,* a catalogue of "all the more prominent workers in the cause … altogether a little over a thousand names."[24]

Meanwhile, the Midnight Meeting Movement had been founded in 1861 for reclaiming fallen women both from London's East End, with its "dirty, draggled vice, open and coarse in its repulsiveness and misery", and West End, where

---

* For example, the Religious Tract Society's *Prayers for Homes for Women and Rescue Associations.* No date, but late nineteenth century.

24 *The Reformatory and Refuge Union Red Book* (1890), Introduction.

immorality "attired in silks and satins, [was] accompanied with the deceitfulness of painted faces and bedizened shame." [25]

In the following year the Movement opened a Mission in Marlborough Street, Dublin, where immediate shelter day or night was offered to those desirous of reform. To wean prostitutes from their lives of sin Midnight Tea Meetings were held, but Maddison disapproved and doubted their usefulness. In both cities large numbers of women converged on the meetings, only to decamp when sober and when "the cravings for liberty and licence" reasserted themselves. Nevertheless, by 1906 the Midnight Meeting Movement had held 2,268 meetings, attended by 115,536 women and girls.[26]

Other Dublin Refuges included the Baggot Street Asylum for Penitent Females (35 inmates); Dublin by Lamplight, Harcourt Street (70 inmates); St. Mary's Refuge, Lower Gloucester Street (established in 1887 for 80 inmates); the Dublin Providence Home, the Rescue Mission Home and the High Park Penitentiary, Drumcondra. The latter, a huge Catholic institution, contained 210 Magdalens by the turn of the century and was run by the Sisters of Our Lady of Charity of Refuge. Far from being "absolutely dependent on the Sisters for everything" (a misleading description applied to them in 1932) these penitents were, in fact, the main support of the Convent. They worked unremittingly in the large laundry attached to the institution, and as the following advertisement indicates, even their daily prayers, being at the disposal of the Asylum's benefactors living or dead, could be turned to profit:

> "At present there are 218 poor penitents in the Asylum absolutely dependent on the Sisters for everything. The Holy Sacrifice of the Mass and the daily prayers of the community and the poor penitents are offered for benefactors living and dead. Donations for the maintenance of this most deserving charity will be thankfully received by the Mother Superior at the Convent. There is a public Laundry attached."[27]

By the 1890s Rescue Work extended throughout Britain, with

---

25 *12th Annual Report of the Midnight Meeting Movement for the Recovery of Fallen Women* (1873).
26 Taylor, *op. cit.*, p.49.
27 *Irish Independent Eucharistic Congress Souvenir Number* (1932) p.59.

most towns containing at least one Magdalen Asylum, and many boasting three or four competing Refuges and Homes. Yet it is unlikely that these institutions did much to solve the "Social Evil" problem. Individuals may have been "rescued" or at least removed from the streets, but inevitably, prostitution itself continued as before.

This was because – increasingly as the nineteenth century progressed – many of the women consigned to these Homes were not of the prostitute class. Some were "first fall" cases, or unmarried mothers whose families (particularly in Ireland) wanted them out of the way. Others were feeble-minded, requiring protection; and many were young girls alarmingly classified as "in need of restraint". Far from being a threat to society most were its victims, their removal affecting no-one but themselves.

Further, of course, the consignment even of genuine prostitutes to Penitentiaries seldom reduced their numbers on the streets, any more than did an individual prostitute's death. So long as poverty continued, and the demand for public women remained, such losses were easily replaced. Maddison dismissed this argument, and rejected the notion that "every Rescue means another fall". Diminishing supply would, in his opinion, automatically affect demand, since a reduction in prostitutes would make such women more costly and difficult to obtain.

Thus the issue of continued demand for prostitutes was barely confronted, so absorbed were moralists with the disgraceful and more visible evidence of supply. And while acknowledging that poverty, overcrowded slum housing and lack of employment opportunities fuelled the activity, Rescue Workers shirked the wider issues, insisting on individual moral (rather than radical social) reform.

Equally significant, the Homes themselves had little impact on prostitution over the period. On the one hand, "long-term" institutions like the Good Shepherd Asylums necessarily defeated their object, by endeavouring to retain inmates for their lives. Places were taken up indefinitely, and numbers of new admissions were reduced, or slowed down. At the same time, in both these and the more numerous "short-term" Homes, conditions were so repellent that the vast majority of inmates, whatever their backgrounds, refused to remain. Absconding without training or character, further demoralised, and now with an added stigma attaching to their name, many one-time penitents undoubtedly returned or succumbed to, a life on the streets.

Had the Homes secured a high turnover of genuine prostitutes, who, after training, were restored to society and found respectable work, the Female Penitentiary System - morally questionable though it was - might have effected some good. As it was, however, a pre-occupation with sin on the one hand, and a fear of "rewarding vice,"[28] on the other, together made conditions in the Homes so intolerable, that few prostitutes chose to be admitted in the first place, and fewer still could be persuaded to remain.

Epitomising that "double standard" in sexual morality we so freely attribute to the Victorians, many Magdalen Institutions (particularly the Good Shepherds) survived longer into the twentieth century than they had existed in the past. Most of their business was, in fact, conducted in the post-Victorian Age. Throughout its history, advocates of the Female Penitentiary System betrayed a continuing fear of women's sexuality, a fear particularly evident in Ireland in the 1930s, when, according to one concerned observer, outcast women were "never so numerous and never so sinful". Further:

> "The appalling demoralisation of our times is evidenced mostly in the decline of that virtue amongst woman-kind which is her chief glory and title to our esteem. To-day in ever increasing numbers "Magdalen" has imitators in her sin. But few will share her penance."[29]

To counter such vice, the ideal of womanhood became more firmly than ever fixed in the celibate nun - and of all religious vocations open to women, none more closely resembled the work of Christ himself, than that of the Good Shepherd Sisters. Significantly at this stage of the new State's existence, these nuns' work - "never more needful" - was seen as patriotic. And since

---

28 As early as 1812 in its 5th *Annual Report*, the London Female Penitentiary Society had found it necessary to re-assure an uneasy public on this point and paint a gloomy picture of life in the Home. See below, pp. 227-8.

29 Rev. Father Kerr, Galway, "The Good Shepherd Nuns at Home", in *The Fold of the Good Shepherd* (1931) p.10.

even motherhood in its "purist" form (without the taint of sex and childbirth) was attributed to them, these women were elevated to heights no normal female, however virtuous, could aspire to or attain:

"In the Home of the Good Shepherd the one [the nun] is ever the "Mother", while the other [the penitent] is always the "Child" and no mother and child on earth are bound together by so pure and holy an affection. Can anywhere on earth be found so touching a relationship ... At times indeed there will be tense moments of suspense when it would seem that the Evil One is going to recapture the soul it had lost. At times these poor victims of sin experience frightful temptations to break away from the Fold of the Good Shepherd; sinful desires will at times arise within their hearts which only victims of impurity can realise ... Then will the anxious care and the patient sweetness of the daughter of the Good Shepherd be re-doubled ... to that Motherly care and attentive guardianship do not multitudes today owe their salvation? Surely there is no grander work for God and soul and the spiritual uplifting of this nation."[30]

Such descriptions, ringing hollow even in the 1930s, have now been wholly discredited. Surviving inmates' accounts of harsh treatment and demoralisation in the Homes have shattered forever the illusion of motherly care. But even without this evidence, the system itself was flawed. Such pious preoccupation with "the fallen" is suspect, and the continued practice of punishing women but not men for "irregular" sex, was both immoral and unjust. The term "patented villains" might, perhaps, more aptly be applied to those engaged in Rescue Work, than to the "loathsome sinners" they empowered themselves to save.

---

30 *Ibid.*, p.11.

2

"Never Free From Their Espionage" The Good Shepherd Magdalen Asylums

"I warn you to be on your guard against their wiles, to fear them, as you would the snares of the serpent. Remember, that while we are studying these poor children in order to know them, they are cunningly, I would almost say maliciously, studying us, and striving to know us. You may be sure, they examine you from head to foot; we are never free from their espionage."

Conferences and Instructions of the Venerable Mother Mary of Saint Euphrasia Pelletier, Foundress of the Generalate of the Congregation of Our Lady of Charity of the Good Shepherd of Angers. (Chapter IV)

The French Congregation of Our Lady of Charity of Refuge was originally founded in 1641, by an Oratorian priest Father Jean Eudes, whose "purity", we are told, "was never sullied by even the thought of evil".[1] This "proof" of his saintliness is curiously similar to that later applied by Thomas Burke to the nineteenth-century inheritors of the founding Father's work. Thus, exposed to the nun who has dedicated her life to the service of God in a Magdalen Asylum, the newly admitted penitent encounters:

"The woman who has never known the pollution of a single wicked thought - the woman whose virgin bosom has never been crossed by the shadow of a thought of sin! - the woman breathing purity, innocence and grace, receives the woman whose breath is the pestilence of hell!"[2]

---

1 A. M. Clarke, *Mary of St. Euphrasia Pelletier, First Superior General of the Congregation of Our Lady of Charity of the Good Shepherd of Angers* (1895) pp.44-49. Fr. Eudes was canonised in 1925.
2 Quoted in Caitriona Clear, *Nuns in Nineteenth-Century Ireland*, p.153.

In 1666, a Papal Bull of Approbation raised the Institute to an Order under the Rule of St. Augustine, with Constitutions framed by Father Eudes. As well as poverty, chastity and obedience, the nuns took a fourth vow, peculiar to the Institute, which obliged them to labour for the conversion of penitent women.

Almost two centuries later in 1835, under the Order's modern Foundress, Mother Mary of St. Euphrasia Pelletier, a Generalate was established, and the Congregation took the name of Our Lady of Charity of the Good Shepherd of Angers, popularly known as the "Good Shepherds".* The fourth vow of this enclosed Order, was zeal for the salvation of souls. The Institute spread so rapidly that at the time of the first Superior-General's death in 1868, 110 Convents (in separate Provinces but attached to the Angers Mother House) had already been established world-wide.

The first English Good Shepherd Magdalen Asylum was founded in Hammersmith in 1841, and was followed in the next four decades by Houses in East Finchley (1850), Glasgow and Bristol (1851), Liverpool (1858), Manchester (1866), Cardiff (1872) and Newcastle on Tyne (1888). These were huge institutions, the penitentiary sections of which were centred on and financed by large commercial laundries, providing occupation for the inmates and a means of their discipline and control. Each of these Refuges, the largest of their kind in Britain, housed between 140 to 235 inmates, while East Finchley could accommodate 330 penitent women by 1935.

As noted above, the Order's first Magdalen Asylum in Ireland was opened in Limerick in 1848, followed by Houses in Waterford (1858), New Ross (1860) and Belfast (1867).[3] The opening of the Government Lock Hospital in Cork in 1869 resulted in the Order's fifth and largest Irish Foundation. The Hospital catered solely for the detention and treatment of state-registered

---

* Those Convents wishing to retain their independence kept the original name of Our Lady of Charity of Refuge. Two of this French Order's Houses were established in Dublin - the High Park Penitentiary (1833) - Ireland's first and largest Convent Magdalen Asylum; and the Gloucester Street Refuge (see p.16) whose closure in 1998 marked the end of the country's Female Penitentiary system.

3   The latter was in response to a request from the Bishop of Belfast, Rev. Dr. Dorian. The Sisters took over an existing Refuge which had been opened in 1851 and was under the management of the Sisters of Mercy: "On account of their large schools and many other avocations, [they] were very pleased to hand this charge over to nuns specially trained for this work." *The Fold of the Good Shepherd, op. cit.*, p.27.

prostitutes; some of whom, while in the institution, were persuaded to reform. The Good Shepherd Sisters were invited to the city to ensure that, following their release from the hospital, these women did not return to a life of sin.

Detailed regulations on the government of such women are contained in *Practical Rules for the Use of the Religious of the Good Shepherd for the Direction of the Classes*, Mother St. Euphrasia Pelletier's personal "Instructions" on the subject. The book was first published in this form in 1898, thirty years after the Foundress' death; at which time its Institute-wide distribution was undertaken - not to propose new practices, but on the contrary, to preserve those that were old. The Preface to the work notes that by that date, the Rules had been observed throughout the Order for over sixty years. They had thus ensured a uniformity of practice in every Congregation, which was strictly adhered to by all members of the Community.

It is clear from the above that the Foundress' Rules governed each of the Irish Houses throughout the period of this study. They continued largely unaltered for much of the twentieth century too. Another work, *Conferences and Instructions of Mother Mary of St. Euphrasia Pelletier*, was in circulation from 1885. This book (from which the *Practical Rules* were selected) was published to commemorate the fiftieth anniversary of the establishment of the Generalate of the Congregation, and was intended for every member of the Order. It was based on the notes of the Foundress' Instructions, taken by the Sisters at Angers over a forty year period. The work was reprinted with the inclusion of some unpublished Conferences in 1907.

The Rules for the "classes" were originally developed in the second quarter of the nineteenth-century, and compared with treatment in contemporary institutions such as prisons, lunatic asylums and workhouses, were not unduly harsh - though perhaps more inhumane. Indeed, Mother St. Euphrasia was careful to stress the need for charity, consideration and great kindness to the penitents. Her awareness of the women as a source of evil, however - never to be trusted and a danger even to themselves - created conflict. This was resolved in part by treating them (regardless of age and how long they had been in the Homes) as "children" - a practice continued into the nineteen-sixties.

"You must serve both as guides and mothers to the children of the classes*; they should find in you, comfort in trials and help in their troubles. The greater the spiritual maladies of our penitents, the greater should be our interest in them. The more inclined they are to evil, the greater should be our compassion for them ...We recommend you once for all, to be charitable to the children ... let kindness be the rule of our conduct, of our language, of our manner; thus the children may render testimony that we are, as we ought to be, true Mothers ...We may say that we owe our vocation to the lost sheep; our Congregation would not exist but for them ... Love all your penitents, whatever their country. Devote yourselves to their happiness, with all possible zeal, and you will rejoice the Heart of Jesus and the Heart of Mary."[4]

Doubtless many of the rules were practical and necessary - dictated by the nature of the work itself, the character and disposition of many of the inmates and the large numbers of women coming under the Order's control. Unlike most other Rescue Homes in the period whose accommodation was limited to 25 or 30 women, the Good Shepherd Asylums generally housed between 100 to 250 penitents at any one time. In such circumstances discipline was necessary for the maintenance of order, and it was important that obedience to the Sisters was strictly enforced. Some of the rules, however, were wholly inappropriate; and by any standards more suited to nuns than those attempting to reform. This was particularly the case with the Rule of Silence, for example, to which not only the penitents but the children in the Order's Industrial schools were subjected for part of the day. Its justification troubled even the Foundress - a concern discussed but soon discarded in the Chapter devoted to the subject:

"We cannot expect our children to have the same religious respect for silence that we should have, yet it is a necessary condition for the surveillance and good order of a class; consequently, it must

---

* Not to be confused with the real children and juveniles placed in the Order's Industrial Schools - youngsters who, from 1868, formed an additional, but entirely separate aspect of the Congregation's work. Extending the euphemism further, those subject to unremitting labour in the laundries (practically the entire penitent population) were referred to as the "Class", and the nuns in charge of them were "Mistresses".

4   *Rules for the Direction of the Classes, op. cit.* (1898) pp.98-101.

be respected, like all the other rules, with scrupulous care. Its observance will be, for the good, a means of advancing in virtue and true happiness; and for the others, a preventive against dissipation and dangerous conversations.[5]

The Rule of Silence* was a major feature of the women's lives and continued well into the second half of the twentieth century. Echoes of Mother St. Euphrasia's views on Silence appear in Rescue Work literature in general, and as in the above passage, lip service is paid to the beneficial effects of this time for reflection, on the penitents themselves. The real purpose of Silence, however, particularly in the Good Shepherds where such large numbers were involved, was to ensure quick discipline and order, and to subject the women intermittently, to greater measures of control. When the women's time for recreation was over, for example, the sign for silence was given - the Mistress (also under the Rule) being recommended to assume a serious, authoritative look "to show that she is decided and watchful."

"When the signal is given for another exercise, the Mistress should immediately leave off her present work, rise, and by a look, direct the march, so that all may be done in silence and good order. It is particularly difficult to maintain silence when the children are being conducted from one place to another, and for this reason, there should be a Mistress at each extremity of the ranks; if there be only one Religious she should place a child worthy of confidence, at one end. In these movements the Mistresses should be all eyes, and very serious, to make the children understand that they must not speak. They should not have to wait because a door is locked or a Mistress late; if such take place, it will be difficult to prevent dissipation."[6]

Coinciding with the 1898 distribution of Mother St. Euphrasia's *Practical Rules* was the publication of a similar set of Guidelines for the many and diverse Rescue Workers operating in England. This was the Reformatory and Refuge Union's *Hints on Rescue Work,* the Handbook for Missionaries and Refuge Workers,

---

5   *Ibid.*, p.129.
*   The Great Silence "begins in the evening at the hour of Matins, and continues until after Prime next morning. No word is uttered during this time, unless the matter be very urgent". A. M. Clarke, *op. cit.*, footnote p.124.
6   *Rules for the Direction of the Classes, op. cit.*, p.134.

referred to above. A similar book, *Notes on Rescue Work*, by the Rev. Arthur Brinkman, had already been published in 1895. It is clear from these works that in many Protestant Homes too, periods of silence were frequently imposed, particularly in the laundries and from 9.30 in the evenings, when the women retired to bed. In some Homes even the staff were discouraged from conversations unless these related to their work.[7]

Unnatural too, were the long hours of prayer and devotion forced on the Good Shepherd penitents, a practice which was not only excessive, but particularly inappropriate for that class of women at whom the Refuges were aimed. Also exposed to this regime was that other group of women who were increasingly persuaded to reform - unmarried mothers, "first fall" cases and girls who had been sexually abused. Quite apart from their backgrounds, inclinations and former habits, many of these tormented souls were of limited intelligence, reports by the end of the period estimating that almost one in three of them was mentally deficient or "feeble minded", even in short-term Homes. Most were barely educated, and few would have possessed any real understanding of the dreary religious rites they were forced to observe. Consequently it was reported that prayers and hymns were mechanically recited, and daily practices imperfectly performed.

Most of those admitted to the Homes found the regime intolerable, and the majority of them, as is demonstrated in the statistics included in this study, left after only a very short stay. The real victims were not these but the long-term inmates, who, after years of atonement, betrayed a morbid pre-occupation with religion and sin. Some apparently, assumed "a pious appearance out of vanity", or to win the approval of the nuns; while others, "with an impulse of fervour" displayed a disquieting tendency to make confessions that were frequent and long. Throughout the period the Good Shepherd Annals contain numerous examples of superstition and ignorance, indulged in by the inmates and fostered, even instigated, by the nuns. Incidents such as penitents sacrificing their hair to effect an ill Sister's recovery, for example, are by no means isolated, and are reported joyously in the records not as evidence of the women's credulity, but of their

7   Maddison, *op.cit.*, p.215.

chastened, holy state.[8] The disturbing symbolism of the gesture (a further assault on the women's sexuality) together with the disagreeable approval of the Sisters, overshadows the absurdity of the intention itself.

To discourage vanity and improper thoughts, uniforms were drab and shapeless, and in most Refuges women had their hair cropped, in hideous contrast to the fashion of the time. Such disfigurement - part punishment and part penance - was particularly approved for that class of women, who, it was constantly alleged, had initially "fallen" through pride in appearance and "love of dress". In early Homes such as the Edinburgh and London Magdalene Asylums, heads were completely shaved to prevent or discourage departures. This practice, inflicted with appalling brutality and for the purpose of chastisement, was still being carried out in the Limerick Good Shepherd, for example, as late as the nineteen-fifties.[9]

It is clear that at times the filthy condition of the women, some of whom "swarmed with vermin", had occasionally demanded such action - though for sanitary rather than punitive purposes. Indeed Maddison urged the desirability of all newly admitted inmates being bathed with carbolic, and their garments purified or destroyed. More ominous still, he warned all workers in Homes to avoid cloths or utensils used by inmates, since "even drinking out of a cup or sitting on a chair has been known to have disastrous results." He recommended not only that workers' and inmates' clothes be washed on different days, but that separate washing tubs be used.[10]

In the Good Shepherd Asylums an individual's identity was further suppressed by the Order's universal practice of assigning new names (sometimes bizarre and masculine) to inmates as soon as they arrived. Ostensibly carried out to ensure the anonymity of penitents, this procedure was occasionally adopted in Protestant Homes too - though against the recommendation of Maddison who thought it more trouble than it was worth.

8   See for example, pages 177 and 197.
9   For the nineteenth century, see Mahood, *op. cit.*, p.80. The more recent example is documented in Mary Raftery and Eoin O'Sullivan, *Suffer the Little Children* (1999); and in the Channel Four documentary *Sex in a Cold Climate*, referred to above.
10 Maddison, *op. cit.*, pp. 112-3.

Magdalen Homes rarely admitted applicants who were pregnant,[11] and inmates found to be in this condition were instantly dismissed. Many Homes insisted, as the century progressed, on new arrivals being medically examined before proceeding from the probationary to the general class; and in 1919 it was claimed that the majority of English Homes "returned to sender" not only applicants who were pregnant, but those who were feeble-minded or diseased.[12] By this time, particularly in England where a diversity of Refuges allowed for classification, there were various Homes in which the unmarried mother could be confined. However, vacancies were limited and subject to restrictions; and since repeated offenders as well as prostitutes were refused admission, women dismissed from Magdalen Homes on account of pregnancy generally had no alternative but the workhouse. Occasionally a former inmate might re-enter a Refuge following her confinement, but this was at the discretion of the governing committee, and subject to a place still being available. It was dependent too, in the event of the infant having survived, on the woman's willingness and ability to dispose of her child.

Most Homes discouraged reference to inmates' former lives, and nowhere was this policy more strictly enforced than in the Good Shepherds. The seventeenth-century Approbation for the original Order had been resisted by Cardinals in Rome on the grounds of contamination - it being feared that contact with penitents would expose the nuns to evil which "communicates itself easily". Father Eudes' response to these and other reservations contained assurances that the Sisters would live entirely apart from the penitents, and mix with them only to instruct them and superintend their work. Further, according to "a Religious of the Congregation" writing in 1933:

"To avoid all danger, Father Eudes had, from the very beginning, strictly forbidden any reference to their past life being made by

---

11 The Rules published in the Annual Reports of most Refuges are quite explicit on this point. The First of the General Regulations of the York Female Penitentiary, for example, states that "No Applicant found to be in a state of pregnancy shall be admitted or retained in the House". See Frances Finnegan, *Poverty and Prostitution, A Study of Victorian Prostitutes in York* (1979) p. 171. Also the London Guardian Society's Rules for the Management of the Asylum, in, for example, the 1884 *Annual Report.* - "VI. No female can be admitted who is pregnant or diseased." p.15.

12 *Rescue Work; an Inquiry and Criticism* (1919) p.23.

the penitents in their conversation with the nuns. This rule is always rigidly adhered to in all convents to this day"[13]

By the twentieth century this uncompromising regulation was particularly cruel, since it was indiscriminate and unresponsive to the changing composition of the Homes. Grimly adhered to, it led to much suffering - especially among those increasing numbers who were not prostitutes but unmarried mothers - forced to give up their babies as well as their lives. Regardless of whether passion, seduction or abuse had been the cause of pregnancy; and irrespective of whether the infant had survived, grieving, post-natal mothers were compelled to suffer in silence, and to submit, without murmur, to the anguish of their loss. Often (particularly in the latter years of the Homes' existence) the child was subsequently fostered or adopted, and necessary formalities would be required. Accordingly, the Laundry Mistress would be warned to be "lenient" with a particular girl, who would then be summoned from her labours, to sign away the infant she had neither seen, nor mentioned, since entering the Home. She would return to her work red-eyed or crying, unusually quiet or "difficult", an object of pity, curiosity or scorn.[14]

The managers of most Rescue Homes were reluctant to let penitents have visitors, claiming that they unsettled the inmates and jeopardised their training and reform. It was alleged too, that having abandoned or "brought" a girl to a Home in the first place, parents had been known to turn up at a later stage to reclaim her, should her presence or earning capacity be required. Accordingly, visits were discouraged or forbidden; and at best limited to exceptional circumstances, to close family members, and to their taking place in the presence of the First Mistress or Matron in charge. Correspondence too, was discouraged, and carefully scrutinised. New arrivals were watched with extra vigilance, and later in the period when probationary accommodation was built, they were isolated to guard against

---

13 *Blessed Mary of Saint Euphrasia Pelletier,* by a Religious of the Congregation (1933) pp.45-46. The author of this Biography was a Sister in the Convent of the Good Shepherd, East Finchley, London.
14 The recollections of a Good Shepherd Sister, recounted to the author in 1986. This nun had been Laundry Mistress in one of the Homes for many years. The fact that the women could "do nothing but cry" for the babies taken from them - a loss which haunted some of them for the rest of their lives - is graphically described in the 1998 Channel Four television documentary referred to above.

improper reference to life outside the Home. To avoid such conversations, which "awaken memories" and "do untold mischief", the Good Shepherd *Rules* advocated strict surveillance at all times. Nowhere was this more vital than in the dormitories, where a continuous <u>great silence</u> was rigorously imposed:

> "They should be obliged to go to the dormitory in silence. The signal to set out, should not be given until the ranks are formed, silence established, and the surveillantes at their posts; each child should be obliged to remain in her own place and advance slowly. Order and silence would be more easily maintained by having but one rank and causing the children to recite a prayer aloud whilst walking."[15]

Without showing they suspected evil, Mistresses were charged to be aware of all that took place. Even where Sisters rose and attended chapel earlier than the penitents, the Dormitory Mistress was required to make meditation in her cell, rather than leave the inmates without surveillance. This cell (into which the Sister locked herself each night) was carefully situated and fitted with a slide opening or grille, so that the whole of the dormitory could be observed at once.[16] Penitents with a tendency to "seek out each other's company" were to be separated, but discreetly, "to avoid exciting suspicions or murmurs". This preventive measure was not always successful, and occasionally throughout the period, women were dismissed for "particular friendships" – a possible reference to suspected lesbianism.[17]

> "We should not, at recreation nor elsewhere, allow two children to be alone ... there should be no corners in which some could hide from the eyes of the Mistress. It is in such places the demon lies in wait for

---

15 *Rules for the Direction of the Classes, op. cit.*, pp.152-3.
16 *Ibid.*, p.155. A footnote preceding this instruction states: "It would perhaps be preferable to have no curtains on the beds. Each child might be obliged to turn her face to the nearest wall, to avoid dissipation whilst dressing and undressing." Footnote p.154.
17 Maria Luddy's assertion (*op. cit.*, p. 131) that "Many penitents were also dismissed for engaging in lesbian relationships, or 'particular friendships' as such were termed, with other women in the home", is something of an exaggeration. In fact, the records contain very few dismissals of this category – the precise meaning of which is, in any case, by no means certain. The Managers of other Magdalen Asylums too, of course, were anxious to prevent the development of close associations in the Homes. The Dublin Female Penitentiary's Second *Annual Report* for example (1818) notes that wards are sub-divided into Dormitories, allowing the Superintendents to watch and exclude "unprofitable conversations".

the children, to tempt them to do wrong ... Then redouble your vigilance ... Watch them in the chapel; watch them at work; watch them particularly during the hours of recreation. In the dormitories let a lamp, as the Book of Customs prescribes, burn constantly during the night. Let your surveillance extend to everything."[18]

Such strictures, observed until at least the 1960s, are strikingly at odds with the Foundress' views on charity; and dispel completely recent claims that Mother Euphrasia "anticipated by a century the most enlightened thought and practice of contemporary social scientists".[19] The fact is, that however enlightened the Rules may appear by the standards of her day (and the matter is debatable) they were neither appropriate nor acceptable 130 years later, when they were still overwhelmingly in force. By then it was widely recognised that such preoccupations were themselves unhealthy, revealing more about the so-called "carers", than the women they controlled. Far from the nuns being subject to the "espionage" of the "children", the reverse was patently the case.

Total silence was also maintained in the Good Shepherd refectories, with half an hour only being allowed for each of the two main meals. Mother St. Euphrasia warned against those Sisters who, being mortified themselves, were indifferent to the needs of others, and recommended good food for the penitents, which should be properly prepared and served. In the interest of prudence, as well as charity, the women should have no cause for reproach in this matter, and complaints, while not encouraged, should be investigated both for the well-being of the "children" and the reputation of the Homes.[20]

Penitents' food was probably better and more plentiful than that provided in workhouses, where, even in the late nineteenth century, the scale of diet was dismally low.* Doubtless it was an

---

18 *Rules for the Direction of the Classes, op. cit.*, p.138.
19 Dust jacket for the reprint of Gaetan Bernoville, *Saint Mary Euphrasia Pelletier, Foundress of the Good Shepherd Sisters* (1963).
20 *Rules for the Direction of the Classes, op. cit.*, p.144.
*   Even so, the rations of all paupers in workhouses were standardised, and any deviation from the dietary regulations required the approval of the Poor Law Commissioners. The fact that until relatively recently many children in Irish Industrial Schools suffered from malnutrition or were permanently hungry, is not an indication that inmates of Magdalen Asylums were similarly ill-nourished – even though in some cases, the same Religious Orders ran both types of institution. Quite apart from the considerations voiced by the Foundress, the sustained physical labour to which penitents were subjected required that they were adequately fed.

improvement too, on the general diet of many of the country's poor. Nevertheless, the most that could be required from any Female Refuge was that meals should be wholesome, substantial and plain. Inevitably in practice, they were economical and unappetising, served with monotonous regularity and a complete disregard of personal taste. It was urged that the diets and customs of each country be observed, and Mother St. Euphrasia conceded that penitents unable to eat certain dishes should be given alternatives, though on no account should their preferences be consulted, or their caprices indulged. She recommended too, the occasional introduction of little extras, especially on feast days. Such treats, while they pleased the inmates, were also designed "to accomplish gaily, an increase of work". Those "employed at more fatiguing work" (such as the heaviest labour in the laundries) required larger portions; and extra plates should be provided so that penitents' leftovers, could be served them at another meal.[21]

An insistence on plates being cleared was not uncommon, even in the post-Victorian era, but was usually reserved for children. Some penitents, utterly desperate or dejected, refused to eat at all. Such tantrums were regarded as evidence of their disruptive tendencies, their desire for attention and their "nervous" and unsettled state of mind. According to one of Maddison's contributors - the Manager of an English Rescue Home:

> "A sullen temper, often shown by refusing food, is best dealt with by silence. When a girl wakes up to the fact that no one takes any notice, nor is troubled (apparently at least) by her self-starvation, she gets weary of her self-imposed martyrdom and learns sense.[22]

Surviving information on the diet of Irish penitents suggests that in the early period at least, rations were relatively liberal and varied; and similar to those provided in English Homes.[23]. The London Guardian Society, for example, described in its 1823 *Annual Report* the weekly food allowance for each of the females in its Refuge:

---

21 *Rules for the Direction of the Classes, op. cit.,* p.149.
22 Maddison, *op. cit.,* p.152.
23 For food allowances in the Sisters of Charity Magdalen Asylum, Donnybrook, Dublin (1840) see Maria Luddy, *op. cit.,* p.130.

"One quarten loaf and three quarters,
Half a pound of butter,
One ounce of tea,
Half a pound of sugar,
Four pounds of potatoes,
Three ounces of cheese,
Three pounds of meat,
Seven pints of table beer.[24]

And at the end of the century, Maddison's *Hints on Rescue Work* contained the following "model" diet for women employed in Homes.

Breakfast
    7 days: bread, butter and coffee.

Dinner
    3 days: meat and vegetables.
    1 day: meat and plain pudding.
    1 day: pea soup with bread.
    1 day: plum pudding.
    1 day: boiled rice with sweets.

Tea
    7 days: bread and butter.

Supper
    7 days: bread and cheese.[25]

In the early twentieth century the Epiphany Laundry Home (in which the women laboured for fifty-five hours a week and also attended classes) boasted a similar diet for its Laundry workers, with bread, butter, dripping and golden syrup featuring prominently.[26] It is unlikely that Good Shepherd Magdalen Asylums provided better fare, particularly in Ireland in the mid-nineteenth century when the Foundations were established, and

24 *Sixth Report of the Committee of the Guardian Society* (1823) p.22.
25 Maddison, *op. cit.*, p.217.
26 Epiphany Laundry Home Leaflet.

conditions (most notably in the New Ross Home) were at their worst.[27]

The records contain little evidence regarding penitents' daily routine, hours of work, and time allowed for recreation. However, there are indications that they laboured in the laundries for most of the day, that many were exploited in this respect, and that other aspects of their "training" and welfare were sacrificed to this all important role. Education, particularly in Convent Magdalen Asylums, hardly existed - an omission revealed in the *Rules for the Direction of the Classes* and demonstrated in the 1901 Census - details of which are discussed below. This source indicates that in spite of having spent years, sometimes even lifetimes in the Homes, many Good Shepherd penitents were unable to read or write. Large sections of the general population too, of course, were illiterate, and some of the inmates were clearly of the "feeble-minded" or ineducable class. But others, quite capable of learning, were denied the opportunity - a policy particularly indefensible by the beginning of the twentieth century.

Published details of the daily routine in short-term Homes on the other hand, demonstrate that though the women worked long hours education was seriously regarded, reflecting a concern for the women's future welfare and their ability to take up respectable work. As early as 1823, for example, the *Annual Report* of the Guardian Society informed its readers that inmates:

> "rise at half-past Five in Summer, and Seven in Winter; and retire to rest at Ten in Summer and Nine in Winter … Family Worship is performed Morning and Evening; and a portion of every day is devoted to teaching those who cannot read, and to the religious instruction of all; a Sub-Committee of the Ladies pay particular attention to this subject."[28]

Life in the Glasgow and Edinburgh Asylums was similar, with most women working a ten hour day, beginning at 5.30 or 6.00 in the morning. In the former institution, as in the Guardian Society, one hour daily was set aside for the education of inmates unable to read;[29] and in the Lincoln Refuge, from 1849 onwards

---

27 For a discussion of the privations faced both by Sisters and penitents in the New Ross Home in its early years, see Chapter 5.
28 *Guardian Society Annual Report* (1823) p.21.
29 Mahood, *op. cit.*, pp.79-80.

two hours every evening was devoted to teaching the girls to read and write.[30]

Comparable details for the end of the period are included both in Maddison's *Hints on Rescue Work* and the above-mentioned reforming pamphlet *Rescue Work; An Inquiry and Criticism*, which was produced in 1919. As with the diets outlined above, however, these timetables represent ideal situations, they advocate conditions that should, rather than did, prevail. Common to both is a grim attention to detail, a fanatical precision in which "every minute has its appointed task", and the penitent no moment to herself. In 1919, for example, by which time in society at large, many class and sexual restraints were beginning to break down:

> "The routine of a typical working day is as follows: All rise at 6.15 and are in chapel at 6.50; breakfast is at 7.10, then all make their beds and tidy their cubicles. At 7.45 they separate for work, some to the washhouse and laundry and some to the house and kitchen. Silence is observed at work ... At 10.0 they sit down for rest and lunch, work again till one o'clock, when they stop for dinner and recreation. At 2.0 the girls go back to work. At 5.0 comes tea-time, then a second recreation, from 6.0. to 8.0 there is work again; then comes the third recreation time, spent in reading or in Scripture class. Supper at 8.30, and then all go to chapel as in the morning. At 9.20 all go to bed."[31]

Maddison's timetables for resident staff are even more detailed. They indicate that in the best of circumstances, employment in the laundries continued from morning till night, with many inmates, such as those responsible for preparing water and making up fires, beginning work as early as 6.a.m.[32]

In some of the Homes conditions were even worse. "St. Faiths" in Lostwithiel, Cornwall, for example (opened in 1861) was run by Protestant nuns - the Wantage Community of Sisters, from Wantage, Berkshire. Here, penitents had single cells, into which they were locked at night, though the building had no fire escapes. They rose at 5.00 a.m. to attend Chapel, and worked in the laundry from 7.30 in the morning, until eight or even ten

---

30 Lincoln Asylum for Female Penitents, Ladies Minutes, 1849.
31 *Rescue Work, An Inquiry and Criticism, op. cit.*, p.24.
32 Maddison, *op. cit.*, pp.70-71.
     For the British Provincial Good Shepherd timetable in this period, see below, p.196.

o'clock at night.[33] The advice of the country's leading Rescue Society, The Female Mission to the Fallen, was clearly being followed:

> "Plenty of work, with a proportionate amount of rest, is one of the best means of forgetting and redeeming a regrettable past."[34]

The distasteful practice of retaining "hard workers" in the laundries and discouraging their departure - even from short-term Homes - is referred to frequently in the literature, and discussed below. In long-term institutions like the Good Shepherds, such women, often dull-witted and easily prevailed upon, were a vital part of the system. Not surprisingly, these drudges were frequently detained in the Refuges for life.

An even more disturbing aspect of Rescue Work (and particularly that carried out in Ireland and associated with the Good Shepherds) was the long-term consignment of unmarried mothers, and other "first fall" cases, to institutions primarily established for prostitutes undergoing reform. The morality of confining even these "outcasts" to such places, while their male associates retained their freedom, sanity and good name, is questionable and has been referred to above. But the subjection of that other class of females, some of whom had not yet even fallen, but were judged by their families to be in need of protection or restraint, was a policy which is difficult to defend. The overall role of the Good Shepherd Sisters in this process is undoubtedly disturbing, particularly the Order's alarming inflexibility, maintained throughout a century of change.

Unlike the vast majority of Refuges (whose Rules strictly limited to two or at most three years, any penitent's length of stay) the Good Shepherds' goal was the reform of these women, but not necessarily their restoration to society. This is made clear in the Foundress' *Rules* :

> "The greater number of our children we know desire to return to the world. The thought that they will be once more exposed to the danger of going astray ... is a sorrow for a Religious. We should then, make every effort to induce them to remain in the

---

33 Article on "St. Faiths", in the possession of Cornwall County Council Library.
34 *Report of the Female Mission to the Fallen* (1867) p.156.

asylum opened to them by Divine Providence, where they are assured of the grace of a happy death ... The departure of a penitent is generally a misfortune; it causes as much grief as her arrival caused joy."[35]

At local level the Order's Annals too, contain evidence of this wish to keep inmates incarcerated for life, permanently suspended in a non-sexual, child-like state and unnaturally guarded from re-exposure to sin. Even worse is the acknowledged desire - hinted at in the above passage, but more openly expressed elsewhere - to see penitents consigned to a speedy death, once their conversion and state of grace had been achieved.[36]

It was noted above that the Order's rules discouraged all reference to inmates' pasts; and the virtual absence of such information in the Records prevents an analysis of the different categories of women entering the Homes. Other sources, however, indicate that two distinct classes - prostitutes, together with those who had never engaged in the activity - were consigned to, or voluntarily entered the Penitentiaries throughout the whole period. It will be shown in Chapter 6 that in 1876, for example, twenty prostitutes, of the most "degraded" character, were ousted from their brothels by a local priest, and hounded into the Good Shepherd Asylum in Cork. It was further alleged that thirty more of their number joined them over the next few days. This celebrated incident, much exaggerated, was reported in the Convent's Annals and in the local press. It was submitted as evidence before the Select Committee on the Contagious Diseases Acts in 1881-82, and described (much embellished) in both the 1895 and 1933 biographies of the Order's Foundress.[37] Additional evidence of common prostitutes entering the Homes relates to the Contagious Diseases Acts, which, as described in Chapter 6, were fully operational in two districts in Ireland from 1869 to 1883 - Cork (with Queenstown) and the Curragh. During that period all the Good Shepherd Asylums admitted women

---

35 *Rules for the Direction of the Classes, op. cit.,* pp.182-3.
36 See below, particularly p. 170.
37 In the 1933 biography, *Blessed Mary of Saint Euphrasia Pelletier, op. cit.,* this incident was mistakenly set in Waterford and attributed to the "extraordinary zeal" of Father Crotty, a local priest and founder of Ireland's second Good Shepherd Monastery. In fact, the priest in question was Rev. Shinkwin of Cork, in whose parish the women were housed. (See below, pp.180-82.)

direct from the C.D. hospitals in Cork and Kildare - hospitals which catered exclusively for diseased prostitutes registered, and repeatedly examined, under the Acts. In spite of their apparent (and often short-lived) desire to reform, there is no doubt about the background of these women, or their undisputed reputation for being the most hardened and vicious of their kind. Occasionally the Order's Annals too, contain details on this category of inmate. A woman's depraved history is contrasted with her later piety, for example; or is included as evidence of her dramatic conversion, or to account for her unusually remorseful death. Some of this material is illustrated in the following Chapters.

On the other hand, many of the women entering the Homes were not prostitutes, and this was particularly the case with very young girls. Quite apart from their confined association with women of the very worst class, their removal to Penitentiaries and Magdalen Asylums must have been psychologically damaging, and have adversely affected their prospects of leading a relatively normal future life. This was less the case in the English Protestant Homes, where the emphasis was on training for future employment, and where, in any case, the period for undergoing reform rarely exceeded two years. But lack of classification, even in these smaller institutions was, by the end of the century, causing Rescue Workers grave concern. In both types of Refuge, young, relatively innocent girls were indiscriminately mixed with common prostitutes, and inevitably suffered both from the connection itself and by association. Maddison summed up the problem which was clearly based on the need to staff the laundries.

"At the majority of Homes the Managers content themselves with receiving any fallen woman under 30 years of age, [provided she is not pregnant, or with an infant]. The cause of this is not far to seek. The Homes have sprung up without method or design, beyond the desire of the founders to do something to save the perishing. They are mostly unendowed, and are therefore dependent for their maintenance upon two sources of income - voluntary subscriptions, and the profits on the Laundry; and the deficiencies in the former have to be made up by the latter. This can only be done by keeping the number of inmates to a certain point; and so, when there are vacancies, the Institution cannot afford to wait an indefinite time for one particular class of girl, but must accept the most eligible of the applicants seeking admission. All this renders the task of classifying the girls and selecting the best Homes for them very difficult"[38]

Examples from two contrasting sets of records show this absence of classification, and demonstrate the permanent damage such a system could impose. In England, the Lincoln and Lincolnshire Penitent Females Home was established in 1848 to:

> "rescue women who have either fallen or are in danger of falling, and to restore them with God's blessing to paths of virtue by providing them with a "Home" where they are placed under Maternal influence and trained in Moral and Industrial habits and fitted for Domestic Service."

A small Protestant Refuge, it contained about 20 inmates for most of the period. Applicants had to be under twenty-five years of age (most were much younger) and genuinely desirous of reform. After completing a month's probation, inmates were admitted for one year (to be extended in special cases) trained, and "placed" in situations found for them by the Home. This was one of those institutions where girls were sent to the workhouse or hospital on account of pregnancy, and re-admitted if the baby died. The records show that even until well into the twentieth century, there was little discrimination between prostitutes and others. They illustrate too, the extreme youth of many of the girls.

In August 1900 for example, 15 year old Lucy Aberdale was admitted, having been rescued from "bad people" in Nottingham, by a Police Court visitor. Her mother was dead and her father in an asylum. She was a "restless" character and later absconded. In the following year Ellen Johnson, a 14 year old from near Grimsby entered the Home. This girl too was already a prostitute, and was described as having been living in "bad houses" for some time.[39]

Thirteen year old Kate Martha Green, on the other hand, belonged to a different category yet she too was subjected to the

---

38 Maddison, *op. cit.*, p.106.
39 Ladies' Minutes of the Lincoln Penitent Females Home, 1900-1901.

same regime. She was admitted to the Home in July 1909 from Peterborough, having:

> "suffered from her father's misconduct in her own home. The man is now undergoing 20 months hard labour on account of his continued misconduct with her and her sister, of which her mother has been aware. Conduct, very good."[40]

This case illustrates, incidentally, the links between Rescue Work in England and Ireland. It had been anticipated in 1870 that penitents at the Cork Good Shepherd Magdalen Asylum would be found situations as domestic servants in England and America, though in fact, such cases were surprisingly few. Employment in the opposite direction was even less common; but occasionally the wives of Irish landlords supported English Homes. Because of the particular circumstances of her case, Kate Green's stay in the Lincoln Refuge was extended to three years; and in July 1912 she was sent to the large estate of Countess Bessborough at Piltown, County Kilkenny. Here she was appointed 3rd laundry maid for the relatively generous salary of £14 per year.[41] A remarkably similar placement had been made four months earlier to a neighbouring Irish mansion. Sarah Tasker, aged 15, was admitted to the Lincolnshire Home in April 1910, after serving a three week prison sentence for theft. Her mother was dead and her father, a farm labourer, was reputed to be the cause of her sister's pregnancy. After two years' good conduct in the Home, she was sent to Knocklofty - the Co. Tipperary estate of Countess Donoughmore. Here, she was appointed 4th laundry maid, and she too received £14 per year.[42]

These young girls, clearly not prostitutes but the victims of their fathers, were nonetheless confined to a Magdalen Home intended for women of the "fallen" class. Happily, both appear to have benefited from the training and protection they received,

---

40 *Ibid.*, July 1909.
41 *Ibid.* As late as 1920, for example, Rescue Homes reported that outgoing girls taking up employment as under matrons in Laundries, received between £12 and £18 a year; general servants from £12 upwards, and cooks from £18 to £26. *Rescue Work* pamphlet (1920) p.50.
    In 1901 the new revised edition of Mrs. Beeton's *Book of Household Management* recommended a yearly wage of £10 to £15 for an under laundry-maid – dependant, of course, on locality and experience. Isabella Beeton, *The Book of Household Management*, p.7.
42 Lincoln Home Ladies Minutes, *op. cit.*, April, 1910.

and to have made use of the opportunity to take up respectable work.

The experience of Mary Connolly, an Irish girl of similar age and category, however, was less fortunate. In 1871 at the age of 12 she was taken to the Good Shepherd Magdalen Asylum in New Ross, and admitted "for protection", on the recommendation of a local priest. Sixty-one years later (by which time she was seventy-three years old) she left the Enclosure for the first time. She went as housekeeper to her niece, but returned after a year. She died in the Home in March, 1941, aged 82.[43] It is possible that she too, far from being a prostitute, was a victim of actual or potential incest. Unlike the two previous cases, however, this woman became totally institutionalised, condemned to confinement lasting almost seventy years, and suffering the surveillance, discipline and fierce indoctrination detailed above. And in contrast to the Lincoln girls whose fellow penitents - whatever their backgrounds - were at least young, short-term inmates, chosen for their "suitability" for reform; twelve year-old Mary Connolly was confined with women of every age and disposition, and whose only qualification was their submission to the Home. A victim rather than a "sinner", she was nonetheless sentenced to a lifetime of remorse.

It is clear from detailed analysis of Good Shepherd penitents (provided in the following Chapters devoted to each Home) that this girl's history is far from unique. Practically all Female Penitentiaries admitted mixed categories. Unlike the Good Shepherds, however, the amount of harm most other Refuges inflicted was limited - in duration at least. It was curtailed by regulations governing inmates' length of stay.

The Good Shepherds not only allowed, they encouraged inmates to remain, detaining them if possible for life. They admitted the depraved, as well as those in "moral danger"; and accepted without scruple, unwanted family members, and women certainly not of the prostitute class. They placed no age limit on entrants, and were willing to receive even "hopeless" cases, who left and re-entered, drifting aimlessly from one Asylum to the next.[44]

---

43 Penitents' Register, Good Shepherd Asylum, New Ross, 5 March 1871.
44 Most lay Refuges refused to re-admit women after they had left. Rule 9 of the London Female Penitentiary, for example, stated: "No woman, after having been discharged, shall be received into the Penitentiary a second time, under any account or pretence whatever."

This willingness to receive every type of applicant (unless pregnant) regardless of character, age or physical condition was remarkable. Many of these women were disturbed and difficult cases, with alcoholism or insanity no doubt affecting those described in the Registers as "demented", "violent" or "mad". Such women had nowhere to turn, and without the Good Shepherds their future was bleak. Some would have sunk in an activity they clearly wished to leave; while others, destitute and at risk from their families, might well have eventually descended to a life of shame. These considerations, and the fact that the Good Shepherds sheltered the abandoned - on society's behalf - must be taken into account. Nevertheless their acknowledgement should not prevent a critical analysis of the Homes, nor seek to minimise the damage done to thousands of women (many of them detained against their will) in the name of religion, and with society's support.

The Good Shepherd policy of admitting all classes of penitent to every Refuge blighted the prospects of hopeful cases and endangered the future of those with least to atone for in their past. For regardless of why they entered the institutions in the first place, the stigma of having been in a Magdalen Home (whose very name denoted its purpose) dogged most women leaving. Former inmates were shunned by respectable society and considered "fair game" by those inclined to vice. By all who knew their past they were regarded with suspicion, and seen as a source of cheap exploitable labour, or worse. Consequently, many penitents succumbed to pressures to remain, while others were so demoralised that having left, their re-admission was inevitable. The policy was flawed even further by a virtual absence of internal classification, resulting in a standard treatment for inmates, whatever the reason for their stay. In contrast, as has been seen, well before the end of the century Managers of English Refuges - aware of the need for such distinctions - favoured smaller specialist Homes, each catering for women and girls of a particular class.

Admittedly, "Consecrated" penitents who acted as auxiliaries to the nuns (a system in operation in each of the Good Shepherd Refuges and described below) allowed for some measure of sub-division. Except in the laundries and other workrooms, however, where ability would have been a determining factor, it is difficult to know on what grounds classification could have been based;

and there is no evidence to suggest that it actually occurred. In any case, no matter what the extent of sub-division, the *Rules* excluded its being linked to "reason for entry" - a subject forbidden to both penitents and nuns.

The most damaging aspect of non-classification was not, in fact, the mixing of categories, undesirable though this undoubtedly was. For here, the effects were minimised by the Foundress' Rules on surveillance, which were drawn up specifically to prevent intimacies, the emergence of "party spirit" and private conversations of any kind. The real evil lay in uniformity of treatment - an unavoidable consequence of such a system. Punitive measures, designed to control the most depraved of women, were applied indiscriminately to all. This is apparent in the Foundress' insistence on the Rule of Silence, for example, her excuse for its enforcement being that it made "good" penitents more virtuous, while preventing "dissipation" amongst the bad.

Implicit throughout the *Rules* is the assumption that penitents are not responsible beings. The extracts already quoted illustrate this point. Consequently, as we have seen, no matter how advanced their age, whatever their marital status, and regardless of their previous way of life, for over a century the women were referred to as "children". Collectively, even in the laundries where they laboured incessantly, and which were the Sisters' main support, they and their activities were referred to as the "class". And penitents were compelled to address all nuns of the Order as "Mother" - a practice not discontinued until 1971.[45] Far from being regarded as degrading or objectionable, this regulation was highlighted in 1931 as a merit of the system. Part of the following passage, written to commemorate the building of the Order's new Chapel in Limerick in that year, concluded the previous Chapter.

> "We cannot fail to notice on entering a Good Shepherd Convent the beautiful spirit that prevails between the Sisters and the unfortunate women to whose rescue and welfare they have devoted their lives ... they show the most degraded of their sex that same sweetness and forbearance which He displayed ... And so much indeed have the Sisters won the grateful affection of those entrusted to their care that they are universally styled as

---

45 "The custom of calling us "Mother" by our girls and children has been discontinued. They now address us as "Sister". Cork Annals, 1971.

"Mothers," while on the other hand, the Sisters always speak of the penitents as their "children". It may be only a white-veiled novice with no vows as yet; and it may be an old white-haired penitent giving back to God but the dregs of a life spent in sin. It matters not. In the Home of the Good Shepherd the one is ever the "Mother" while the other is always the "Child".[46]

This imposition of childhood is apparent too, in the nuns' own records (most notably in the *Rules* of the Foundress) in the harsh discipline to which the women were subjected, and in the fact that they were constantly watched. To some extent this was the case in other Homes too, but since Good Shepherd penitents were neither equipped nor encouraged to leave, for many inmates, childhood endured into old age. Not surprisingly those remaining in the Homes for lengthy periods were adversely affected, progressively institutionalised with every long-term stay. Indeed, the records indicate that the more protracted the initial "rescue", the greater was the risk of permanent dependence on the Homes. Eighteen year old Nora Gallaher, for example, was "brought" by her aunt to the Limerick Asylum in February 1877; and "sent out" during a Retreat ten years later. After an interval of two years she was re-admitted, and though "Addicted to particular friendships for years", she died "most happily" in the Home in September 1939, having served 62 years penance.[47]

Continued emphasis on sin and remorse must have further damaged the women; and in spite of the Foundress' lip-service to charity, the detection of evil and an awareness of guilt was obsessively urged. Doubtless some women's behaviour required harsh measures - the Registers listing many of them as "bad spirit", "prone to evil", "deceitful" and "sly". Others, however, were "docile", "meek", "obedient" or "good"; and morbid talks like the following, especially recommended by the Foundress, were not only unwarranted, but positively harmful for those who were depressed, suicidal, or anxious to do well.

"Another day you can speak to them in an instruction of the great evil of sin, and the suffering we have to endure in purgatory; and

---

46 Rev. Kerr, *op. cit.*, p.10.
47 Names of Penitents Received Since the Foundation of the Monastery of the Good Shepherd, Limerick, 21 February 1877.

dwell upon how fortunate we are to be able to save ourselves from this suffering by practising mortification in this world."[48]

For women not contemplating the religious life, the prospect of total confinement in such institutions must have been daunting. It may well be that those who were "saved" until released by death, were more to be pitied than those who remained unrescued, and destitute, outside.

Women who entered the Homes voluntarily, of course (though the alternatives they faced must qualify the notion of "free will") retained some possibility of leaving. Legally, as was the case with all the penitents, they could not be restrained against their will, and in theory at least, they could quit the Asylums whenever they chose. The records indicate, however, that at the very least inmates could be pressured into postponing departure (until seeing the priest, for example) during which time every effort was made to persuade or frighten them into a change of mind. Such methods had been common practice from the Order's beginnings. We are told that at the Mother House in Angers for example:

> "Mother Pelletier had a wonderful ascendancy over sinners. How often it happened that a poor child had been bent on returning whence she came. The Mistress had used every argument to induce her to remain in safety. As a last resource Mother Pelletier would send for the misguided one, and with that penetrating look of hers, and a few brief but kind words, would quell the dangerous desire."[49]

At other times "one or other of the penitents" went to her and begged repeatedly to be allowed to leave:

> "Our Mother would not give her consent; gently and firmly she represented to the poor girl that her only chance of safety was to remain here; that were she to leave, she would infallibly lose her soul. Her words never proved wrong. Those who listened to her kindly warning, found her prediction come true; some died a holy death, others are still amongst us, having consecrated themselves to God for the remainder of their days."[50]

---

48   *Rules for the Direction of the Classes, op. cit.,* p.146.
49   *Blessed Mary of Saint Euphrasia, op. cit.,* pp.113-14.
50   A. M. Clarke, *op. cit.,* p.359.

Such scenes undoubtedly occurred too, in short-term Protestant Homes - though with less tragic results - one Superintendent of a Refuge reporting to Maddison in the 1890s:

> "When a girl desires to go, she asks to see me, states her reason, and her *unreason* . I exhort her, persuade, entreat, and warn to the best of my power. Sometimes she will give in at once, and one thus perceives she was craving for a little extra attention or sympathy; sometimes, when I have exhausted myself with talking, the answer still comes, 'Please, I wish to go'. Then the Warden sees her, tries what he can do, and often succeeds; but if we all fail, there is nothing left but to let the poor wanderer go on her own wilful way once more. It is wonderful the pleading they will sometimes resist; lady after lady will (during the four days' notice which we expect from them in order to prevent their acting on impulse) find opportunities of trying to win back the wayward creature, but in vain. 'Yes', she will say, 'I know it is all for my good, and it's very kind of you, but I ain't a-going to stop.' "[51]

Even more exposed to a lifetime of penance than those who had entered the Asylums voluntarily, however, was that vast category of inmates (about fifty per cent of the total over the period analysed) who were neither "recommended" nor entered the Good Shepherds, "of their own accord". They were "brought" to the institutions - by priests, relatives, or friends; but how unwillingly, and under what constraints they were kept in the Homes, will never be known. Many of these were undoubtedly ignorant of their legal status, with very young inmates, and increasing numbers of "simple minded" women being especially vulnerable in this respect. According to the records, various penitents "absconded", "scaled the wall" or "ran away" - evidence not only of their enforced confinement, but their desperate state of mind. Such escapes, defying constant surveillance, locked doors and high boundary walls, risked punishment if unsuccessful. Analysis of the way in which women left the Homes shows that only 3 percent of those for whom such information is recorded quitted the Good Shepherds in this way. There is no indication of how many women failed in such attempts, or what happened to those who were caught.

---

51 Maddison, *op. cit.*, p.129.

This illegal detention of women continued for more than a century. In 1970 the *Reformatory and Industrial Schools Systems Report*, for example, (referred to hereafter as the Kennedy Report) observing that 70 girls between the ages of 13 and 19 were currently detained in Convent Magdalen Homes by the Courts, commented that the legal validity of this procedure was doubtful. If these official cases were questionable, what of the many older women still in the Homes at that time? Women who had been placed in the Asylums many years earlier (by their families or priests rather than the State) and who continued to be improperly detained? And what of the thousands of others over the period who, for varying lengths of time, had been held against their will?

An awareness of their rights would hardly have affected those conditioned to their treatment and taught to view themselves as lost. And as for former inmates – those survivors of the system who had returned to the world - few wished to draw attention to their past. Ashamed and dispirited, they lacked the confidence, the education and support to make themselves heard. Even had they done so, it is doubtful if a public so indifferent, so prepared to tolerate the system in the first place, would have intervened on their behalf. If, as has been demonstrated by recent exposures of brutality and abuse, charges against Religious Orders were systematically suppressed as late as the nineteen-eighties and widely disbelieved a decade later, it is unlikely that in an earlier period credence would have been given to such a discredited group. Finally, fear of the police who sometimes returned girls to the institutions added to the silence which generally surrounded the Homes.[52]

Nevertheless, the idea that society was blameless - that Magdalen Asylums were so shrouded in secrecy that the public was unaware of what was taking place - is a myth. These vast institutions, though forbidding and inaccessible, were part of the community from which they emerged. They were founded in response to local conditions and demands for reform; and the success with which funds were raised and laundry orders received, reveals a system both supported and approved. A conspiracy of silence may have marked the disappearance of individual women; and the fact that others were permanently lost sight of, may have

---

52 Evidence of the police acting in this way has been well documented in recent autobiographical accounts of life in these institutions. See particularly *Suffer the Little Children, op. cit.*

been attributed to "emigration", for example, by relatives resolved to hide their shame.* Undoubtedly too, practices within the Homes advanced this process, or at the very least, allowed it to occur. The assignment of new names, the discouragement of external contacts, and strict rules forbidding all reference to the women's pasts, obscured their identities, blurring the existence of those who had been put away. For many of the women, denied or disowned by their families, an alarming anonymity prevailed, and to the outside world at least, they had almost ceased to exist. Whatever the extent of such practices, however, and regardless of how hushed-up these institutions were; the reality is that society – the world outside – continued to furnish Magdalen laundries and their Convents with both penitents and nuns. The purpose of these institutions was clearly accepted, approved of, and very widely known. Prostitutes, and later unmarried mothers, were openly targeted, and until very recently parents corrected their children with the threat of Magdalen Homes. Laundry advertisements emphasised the penitential aspect of these Refuges, and annual sermons and newspaper articles repeatedly appealed for funds. Above all, of course, and most conclusively, much of the country's washing was taken to these Convents; with no-one supposing it was laundered by the nuns. Advertisements such as the following, appearing in 1895, 1931 and 1932, are quite explicit:

"The Magdalen Asylum Laundry. [Waterford]
The Community of the Good Shepherd beg to inform the public that in the new Magdalen Asylum Laundry, under their care, washing is done most carefully and satisfactorily as can be testified by the gentry of both County and City. The Community earnestly solicit the County and City Clubs, and also private families to send their washing, as the work in the Laundry at present is not sufficient to keep the penitents employed, and is besides, inadequate for the maintenance of the daily increasing numbers who make application for admission. The Magdalen Asylum Laundry van will call to any place in and around the City for washing, and will deliver it in due time when done."[53]

---

*   This is also alleged to have occurred with "insane" individuals, secretly deposited in mental institutions from which they would never emerge. At least in their case, however, there was some semblance of safeguard, since a doctor's signature was required before committal could take place.

53   *The Waterford Chronicle*, 14 December 1895.

"Convent of the Good Shepherd, Limerick.
The Religious of the Good Shepherd ask pleadingly for the patronage of the kind public for their Laundry. It is the sole means of support for over 150 poor penitents, sheltered and cared for without other grant or means than what their own Industries afford them. High-Class Laundry Work. Gentlemen's Collars a Speciality. Hair Mattresses Re-Made."[54]

"The Magdalen Asylum,
Lower Gloucester St., Dublin.
The charitable are asked to kindly remember the above Institution. It shelters one hundred and twenty-five penitents, who pray several times daily for their benefactors, living and dead. Persons making their WILLS are earnestly requested to remember this truly Charitable Institution, which is still heavily in debt."[55]

Finally, no matter how enclosed these institutions were, outsiders other than priests and doctors were occasionally employed. Particularly in the later period, laundry equipment, for example, required maintenance, and workmen such as electricians (under constant observation) were necessarily admitted to the Homes. Inevitably, rumours circulated, and speculation was rife. Stories persisted of girls being put in the Good Shepherds and never re-emerging, and records of life-time confinements, as well as recent autobiographical accounts, confirm this popular view.

Also confined for life, the nuns too, of course, were institutionalised; but these women, who exercised such power over their charges, command little sympathy. Theirs was a self-imposed exile, from a world which revered, rather than rejected them - they were exalted, rather than despised. These were not grieving, post-natal mothers, frantic for their babies and made cruelly conscious of their shame. Nor were they made to feel self-loathing and disgust. On the contrary, they were "angelic" - "perpetual virgins", whose salvation was secure. They were supreme even amongst other female Religious since, as the public was informed in 1931:

---

54 *The Fold of the Good Shepherd, op. cit.*
55 *The Irish Independent Eucharistic Congress Souvenir Number,* 1932, p.91.

"... The order of the Good Shepherd most closely approaches the ideal ... to reclaim the outcast, to raise up the fallen, to seek out the lost sheep - the "sinful women" of our time - never so numerous and never so sinful as to-day; to inspire hope in hearts that had despaired of purity and pardon; to stretch out a helping hand to souls sunk in the lowest depths of sin and vice, and raise them to the heights of penitent love - that, we think, is the most Christ-like work of all."[56]

---

56 Rev. Kerr, *op. cit.*, p.9.

3

The Good Shepherd Magdalen Asylum, Limerick

Limerick's original Magdalen Asylum was opened in 1826 by Rev. Maurice Fitzgibbon of St. Michael's parish. Situated in Newgate Lane, it was managed by a Mrs. Meade; and prostitutes sometimes entered the Refuge from the nearby city jail.

Shortly afterwards, the penitents were moved to a more suitable premises on the site in Clare Street that would eventually house the Provincial Monastery of the Congregation of the Good Shepherd. A Miss Reddan, the owner of an adjoining property, is regarded as the foundress of this small lay Refuge, since she established a Rule for the inmates, and provided a laundry for their support. By the early 1840s the Home was probably operating on similar lines to those of Rev. Dowley's Refuge in Waterford (discussed in the following Chapter) opened in 1842. Certainly, both sets of penitents were subsequently to have difficulty adjusting to the Good Shepherd take-over, which suggests that in Limerick, as in Waterford, the women had been accustomed to a less repressive rule. This is indicated both in the Limerick Annals, and in the 1933 Biography of the Foundress, which notes that the Order's first eighteen months in Limerick:

> "saw strenuous work; a house, formerly a factory acquired, land obtained for further extension, and the penitents formed to a stricter regime than they had been accustomed to in the days that were gone."[1]

Although occupied with Rescue Work, Miss Reddan had for some time been drawn to the Mercy Order, and wished to become a

---

1 *Blessed Mary of Saint Euphrasia, op. cit.*, p.332.

nun. In this she had been discouraged or possibly forbidden, by the Bishop of Limerick, Dr. Ryan, who believed that without her assistance and property, the penitents would be dispersed. During a visit to London in the mid 1840s, however, she became familiar with the work of the Good Shepherd Sisters in Hammersmith, whose Convent had recently been established under its first Superior, Mother Mary of St. Joseph Regaudiat. Miss Reddan was convinced that this Order should take over her Limerick Refuge, and eventually secured the approval of the Bishop. A successful application was made to the Angers Mother House, and on 18th February 1848, three Sisters - the Foundresses of the Good Shepherd Mission in Ireland - arrived in Limerick. The repercussions for Irish society were far reaching, as the French Order was to be the driving force in the country's Magdalen Movement for almost a century and a half.

Mother Mary of the Visitation Smith (a native of Preston, Lancashire) was Prioress of the Convent of St. Omer in France when she was named Superior of the Irish Monastery. Sister Mary of St. Magdalen Holden was transferred from the same Convent; and Sister Mary of St. Agnes was selected from the Hammersmith Home.

Determined to keep her property under his own influence, the Bishop now pressed Miss Redden to join the Good Shepherds rather than the Mercy nuns; and she dutifully became a postulant. This proved so unsuccessful that she was eventually allowed to enter the Mercy Convent in Kinsale. After being professed she founded a House in San Francisco where she soon afterwards died.[2]

Meanwhile the Limerick Sisters had acquired an abandoned weaving factory and some land adjacent to Miss Reddan's property in Clare Street. Part of this factory was converted to a chapel; and from that time onwards, the penitents, like the Sisters, were completely enclosed. The Annals record that in the early days, though respectful to the Sisters, the girls had difficulty in adjusting to the new regime. Soon however, by their "regularity, piety, industry and truly extraordinary spirit of penance", they became a great source of consolation to the nuns.[3]

---

2   A. M. Clarke, *op. cit.*, p.304.
3   Typescript of Annals of the Limerick Good Shepherd, p.5.

After eighteen months in Ireland Mother Mary of the Visitation Smith was recalled to Angers, and appointed Superior of the Convent in St. Louis, Mississippi. She survived in this difficult post for less than two years and died in March, 1852. She was replaced in Limerick by Mother Mary of St. Louis de Baligand, a member of the Bavarian aristocracy, and "a valuable addition" to the Congregation, which she had entered when aged only sixteen. According to the Annals, soon after her arrival the new Superior introduced embroidery and lace work for the most able penitents, a young Belgian lace-maker Emilie Van Neuvenhoven being imported to instruct the girls. Fearing the effects of competition from an Irish-based industry, the Belgian Government sent an emissary to recall the young woman, but since she was found to be already "clothed in the Habit of the Congregation", she was left in peace.[4]

During this period the Order was expanding as rapidly as its individual Foundations, and there were already fifty-three Good Shepherd Convents established by the end of 1854. The recruitment of Novices could hardly keep pace with these developments, yet in spite of the strains on the Mother House its Foundress resisted demands for change. By this time many Bishops outside France, including Cardinal Wiseman of Westminster, wanted Novices trained in their own jurisdictions. In response to pressure Rome advised a division of the Institute into Provinces, a direction which, though unwelcome, could hardly be opposed by the Foundress since the Order came under the sole jurisdiction of the Holy See. While the debate was in progress Cardinal Wiseman urged the Hammersmith Sisters to break completely with Angers. Mother St. Euphrasia, alarmed at the prospect of a total detachment of the English Houses (now including Convents in East Finchley, Glasgow and Bristol) was forced to make an important concession. While the Mother General retained her right to appoint all Provincials, and equally important, to name the Superior of every House, the Cardinal would select England's Provincial himself. He named Mother

---

4   *Ibid.* Emilie Van Neuvenhoven (Sister Mary of St. Philomena) was listed on the 1901 Census, and at 80 years of age was the oldest Good Shepherd nun then in the Convent and the Province. The Census also records that of the 101 inmates in the Magdalen Asylum, only 3 were engaged in lace-making, the majority of the remainder being classed as laundry workers. See below, page 80.

Mary of St. Aloysius Fillit, of the Hammersmith Covent, Provincial for the Monasteries of Great Britain and Ireland. Since Superiors holding such office were now required to visit the Houses under them at stated intervals, she made her first visit to Limerick in 1856.[5]

In 1860 Mother Mary of St. Louis de Baligand was appointed Superior for Aix-la-Chapelle, her illustrious position being indicated by the fact that her journey (on which she was accompanied by her spiritual director, Rev. Dr. Meechan) was paid for by her admirer the Earl of Dunraven. Her successor was Mother Mary of the Immaculate Conception Lockwood, a wealthy English convert to Catholicism, who was appointed from the Glasgow Monastery where she had been Superior for six years.

Following the foundation of the Order's third Irish Monastery (New Ross in Co. Wexford) Ireland became a separate Province in 1860, with the Limerick Convent as Provincial House. In spite of this elevation, however, there was clearly some resistance from Angers, particularly concerning the training of Novices. The Limerick Annals record that with many good vocations being lost to the Congregation through parents and spiritual directors opposing the training of postulants abroad, requests for an Irish Novitiate became ever more pressing. The eventual naming in 1861 of the Limerick Monastery as Provincial Novitiate, ensured that by the late eighteen-sixties, Irish Houses could be staffed by Irish Sisters, trained at home.

These changes undoubtedly affected relations between the Irish and English Provinces, now no longer linked; and between the Irish Province and Angers. Possibly too, it changed the outlook and direction of the Irish Order, which, exposed to fewer external influences, seems to have become more narrowly inclined. The repercussions of this process inevitably filtered down to the penitents, affecting attitudes to them and the treatment they received.

5   Typescript of Limerick Annals; and *Blessed Mary of Saint Euphrasia, op. cit.*
The Irish Province, which at the time of her death in 1868 had Monasteries in Limerick, Waterford, New Ross and Belfast, was never visited by Mother St. Euphrasia Pelletier. In 1844 she had journeyed to England for a ten day visit to the Convent in Hammersmith - which, in spite of uncertain beginnings, was by then doing well. As noted in Chapter 5, the apprehension with which the new Mission was regarded in Angers is evident from the fact that in November 1840 its two founding Sisters were obliged to resort to secular dress before leaving France. Four years later the Mother Foundress refused to take such a precaution.

Unlike the other Irish Houses, which were all to be located on the outskirts of towns and capable of easy expansion, early development at the Limerick Convent was hampered by shortage of space. Within four years of the Founding Sisters' arrival, the Community had increased to eight; and it was necessary to build eleven cells, a small infirmary, a hall and a parlour for the use of the nuns. By the mid eighteen-fifties, it was the penitents' accommodation that caused concern. There were already 75 women in the Home, yet further expansion seemed impossible. The only ground available had been ear-marked for the new Chapel - the existing structure being "excessively overcrowded" and inappropriate for its use. To overcome this difficulty Mother Louis de Baligand decided to "excavate deeply", and build the refectory, kitchen and other rooms needed for the "girls", under the proposed new Church. This work was begun in 1857 and completed in 1859.

However convenient for the Order (the plan was "pronounced a success by all") for the confined and work-driven women this semi-underground existence, even for part of the day, must have been grim. Worse was to come. Also in 1859 the Irish Order's first extra-Magdalen activity, St. Joseph's Reformatory School for girls was opened. The absence of available accommodation proved no obstacle to a Community bent on availing itself of such a profitable line. Since the young offenders were funded by the Government, their quarters required official approval, and were subject (in theory at least) to periodic inspection and control. With no such regulations applying to the penitents, who, as "voluntary" cases, were not supported by the State, the new venture resulted in the women having to change their quarters in favour of the new category. Such upheaval:

> "Caused even greater hardship and inconvenience to the Sisters working in the Class, but all suffered cheerfully, and another piece of land was acquired with a view to future building."[6]

It would seem that the women too, were inconvenienced, as within a decade of these developments the hardship they were caused affected their health. Between January 1860 and

---

6   Typescript of Limerick Annals, p.8.

December 1869, 225 penitents were admitted to the Limerick Asylum, some of them on more than one occasion. During this period, 31 of these admissions (14 per cent of the total) were either sent out to hospital, or died in the Home after a relatively short stay. Others, having entered in the previous decade, were also sent to hospital or left through ill health during these years. Nineteen year old Margaret Lynch from Galway, for example, left for hospital soon after her arrival in May 1860;[7] Mary Gubbins, a 24 year old Limerick woman who entered in June 1861 was later "sent to the union hospital";[8] and two other young penitents - Joanne Farrell aged 18 from Co. Limerick, and Eliza Fitzgerald aged 21 from Co. Cork - each of whom had been registered in July 1861, suffered the same fate.[9] Catherine Hayes aged 20, was admitted in July 1862 and died at Barrington's Hospital within a year; and three weeks after being registered in the Home in October 1862, eighteen year old Bridget Walsh from Tipperary, was sent to the union hospital.[10] A Limerick girl, Bridget Hastings aged 18, left for the hospital in June 1863 after a stay of one month; and 16 year old Mary Kennedy from Ennis, was sent to hospital in November 1863 after 5 months in the Home. The detention of Margaret O'Brien aged 19 from Carlow, was even shorter. She was sent to the workhouse hospital in August, 1863, after only 10 days.[11] A 28 year old penitent Margaret Molloy, was sent to hospital in May 1865 having spent three years in the Home; and in the following year (April 1866) after slightly more than a year in the Home, 20 year old Rose Crowley also left for the hospital.[12] Seven months later, 33 year old Winifred Broderick from Galway, and 19 year old Ellen Ryan from Limerick were both sent to hospital, each having been in the Home for only six months; and in May 1868, 28 year old Kate Hartigan of Cork went to hospital after one year's penance.[13] Nineteen year old Anne Browne of Limerick was admitted to the Home in January 1868, and some time afterwards was "sent to St. John's Hospital"; and Bridget Daven,

---

7   Limerick Register of Penitents, 7 May 1860.
8   *Ibid.,* 17 June 1861.
9   *Ibid.,* 21 and 23 July, 1861. The particular hospital to which these two women were sent is not recorded.
10 *Ibid.,* July and 10 October 1862.
11 *Ibid.,* 20 May, 18 June and 23 July 1863.
12 *Ibid.,* 5 May 1862 and 3 March 1865.
13 *Ibid.,* 3 and 27 May 1866, and 29 May 1867.

a 30 year old woman from Queenstown admitted in July 1866, went to hospital 9 months later.[14] Thirty year old Catherine Flannigan from Glin was another short-term penitent. She was sent to hospital in August 1868 after five months in the Home.[15]

In the following year Mary Kennedy from Ennis, now aged 17, returned to the Home and was sent to hospital after 2 months; 20 year old Kate Ford from Waterford required hospital treatment after only 5 days; and 27 year old Eliza Donaven, admitted in December 1869, was later sent to hospital.[16] Three women were sent straight from the Home to the nearby Lunatic Asylum. Twenty-seven year old Mary Scanlon from Kerry was transferred in May 1862, after a stay of less than a month; 24 year old Mary Hayes was transferred in April 1865 after sixteen months, and Sarah O'Neill, a 17 year old from Dublin was transferred in April 1867 after spending seven months in the Home. All three were recommended to the Penitentiary by priests.[17]

Other women died in the Home. Admitted to the Refuge before the arrival of the Good Shepherd Sisters,[18] both Mary Wolfe and Abbey O'Lairy, for example, died of consumption in 1862; and in 1864 the same disease carried off two other early penitents, Honoria Hewson and Maryanne Godfrey. Also in 1864 Margaret Ryan died in the Refuge from "throwing up blood". She had been sent to the Home from Limerick workhouse sixteen years earlier when she was aged thirty-four.[19]

---

14 *Ibid.*, 3 January 1868 and 3 July 1866.
15 *Ibid.*, 5 March 1868.
16 *Ibid.*, 15 February, 3 August and 15 December 1869.
17 *Ibid.*, 3 April 1862, 19 December 1863 and 27 September 1866.
18 The Registration of the pre-Good Shepherd penitents is complicated by the Order's take-over in 1848. The first Register begins 1 May 1828, and is titled "Names of the Penitents who were in the Magdalen Asylum Before the Sisters of the Good Shepherd Took up the Charge". Following entry number 218, the Register is titled, "Names of Penitents who were in the Magdalen Asylum when the Sisters of the Good Shepherd took up the charge, 1848". This section ends in 1847 with entry 248. From this point, the Register (beginning again at No. 1) is entitled, "Names of Penitents Received Since the Foundation of the Monastery of the Good Shepherd Limerick 1848" - the last entry in this book being 16 December 1879. Register No. 2 covers the period December 1879 to 9 March 1909 - the final entry in this book being No. 2,686. A total of approximately 3,000 women were thus admitted to the Home during the eighty year period. An additional "Entrance Book of Penitents" for the early Refuge contains some information not transferred to the Good Shepherd Registers. That for Abbey O'Lairy, admitted in 1840, and Margaret Ryan, admitted in 1848, occurs in this source. For the above five women the year, but not the month or day of registration is recorded.
19 *Ibid.* Mary Wolfe was admitted in 1844, Honora Hewson in 1837 and Maryanne Godfrey in 1846.

In most cases, however, cause of death was not given. Nineteen year old Kate Davern from Tipperary, for example, was admitted in July 1862, and 37 year old Bessie Lawlor from Wexford in April 1864. The records merely state that they died in the House - presumably shortly afterwards.[20] Joanne Smith from Limerick was admitted in November 1860, and died in March 1863, when she was only 27.[21] Two other women survived only 3 years' penance, both of them aged 29 when they died - Mary Robinson from Limerick (in April 1865) and Mary Keating of Tipperary, (in April 1866).[22] Twenty year old Marie Derze (?) from Listowel, Co. Kerry was admitted in June 1864. She died in the Home after less than three years; and Mary Quinlan, an 18 year old when admitted in 1868, died 14 years later when she was still only 32.[23]

It is clear that some of these women were ill on arrival, their departure for the union hospital in particular, indicating pregnancy or venereal disease. Nevertheless, the number of deaths in the institution during this decade, and the frequency with which women left for hospital was unusually high; and poor accommodation may well have been a contributory factor. Ill-health and depression were inevitable in such a system. In Limerick (and later in the New Ross and Waterford Homes) eventual improvements to the penitents' living quarters, or the provision of entirely new accommodation, eased the women's lot. Essentially, however, their lives were hardly changed. They continued in absolute confinement, the young, the middle-aged and the elderly; sleeping in huge silent dormitories, forbidden to speak and under the surveillance of a nun. Likewise, the introduction of modern laundry equipment (often the most up-to-date in the country) - though installed to maximise profits and resulting in a greater flow of work, must nevertheless, have lightened the women's load. Such changes, however, were small compensation for the stripping of sexuality and the loss of a normal life.

It was widely believed in the later nineteenth century that women of this class were less sensitive to pain than were their more virtuous sisters. The influential Dr. William Acton had

---

20 Limerick Register of Penitents, 12 July 1862 and 29 April 1864.
21 *Ibid.*, November 1860.
22 *Ibid.*, 9 May 1862 and 2 May 1863.
23 *Ibid.*, 2 June 1864, and 17 April 1868.

endowed their kind with "iron bodies"; and it was generally observed that "the fallen", possessed none of the "finer" feelings attributed to others of their sex.[24] We know little of the penitents in the Limerick Magdalen Asylum, nor why they entered such a Home. There is no reason to suppose, however, that women pressed into giving up their babies, deprived of a normal existence and tormented with the enormity of their sin, were less inclined to grieve, less prone to despair and less subject to ill-health, than were other victims of the so-called "Rescue" movement. For a few of these women, detailed evidence occasionally survives, and some of this material appears in Chapters 5 and 6. The Foundress' own comment on ill-health is revealing:

> "See that no one is ill without the Mistress knowing it; and when they are suffering, do not exact from them the same amount of work." [25]

It will be shown that each of the Good Shepherd Monasteries in Ireland was established with only between three to five nuns, a practice normal in this period of the Order's history. As penitent numbers increased, and the work diversified, more Sisters were required both to set up new Foundations, and to staff existing Homes. Following Ireland's Provincial status Convents all over the world (and particularly Australia) gained from the new Novitiate. Initially, however, it was the Irish Foundations that benefited most, and their expansion can be traced by the numbers of Sisters in individual Houses over the period.

We have seen that a group of only three nuns founded the Limerick Monastery in 1848. By 1901 there were 79 Religious

---

24 For a summary of Acton's attitudes see Finnegan, *op. cit.*, pp.2-6.
   In the Irish context, Cork Priest Rev. Maguire had this to say on the highly controversial fortnightly examinations to which registered prostitutes were subjected: "I cannot fancy that for a woman who goes and barters away her virtue and commits all sorts of excess, there is any degradation, because there is no limit to the vile excess which women are driven to." *Royal Commission op. cit.*, 6 May 1871. As noted below, he was probably the most misogynistic of the witnesses giving evidence. Reporting to the Select Committee of Enquiry eleven years later, on the other hand, J. B. Kingston, a Protestant Rescue Worker from Cork, gave the opinion of two local prostitutes: "One of them said to me that they had a great fight to get her on the table, and now that they had succeeded in that she did not care what end became of her. Another said, not three weeks ago, that she was taken over to the hospital ... to undergo an examination; and now she said she had just as soon be dead, because it was the most disgusting thing she ever knew."
   Select Committee, op. cit., 1882 (2531).
25 *Rules for the Direction of the Classes, op. cit.*, p.160.

listed on the Census, some of these being Novices (see below). The Waterford Foundation began in 1858 with 5 Sisters. By 1901, with four separate Sections in the Enclosure, there were 38 nuns. New Ross too, had started with 5 Sisters, and by 1901 there were 26 listed on the Census. Belfast, originating with 3 Sisters in 1867, housed 26 by 1911[26]; and finally, the Cork Monastery, starting off with 4 Sisters in 1870, contained 39 by the end of the century.

How many of these women, who had been drawn to the particular work of the Institute, and had contracted to "labour in a special manner for the conversion of sinners", were actually working with the "fallen"? The answer is, surprisingly few. Many Good Shepherd Sisters, in fact, had virtually no contact with the penitents; and in spite of their fourth vow and their attraction to the work, were assigned to other roles. Few, of course, were appointed to that Office of supreme importance, First Mistress of Penitents:

> "This religious should be solidly grounded in virtue, and profoundly attached to the works of her vocation; she should be animated by a great zeal for the salvation of souls, and apply herself more than others, to live by Faith ... She alone shall be charged with the direction of the class, the other Mistresses being subject to her authority in all that regards their employment. It is absolutely necessary that it be so. There shall be in each class only one directress viz.; the first Mistress. Not to hold to this point would be to lay the foundation of a thousand miseries, we earnestly recommend fidelity to it."[27]

Only the First and Second Mistresses, and other Sisters appointed to the class (such as the Dormitory and Laundry Mistresses and their Assistants, the Infirmarian and those Religious charged with surveillance, etc.) were in constant contact with the penitents, and these were the women who ruled their daily lives.

Other Sisters were regarded as more usefully employed elsewhere. Mother Louis de Baligand, for example, possessed "a brilliant mind, sound judgement and distinguished manners" - all of which would be wasted on penitents but highly prized in other aspects of the work. In her case, linguistic ability had influenced

---

26 *Holy Rosary Parish Golden Jubilee Souvenir - 1898-1948*, pp.15-18.
27 *Rules for the Direction of the Classes, op. cit.*, p.59.

the choice. While working at Angers she had been Mistress of the English Novices (and later of those who were German and French) before being named Superior of an American Foundation, prior to her Irish appointment.[28] She could have had little contact with the penitents throughout her monastic career. The same is true of the two Devereux sisters who were prominent in the New Ross and Cork Missions, and were appointed First Mistresses of Industrial Schools, before being named Superiors very early in their Convent lives. Like Mother de Baligand, whose contacts were such that she could call on exiled Royalty for help with a Bazaar;[29] and Mother St. Magdalen Devereux, whose friendship with Countess Murphy was to prove so hugely beneficial to the Order in Cork, such women were prized as much for their important social connections as for their wealth, education and administrative skills. Sister Mary of our Lady of the Sacred Heart Coppinger, on the other hand, also from an unusually distinguished background, was to spend her life in the Penitents' Section. During her Novitiate the young woman was named First Mistress of Penitents at Cork - a unique position in view of the Foundation's association with the Contagious Diseases Acts; and a post which she held for over half a century. She was selected for this important role by the new Mother General, Mother Mary of St. Peter de Coudenhove, who was then visiting Ireland.[30]

Unauthorised Mistresses - those assigned to other work - were firmly discouraged from entering the "Class". This was not only to ensure the isolation of the different Sections (an abiding concern of the Foundress) but to uphold the strict hierarchy in operation in the Homes. Equally important, untrained Sisters or those inexperienced in this special work, might not only endanger themselves but put the object of the Institute at risk. This is made clear in the *Instructions:*

> "We recommend those of you who are not occupied in the classes
> to refrain from going to them or speaking to the children

---

28 Typescript of Limerick Annals, p.3.

29 To meet the costs of extensions to the Convent buildings in 1852, friends and benefactors of the Sisters organised a Bazaar. Mother de Baligand wrote to her friend Queen Amelia, wife of the exiled Louis Phillippe of France, who responded with a "magnificently embroidered vestment" worked by herself; and some exquisitely embroidered "sacs" in which Easter Eggs had been presented to the Royal family. *Ibid.*, pp.4-5.

30 Cork Annals, at the time of Sister Coppinger's death in 1927.

without permission. Be sure if you are not named for a class the grace to do good in it is wanting, nor can you [do so] without great prejudice to yourself unless you have the blessing of obedience. The children know that in acting thus you are disobedient. On the contrary, a religious who keeps to her duty and who avoids, as far as she can, being seen, and speaks only to those she is authorised to speak to, wins respect, and if she be some day named mistress she is received with esteem and gladness.[31]

Included in the above statistics for Irish Houses at the turn of the century, then, were nuns not appointed to the "fallen" - Sisters with no experience of the penitent class. They may have been administrators, assigned to Convent or other duties, have worked with the "Industrial" children or with the "Preservation" girls. In the Waterford Asylum a superior category of contemplative penitents, the "Magdalens", required special supervision (see below); and in Limerick, some of the Religious were appointed to direct the Novitiate Class.

Lay Sisters too, were included in the above statistics, but their duties would rarely have brought them into contact with the penitents. These were women who had a vocation for the religious life and may well have been particularly drawn to the object of the Institute. But they were recruited from the humbler ranks of society. Their education was generally inferior to that of the choir nuns, their dowries (if any) were smaller, and their backgrounds - necessarily respectable and by no means impoverished - were lowly, rather than rich.[32] Though apparently never precisely defined as such, they were, in effect, the domestic servants in the Convents, performing those duties deemed inappropriate for choir nuns, who had entered the Order from a higher, and wealthier social sphere.

In common with all large establishments in the period, most Convents relied on domestic staff for comfort and cleanliness. The privacy of the enclosure, however, seemed violated by such intrusions; and it had long been held more proper to have none but Community members in such intimate contact with the nuns. Such a solution (and the Good Shepherd Order was by no means

---

31 *Conferences and Instructions, op. cit.*, pp. 373-4.
32 For a comprehensive discussion of this subject, see Clear, *op. cit.*

unique in this respect) had the additional virtue of accommodating vocations from the humbler classes of society.

It is sometimes assumed that penitents were made to clean the Good Shepherd Convents, which are always remembered as being spotless. This may have been the case in the closing years of the Foundations, when the laundries had ceased to operate; and the "ladies" (no longer kept at washing) were not totally confined. But at least until the 1960s, and probably later, it is doubtful if penitents ever stepped inside the Convent walls, such violation being not only unnecessary, but traditionally proscribed.* Familiarity with the layout of each Monastery and reference to the Institute's Rules, makes it clear that such women were completely segregated from the nuns, their presence, as we have seen, having always been regarded as a source of contagion. Consequently, penitents had no access whatsoever to the interior life of the Convents, the buildings of which were entirely separate or closed off from the women's quarters, and serviced exclusively by lay or domestic nuns. This is indicated in the *Rules for the Direction of the Classes:*

> "You all, while you are in the Institute, labour for the salvation of souls ... Our sisters engaged in the kitchen, in the bakery, in the garden, in the vestry, and in the linen rooms ... are all working for the salvation of souls. They practice the fourth vow as much as the superiors and the first mistresses of penitents. Had you no other occupation than dusting the stalls, sweeping the house, washing the dishes, it should be done with purity of intention and holy zeal. Be persuaded, moreover, that in a religious house, one who is faithful in the fulfilment of a humble office, often renders more service than another with a much higher order of mind."[33]

Caitriona Clear notes that between 1861, when records of entrants began, and 1900, the proportion of lay Sisters to choir nuns in the Limerick Good Shepherd was 36 per cent - an unusually high figure compared with other Convents in the period, and no doubt attributable to the varied projects run by

---

* Certainly by the 1950s, however, the "Industrial" children were being used to clean Convent corridors and staircases, and even parts of the Chapels. See, for example, Margaret Matley, *Always in the Convent Shadow* (1991) - an account of childhood in the Cork Good Shepherd Industrial School.

33 *Rules for the Direction of the Classes, op. cit.*, pp.55-56.

the French Order.[34] Comparable material for the other Good Shepherd Congregations in Ireland has not been made available, but it is unlikely that for them this figure (more probably determined by the Novitiate than the laundries and other activities) was ever achieved.

Detailed contemporary descriptions of the purpose-built new Waterford Convent, for example (completed in 1894) reveal that in spite of the Order's attachment to poverty and humility, hierarchical structures, based on wealth, privilege and rank, were firmly in place. Separate accommodation was provided for the lay Sisters, and in much of the Convent life a proper distinction was preserved. The ground floor - housing a refectory and a communicants' room, each 40 ft. long; three large reception rooms and the Superioress' room - contained a separate wing devoted to the "culinary department". On the first floor were two separate infirmaries, the Superior's room and spacious cells. Significantly, accommodation on the second floor included a large dormitory, oratory and cells. As in any wealthy establishment of the period, a back staircase, smaller and less ornate than that in the front of the Convent, ensured that humbler members of the Community could go about their domestic duties almost unseen.

A division of labour was inevitable. Choir nuns, preoccupied with religious duties, and absorbed by administrative, intellectual or training pursuits, could hardly be required to undertake the additional burden of menial domestic work. Equally important, many of them were ladies, who had been cared for by servants before taking the veil. They were not accustomed to rough labour, nor, in spite of their vow of poverty, was it something they were required to perform. There was little social equality in such Convents; and as in other Orders, women of wealth and distinction had an almost separate existence from the daughters of the poor. Sisters whose money had profited the Congregation, and whose families and prestigious social connections might still be of use, were often swiftly elevated, as befitted their education and class.

It has been noted that the duties of lay Sisters kept most of them in the Convents, and that many other nuns too, were totally excluded from the Penitents' Section. When all these women are

---

34 Clear, *op. cit.*, p.82.

deducted, the numbers of Sisters controlling the "fallen" must have been small. Of the 38 Religious in the Waterford Foundation at the turn of the century, for example, some (probably about one quarter) were lay nuns; while others, like the Superior and her Assistant, had no direct responsibility for the penitents, but governed the Monastery as a whole. Various Sisters were occupied in the Convent itself; a significant number were allocated to the Industrial School, and one or two worked in the totally separate "contemplative" Magdalen Section. With so few Sisters remaining to work with the penitents (by whom they were greatly outnumbered) one wonders how these women were so effectively controlled.

The records contain no evidence of riots, mass breakouts, serious disorder or nuns being attacked. Yet many of the women, scarred by experience and deeply disturbed, must have been difficult to manage. Others - depressed, pining for their babies, or frantic to escape - resorted to tantrums, window-smashing and refusals to work.[35] Total confinement and constant harping on sin and penance must have aggravated their condition, which in that abnormal setting was intensified by overwork, sexual deprivation and a future without hope. Some inmates, "passionate" or "half-insane", were clearly unbalanced - or made to be so; while others were described as "demented" or "unhinged" - perhaps through craving for drink. [36]

Some (often older than the average on admission) were dangerous. Mary Jane Bailey, for example, was 47 when she "voluntarily" entered the Waterford Home in 1890. Eight years later, allowed to leave at her own request, she was described as "very violent". In January 1898 a Mrs. Parker, 48 and "a very dangerous character in general" spent only three weeks in the

---

35 This was particularly the case by the mid-twentieth century when unmarried mothers, rather than prostitutes were targeted for "reform". Eye-witness accounts of this behaviour are contained in the television documentary, *Sex in a Cold Climate, op. cit.* The continued dismissals for "bad conduct" suggest that throughout the whole period individual women refused to conform; and occasionally, minor but potentially explosive incidents occurred. In January 1876, for example, a Limerick penitent named Higgins was sent out for "story carrying and for throwing a goffering iron at one of the children, quite close to one of the mothers." - Annals of the Limerick Good Shepherd Asylum, January 1876.

36 Similar cases occurred in the York Female Penitentiary (see Finnegan, *op. cit.*); and in the Lincoln Home. In 1873 Betsy Agnes Ellis, for example, "Left for Boston [Lincolnshire]. Her reason for doing so, was that she could not do without the drink to which she had become accustomed." Lincoln Home Ladies Minute Book, 1873.

Home; and Mary Osburn, aged 40 stayed for an even shorter period in the same month. She too, had a "violent temper".[37]

These descriptions, taken from the Registers of Penitents, make it highly improbable that any "children" however trusted, gained access to the Convent itself. An awareness of danger, explicit in the *Rules for the Direction of the Classes*, is nowhere more apparent than in the order charging the Dormitory Mistress to lock herself into her cell each night. A wise precaution, and a chill reminder of the Sisters' need for constant vigilance.

Two sources - the Foundress' *Rules* and the records of individual Irish Houses - indicate that control was partly maintained through compromise and the avoidance of confrontation. It was, as we have seen, the Order's object ("sadly, too rarely achieved") to retain women in the Homes for life. The salvation of souls necessitated such a measure, since only those sheltered from temptation and protected from sin, could die in a state of grace. Every effort was made to achieve this goal, and it has been noted that a penitent's departure caused as much sorrow as her arrival caused joy. Nevertheless, no matter how cherished by the Good Shepherd Sisters was each of the rescued sheep (a Biblical image particularly favoured by the Foundress and common to Rescue literature in general[*]) a single "bad spirit" or "wolf in the fold" must never endanger the flock. Mother Euphrasia was adamant in this matter:

> "We sometimes meet with *bad natures* in which no good sentiment can be awakened. They spread around them corruption and revolt; sometimes ... deceiving everybody by an appearance of virtue. Such persons are capable of acquiring a certain influence of which they make use to lead their less intelligent companions into faults; they prevent good, cause much sin, and destroy the spirit of a class. As soon as discovered they should be dismissed; they will do less harm in the world than in our houses; we could never hope to convert them unless they be very young and that the Mistress clearly detects their evil dispositions."[38]

---

37 Waterford Register of Penitents, 19 September 1890, and 10 and 18 January 1898.

* The motto of the Reformatory and Refuge Union, for example, was "To seek and to save that which was lost"; and engravings such as Fig. 2 were very popular and were hung in the Good Shepherd Convents.

38 *Rules for the Direction of the Classes, op. cit.*, p.200.
Managers of English Homes encountered similar problems, one of them warning in 1901 that the influence of some girls could disrupt a Refuge. "They often wilfully irritate and annoy each other ... they insinuate things that are untrue and sometimes secretly incite to discontent or even rebellion. The insidious girl is a great source of danger with others." *Report of the Annual Conference of the Reformatory and Refuge Union*, 1901, p.17.

The Penitents' Registers show that this advice was closely followed, particularly with regard to those women who had entered the institutions voluntarily. In April 1877, for example, Limerick penitent Mary Costello aged 30, after only a week in the Home "would not remain in the Asylum." Three days later she was re-admitted, but within 48 hours had "destroyed her jacket and insisted on being let out." Later that year Mary Higney, another 30 year old "had to be allowed out after giving way to passion and great party spirit". She had been in the Asylum several times.[39] Similarly, 25 year old Johanna Shelly, from Carrick-on-Suir, managed to quit the Waterford institution in 1891 after only four months. In this case, the nuns were suspicious - noting in the Register that she was "A Simpleton or pretending to be one". A final example is 17 year old Margaret Best from Co. Cork, who was admitted to the Limerick Asylum in 1877 but was dismissed for "using bad language, which she did, in order to get out."[40]

Others were dismissed or "expelled", with comments in red ink to show they must not be re-admitted - though they frequently were. Thus thirty-nine year old Bridget Gissane was "sent away for <u>bad conduct</u>", soon after entering the Limerick Asylum in August 1875. She had been in the Home before and was a "bad Spirit, and done much harm to others." Having pawned some of the Asylum's clothes she was <u>Not to be taken again</u>. Shortly afterwards, however, she was re-admitted, only to be expelled again in the following year.[41] Others were barely registered before leaving. Thirty-two year old Anastasia Hussy, for example, was admitted to the Waterford Asylum in October 1873, having "entered voluntarily". Her conduct must have been unusually outrageous, as she was "dismissed same day."[42]

Reasons for dismissal (excluding those relating to health) ranged from "bad conduct" - the most common; to "inciting others to leave" - the most feared. Most shocking was "particular friendships", a tiny proportion of the whole; and most mysterious was "party spirit". Many women left "of their own accord", without, apparently, taking up a situation or joining family or friends. This indicates a measure of self-determination for some

39 Limerick Register of Penitents, 20 and 21 April, and 3 May 1877.
40 Waterford Register of Penitents, 19 August 1891, and Limerick Register of Penitents, 3 September 1877.
41 Limerick Register of Penitents, 5 August 1875.
42 Waterford Register of Penitents, 24 October 1873.

penitents, possibly related to how such women arrived. While 43 percent of inmates entered voluntarily, however, and 34 percent departed in this way - only 21.3 percent of those for whom this information was recorded, both arrived and left "of their own free will". This information is contained in Tables 1 and 2 at the end of this Chapter.

It has been noted that occasionally inmates risked attempted escape by scaling the walls. Generally, however, women who were determined to leave engineered their own expulsion (or tried to do so) - a practice which continued throughout the history of the Homes.[43] Thus between October 1876 and May 1877, three Limerick penitents (in common with 30 year old Mary Costello referred to above) were sent out for insubordination and "tearing their clothes".[44] Each had been in the Asylum before.

Though such dismissals formed a high percentage of departures - 101 out of 518 in the Limerick Asylum between 1848 and 1887, for example - it had been the intention of the Foundress that they should occur rarely, and only in extreme circumstances. Dismissals were, after all, an indication of failure; they worked to the detriment of both the Sisters' and the Class's morale; and because of the scandal and ill-feeling they caused, they put the reputation of the Homes at risk. Mother St. Euphrasia preferred compromise, advocating that ringleaders should, where possible be placated and harnessed to the Order's cause. Her instructions on the subject betray an awareness of potential danger and indicate how some "auxiliaries" were chosen for their work:

"In almost every class there are children who exercise a certain influence over their companions; to try to destroy this influence would be useless. It is much better to win such children to our side and turn their power to good account."[45]

---

43 Most recently, those few women who have talked of their experience in Magdalen Homes have listed tantrums, refusal to work, eat, or obey rules as the usual method of defiance in the hope of dismissal. Such measures provoked punishment - often "vicious" - of which, of course, there is no mention in the records. See particularly *Sex in a Cold Climate*, op. cit., and *Suffer the Little Children*, op. cit.

44 Limerick Register of Penitents, 14 October and 25 November 1876, and 16 April and 3 May 1877.

45 *Rules for the Direction of the Classes*, op. cit., p.82.

Carefully delegated authority then, a limited sharing of power
with "auxiliaries" whose personality and influence made them
dangerous enemies but useful allies, helped the Mistress to
preserve order in the Class. Such women, "recompensed" with
badges of Sodalities, or acquiring "Child of Mary" status, were
given special treatment and discouraged from leaving. They were
not, however, exempted from surveillance.

These measures applied particularly to the "Consecrated"
penitents, who, before being admitted to take the habit, were
subjected to a lengthy trial of piety, devotedness and submission.
Once Consecrated, no efforts were spared to sustain their fervour
and they were frequently instructed in the practice of virtue, apart
from the other women. Though urged to show the Consecrates
confidence and even "to treat them with a certain deference",
Mistresses were, nevertheless, warned to watch them closely, to be
aware of their defects, and above all, not to permit them to
domineer or govern the Class. Prudence and great tact were
required when dealing with these women, it being recognised that
public reproach or reprimand could turn them against the
Mistress, with disastrous consequences for the whole of the
Class.[46] Occasionally a Consecrated penitent fell from grace, in
which case her former privileged status was rarely restored.
Twenty-one year old Mary Warren, for example, had been
admitted to the Limerick Asylum in August 1872 and a few years
later took the black dress and "received the name of Thais of the
desert". She lost the black dress in 1879, and never recovered it,
though she remained in the institution for a further fifty-eight
years, eventually dying in the Home in February 1937.[47]

Apparent in Mother Pelletier's guidance is the realisation that
power in the Asylums was tenuously held. Penitents with violent
tempers, for example, must not be upbraided in public, and
should be reprimanded only when their passions were cooled.
Above all, both for the dignity of the Sisters and the peace and
well-being of the Class, open confrontation was always to be

---

46 *Ibid.*, pp.119-120.
47 Limerick Register of Penitents, 8 August 1872. This woman is probably "Mary
    Warrell" on the 1901 Census, at which time the ex-Consecrate was definitely in the
    Home. Although of the right age, her place of birth, listed as Co. Dublin in her
    original entry in the Penitents' Register, is recorded as England in the later source.
    She is one of the 15 penitents described in the Census as a seamstress.

avoided - even if wrong-doers went unpunished. Control was maintained too, of course, by means of discipline, silence, surveillance and work. Since those entering the Homes were already disposed to penance, feelings of guilt (sedulously nurtured) furthered the process of subjugation and strengthened the Sisters' rule. Above all in these institutions, religious indoctrination was an effective form of power.

The Religious of the Good Shepherd were forbidden to strike the penitents, to deprive them of food, to give them fatiguing penances (such as holding the arms in the form of a cross) or to place them in solitary confinement.[48] Sisters were advised to ignore the faults of penitents whose "evil dispositions lead them to provoke us, just to be punished"; and were warned against the dangers of appearing glad to inflict a punishment. Further:

> "We must also beware of punishing an entire class for the faults of a few; it might have very serious consequences. Poor children, who have worked all day, and who have made every effort to satisfy their mistresses, should not be treated like the disobedient ones."[49]

"Recompenses" too, were used to control the women - a walk in the garden for example, being much appreciated in the French Mother House. These and similar treats not only gave pleasure, they created a love of duty and authority.

Such were the Foundress' regulations governing the control of the Class. The fact that for one and a half centuries so many women were ruled by so few, is a measure of their success.

Nevertheless, the mid 1870s was a difficult period for the Limerick Asylum, with escapes and expulsions occurring more frequently than usual, and few new admissions remaining in the Home. There were nine registrations in April 1874, for example, only four of which were satisfactory. Seventeen year old Nora

---

48 *Rules for Direction of the Classes, op. cit.,* pp.114-115.
   From the evidence of former inmates it is clear that in Ireland, at least, such regulations were not always adhered to. In the 1950s the Reverend Mother of the Limerick Good Shepherd, for example, appears to have been quite brutal - the shocking abuses occurring in the institution under her control being described by Brigid Young in *Sex in a Cold Climate, op. cit.* Other references to ill-treatment by the Good Shepherd Sisters occur in *Les Blanchisseuses de Magdalen* – the 1998 France 3/Sunset Presse television documentary (see below), *Suffer the Little Children, op. cit.* and Matley, *op. cit.*
49 *Rules for the Direction of the Classes, op. cit.,* p.111.

Madigan from Limerick went to hospital a week after she arrived; and both 22 year old Joanna Ryan, who had been in the Asylum before, and 34 year old Mary Donovan from Limerick, were expelled "for bad conduct". A Dublin woman "McDonnell", aged 27, "escaped from the Asylum" in the following August; and Ellen Dodd aged 18 and from Co. Kerry, was expelled for Bad Conduct within a few months.[50]

There were only eight admissions in June 1874, six of which were disastrous. Twenty-five year old Cork prostitute Anna Gamson, for example, was recommended to the Home on 5th June by Mrs. Walsh, nurse at the "Queen's [Lock] Hospital, Cork" (see pages 212-15). Almost a year later, she was "expelled".[51] Jane Stapleton, a twenty-six year old woman from Cashel who left at her own request, beat up the van driver when she was refused re-admission;[52] and 26 year old Joanna Grady was expelled for bad conduct" within a few months of her arrival.[53] Bessie Foley, a 20 year old from Tipperary "escaped" after two months in the Asylum, and 13 year old Mary Pinder from Co. Galway (referred to in Chapter 7) was sent out for beating and "knocking down" one of the penitents, a month after she arrived.[54] Twenty year old Mary White from Tipperary, a former inmate of the Waterford Good Shepherd, had to be "sent away for insubordination";[55] and in July Ellen Tobin, a 25 year old woman from Limerick was admitted - only to be sent out after eighteen months for "being insane".[56] Shortly after her arrival 16 year old Joanna Carroll from Co. Limerick "escaped";[57] and over the next few months five local girls, 18 year old Ellen Mahony, 17 year old Mary Redding, 15 year old Mary Roache, 16 year old Mary Rainsford and 24 year old Catherine Dillon, all departed in the same way.[58]

Catherine Quin, a 17 year old from Cashel was admitted in September. She remained for 6 years before being sent home

---

50   Limerick Register of Penitents, 5, 7, 9, no date, and 13 April, 1874.
51   *Ibid.*, 5 June 1874.
52   *Ibid.*, no date June 1874.
53   *Ibid.*, 1 June 1874.
54   *Ibid.*, 1 and 11 June 1874.
55   *Ibid.*, 27 June 1874.
56   *Ibid.*, 6 July 1874.
57   *Ibid.*, 9 July 1874.
58   *Ibid.*, 13 and 26 July, 17 and 29 August and 13 September 1874.

"Not to be admitted again. Had very bad spirit in the Class."[59] In October 1874, 17 year old Mary Monaghan came from the City Jail. She was expelled for bad conduct a few weeks later. Ellen Kennedy, aged 17 had to be sent to the union hospital 5 days after admission; and the same fate was in store for Margaret Sullivan, of Tralee, though she remained in the Home for just over a year.[60] In November Mary Heggeny aged 24 from Limerick, was received for the fourth time but sent out for insubordination; and also in that month Mary Fitzgibbon was admitted but soon afterwards expelled. Still in November, Joanna O'Grady, a 26 year old Limerick woman was admitted for the third time, only to be expelled two months later; and in the following week, Ellen Barring, a 22 year old, came direct from the jail and was "very insolent". She had been in the Home twice before. [61]

In January 1876 the Rev. Mother of the Presentation Convent in Listowel sent a blind woman, Bridget Shanahan to the Limerick Asylum. Whether or not she was a proper subject for a Magdalen Home (she was 38 years old and her parents were dead) she was expelled in the following year for bad conduct. The nuns were pleased to be rid of her, as "She gave great scandal by cursing", and the Mother Provincial paid her fair home."[62] Coinciding with her stay was that of Winifred Riordan, a 32 year old Limerick woman with similar tendencies. She too was expelled in 1877, having been:

"idle, passionate and sullen, and cursing and blaspheming the old penitents with whom she could not agree."[63]

It was noted in Chapter 2 that compared with Refuges in England, the number of women placed in situations or found work of any kind straight from the Irish Good Shepherds was consistently low. There were fewer outlets generally in Ireland for domestic servants, and particularly for those from such a dubious

---

59 *Ibid.*, 14 September 1874.
60 *Ibid.*, no date October 1874; and 13 and 23 October 1874.
61 *Ibid.*, 2, 20 and 28 November and 1 December 1874.
62 *Ibid.*, 22 January 1876.
63 *Ibid.*, 26 February 1876.

source. Contemporary observers reported a strong prejudice against ex-magdalens; (see, for example, pp. 167-8) and inevitably, those that were given employment were commonly over-worked and under-paid. Such prejudice was possibly exaggerated to account for the relatively few penitents leaving for situations once the Sisters took over the Homes. This was particularly the case with the Limerick Convent Asylum, whose record of placements compared unfavourably with the earlier lay Refuge run by Mrs. Meade and Miss Reddan, and whose figures in this respect continued to decline.

In May 1828 the first inmate of Limerick's original Refuge was admitted, and in 1832 she was sent out to a job which its Managers had procured. During that four year period 59 other penitents were registered in the Home, 30 of whom - an astonishing 50 percent - left for situations. Since the avowed purpose of Rescue Work was the reclamation of the fallen and their restoration to society after training and reform, such a result (never repeated) was to be expected, and was clearly a success. Obviously, lay Managers like Mrs. Meade were in a better position to place the women in service than were the nuns who subsequently arrived. Newcomers to the city and confined to the Enclosure, the Sisters could rarely have had the contacts, initially at least, to compete with such results. However, it seems likely that their failure to do so, stemmed more from reluctance than inability. Throughout the period various priests (such as Rev. Shinkwin in Cork, Rev. Condon in Limerick and Rev. Aylward in New Ross, for example) together with lay people such as Miss Farrell (referred to below) were extremely active in recommending fallen women to the Homes - their names recurring in each of the Convent's Registers. Had the Good Shepherd Sisters been committed to restoring their penitents to society, they could have called on these and similar individuals to help in this vital last stage of the Rescue process. Such, however, was not the object of the Order, and the dwindling numbers of women provided for in this way reveals how unimportant rehabilitation was. Such facts support Michael McCarthy's observations introducing Chapter 7 - namely that Convent Magdalen Asylums, by maintaining their staffs (i.e. the penitents) engaged in lucrative laundry work, rather than in the reduction of immorality.

Between the arrival of the nuns in February 1848 and October 1877 (the final year analysed for this particular Home) a total of 897 women were admitted to the Limerick Magdalen Asylum, approximately 40 percent of them returning to the institution at least once. Table 1 lists how the women were admitted to the Refuge. In the Penitents' Register for this institution, those entering voluntarily are described as "came of own accord". For 220 women (approximately 25 percent of the total) this information was not recorded. Of the remainder, 41 percent of the women were sent to the Asylum by priests, many of whom worked in local parishes.

Table 1
By Whom Recommended: Limerick Good Shepherd
1848-77

	Total 677	Percent
Own Accord	332	43
Priests	317	41
Nuns	45	6
Ladies	20	3
Workhouse/Hospital	10	1
Other Good Shepherds	10	1
Prison	8	1
Female Relatives	8	1
Other	20	2.5

Table 2, which lists the major reasons for inmates' departure over this thirty year period, shows that in marked contrast to what had occurred before the nuns took control, only 43 inmates (5 per cent) left for a situation. "Left of own accord" refers to those women who were determined to leave, and were frequently described as "very hasty", or "in a bad disposition". Unlike those listed in Category 4, they were neither sent for, nor returned to friends.

Table 2
Reasons for Leaving Limerick Good Shepherd:
1848-1877

	Total 897	Percent
Left of Own Accord	306	34
Expelled	175	19
Hospital	102	11
Left for Family / Friends	61	7
Died in Home	66	7
Escaped	52	5
Left for Situation	43	5
Other	73	8
Not Given	19	2

Table 3 shows how long penitents stayed in the Limerick Asylum, though this information is available for only 327 penitents. The average length of stay of those for whom evidence survives was 3 years. Almost two thirds of the inmates, however, left within six months of their arrival.

Many inmates, of course, departed from the Home (or died) after 1877 - the final year for which Admissions in the Limerick Penitents' Registers were analysed. Admissions, therefore, are from 1848 to the end of 1877 - but there is no cut-off point for date of departure.

Penitents' religion - overwhelmingly Catholic - was carefully listed in all the Irish Houses, and those few Protestants who were admitted were generally converted to Catholicism. Thus 1872, the year of the first admissions to the Cork Good Shepherd, for example, was marked by three of the penitents being "baptised and received into the Catholic Church."[64] Confirmation of Catholic inmates occurred more frequently, as was the case in 1885, for example, in the New Ross Home. Here, twenty-one year old Kate Ryan, who had been in the Refuge for two years; Mary Molloy, a 17 year old brought to the Asylum by her father; and 16 year old Lizzie Barrett were all confirmed that year. In

---

64 Annals of the Cork Good Shepherd Magdalen Asylum, 1873.

Table 3
Length of Stay in Limerick Good Shepherd for
Penitents Admitted Between 1848 and 1878.

	Total 327	Percent
Under 1 week	35	10.6
1-2 weeks	24	7.4
2-4 weeks	48	14.8
1-2 months	45	13.8
2-6 months	50	15.3
6-12 months	38	11.6
1-2 years	26	7.9
2-5 years	29	9.0
5-10 years	12	3.7
10-15 years	5	1.6
15-20 years	-	-
20-30 years	5	1.6
30-40 years	-	-
40-50 years	3	1.1
50 years +	5	1.6

1905 the New Ross Sisters recorded an even greater triumph - the Baptism of a penitent (sent by a zealous priest from Gorey) who had been in the Home for over a year:

> "She was rather advanced in years and all belonging to her were Protestants for generations ... great was the delight of the Mistresses and of the whole Community to claim another soul from Satan and present it to the Good Shepherd." [65]

In the Limerick Asylum only one Protestant was recorded throughout the period, and one woman had no religion listed. But in November 1876, Ellen Donaher aged 16, and her sister Bridget, aged 17, were admitted "of their own accord". They were from Waterford where their mother was still living. Seven months later the two girls left. Bridget went to Waterford; and although

---

65 New Ross Register of Penitents, 23 August 1883, and 16 June and 13 July 1885. Also New Ross Annals, 1905.

she was re-admitted to the Limerick Home in 1881, she was dismissed after three years. Ellen, who had resorted to tearing her clothes to gain her freedom, returned on the same day; but in 1878 she left for the Protestant Refuge in Cork. After three years: "she returned again very penitent and very sorry for what she did", and stayed in the Home until 1883.[66]

Age on admission to the Limerick Magdalen Asylum ranged from 13 years (two girls) to 60 years (one woman). For 140 inmates (16 percent of the overall total) this information was not recorded. The remainder (756) are included in Table 4, which shows that the vast majority of admissions (80 percent of those for whom there is information) were under 30 years of age. Forty-seven percent were in their twenties when they were registered, and almost one third of the inmates were admitted in their teens.

Table 4
Age on Admission: Limerick Good Shepherd 1848-1877.

Years	Total 756	Percent
13-19	246	32
20-29	358	47
30-39	119	16
40-49	26	3
50-59	5	0.7
60	2	0.2

With regard to marital status over the period, 862 of the women (96 percent) were single; 28 (3 percent) were married and four women were listed as widows.

Contemporary observers noted that many fallen women were either orphaned or had only one parent - a factor often believed to have contributed to their involvement in prostitution. This

---

66   Limerick Register of Penitents, 25 November 1876.

pattern is certainly confirmed in the York, Lincoln and Irish records, though as Walkowitz suggests in her study of prostitution in the West of England, such information - providing at once an excuse for taking part in the activity, and anonymity - should perhaps, be treated with caution.[67] According to the Limerick records only 85 penitents (16 percent of those for whom this information is given) had two parents living at the time they were registered. 227 of the women (44 percent) were listed as orphans, and for 208 entrants (40 percent) one parent only, was recorded.

It will be shown that in all the Irish Houses, penitents were drawn from increasingly wider areas as the century progressed, the extent to which this was a deliberate policy being examined in the following Chapter. In Limerick over the period as a whole, for 106 women (12 percent of the overall total) this information was not recorded. Of the remaining 790, approximately 55 percent came from the city and county, with most of the remainder being drawn from the surrounding counties of Cork, Tipperary, Kerry and Clare.

Table 5
Birthplace of Limerick Penitents: 1848-1877

	Total 790	Percent
Limerick City	307	39
County Limerick	123	16
Surrounding Counties	208	26
Other	152	19

The 1901 Census Enumerator's Notebooks (the earliest surviving for Ireland) give an overall picture of the Limerick Monastery at the turn of the century. Seventy-nine nuns were resident in the Home on Census night; their ages ranging from 19

---

67 Walkowitz, *op. cit.*, pp.16-17.

years (2 Novices) to 80 years (Emilie Van Neuvenhoven, the former lace maker from Belgium, referred to above). The fact that this Convent contained the Provincial Novitiate accounts for the unusually high proportion of young Sisters listed, with forty-six of the Religious (58 percent) being under forty years of age.

The Home contained 101 penitents. Although it has been noted that two 13 year olds had been admitted to this Asylum during the course of the period examined, at the time of the Census, the youngest inmate was 16. The oldest penitent then in the Home was aged 79; and 54 percent of the women were in the 20-40 year age bracket. Table 6 gives the ages of nuns and penitents in the Provincial House at the time of the Census.

Table 6
Ages of Limerick Nuns and Penitents: 1901 Census

Years	**Nuns** (Total 79)		**Penitents** (Total 101)	
	Number	Percent	Number	Percent
16-19	2	3	10	10
20-29	24	30	24	24
30-39	20	25	30	30
40-49	14	18	14	14
50-59	8	10	13	13
60-69	9	11	7	7
70-79	1	1	3	3
80-89	1	1	–	–

The Census records that of the 79 nuns then in the Convent, 30 spoke Irish as well as English, the majority of these being in the younger age brackets. All could read and write and all were, of course, unmarried. In the Magdalen Asylum all the inmates were Roman Catholics; and apart from 6 widows, all were single. Compared with the Waterford Home the recorded literacy level in the Limerick Penitentiary is surprisingly high. According to this source, only 6 of the women were unable to read and write, and only one could read only. Twenty-one of the penitents could speak Irish as well as English.

Apart from the Belgian Sister and one whose birthplace was South America, all the nuns in 1901 were Irish-born. In the Magdalen Asylum, 93 of the 101 penitents had been born in Ireland. Four had been born in Scotland, 3 in England and 1 in Germany.

Table 7 shows that at the turn of the century, both nuns and penitents were still being drawn from Limerick or the surrounding counties, with the percentage distribution in the two categories of women being practically identical. By this time, however, penitents were arriving from further afield than had been the case for the overall period. Whereas in Table 4 only 19 percent of the women had come from outside Limerick and its surrounding counties, by 1901 this proportion had increased to 37 percent.

Table 7
Birthplace of Nuns and Penitents: 1901 Census

	Nuns (Total 79)		**Penitents** (Total 101)	
	Number	Percent	Number	Percent
Limerick	18	23	24	24
Co. Lim.	6	8	8	8
Neigh. Cos.	25	32	31	31
Other	30	38	37	37

Also in 1901, St. Joseph's Reformatory contained 38 "pupils" aged between 8 and 17, together with 4 lay staff. St. George's (the Industrial School attached to the Provincial House, and discussed below) contained 122 girls aged between 5 and 16 years. A Portress was also listed.

The inmates of the Limerick Magdalen Asylum were described as "Employed Females" in the 1901 Census. While most of the women worked in the laundry, others were clearly involved in the maintenance of the Penitentiary itself - a further indication that the lay Sisters were centred almost wholly in the

Convent. One inmate, Margaret Keane a 79 year old from County Clare was described as an invalid and had no occupation. She spoke Irish as well as English, but could neither read nor write.

Although the Convent was responsible for the revival of lace-making in Limerick, it is clear that contrary to popular belief, few of the penitents - at the turn of the century at least - were engaged in such delicate work.

Table 8
Occupation of Limerick Penitents at 1901 Census

	Total	Percent
Laundress	70	70
Seamstress	15	15
Domestic Servant	6	6
Quilter	3	3
Lace Maker*	3	3
Dressmaker	2	2
Nurse	1	1
Invalid	1	1

*   For a discussion of this revival, see Ada K. Longfield, *Guide to the Collection of Lace*, National Museum of Ireland, pp.34-6.

Fig. 3, a mid-nineteenth century painting of four inmates of the Hammersmith Foundation, illustrates the costumes then being worn by the Sisters and Consecrates of the recently established Generalate. Comparison with the 1932 Strasbourg Good Shepherd photographs (Figs. 11 and 12) demonstrates that after almost a century there had been little change. Not surprisingly, the Sisters' habits remained the same; but the unaltered garb of their Auxilliaries is an indication of how the Order clung to its traditions. Even more striking in these 1932 photographs is the outmoded attire of the ordinary penitents - effectively designed to hide the women's shape and discourage "love of dress".

From the evidence of former inmates of the Good Shepherd Asylums in Ireland, it would appear that a generation later - by the late nineteen-fifties - such antiquated outfits, so symbolic of penance, were still being worn. These women remember the strips of calico tied tightly round their breasts, the white bonnets of some long-term inmates, the rough and shapeless garments and the ugly, heavy boots.

Above all, and particularly those from Limerick recall the despair - the fear of never leaving - and the life of "living hell".

4

"A Citadel of Piety"
The Good Shepherd Magdalen
Asylum, Waterford.

"... and, last and significant appendage to the [Waterford] list, a convent of the Good Shepherd, with 39 nuns, and in which there is a Magdalen Asylum with 120 selected inmates. Associated with this Magdalen Asylum, and conducted by the same nuns, is a State-supported "industrial" school, drawing £3,173. 9s. 9d. per annum of public money for its 170 vagrant little girls. I do not think it is right that an "industrial" school and a Magdalen Asylum should be conducted by the same community of nuns."[1]

Edmund Downey's *Illustrated Guide to Waterford,* published in 1915, states that the City's Magdalen Asylum (later under the care of the Good Shepherd Sisters) was originally founded in 1799.[2] If so, the Home pre-dates all but four Asylums for fallen women throughout the whole of Britain, these being, as noted earlier, the London Magdalen Hospital, 1758; the Dublin Magdalen Asylum, 1767; the London Lock Asylum, 1787; and the Edinburgh Royal Magdalene Asylum, 1797. Such a distinction, though not impossible, is not referred to elsewhere.

All other sources give 1842 as the year the small Home opened, a more probable date for a Refuge of its kind. By then the Rescue Movement gripped the middle classes, particularly in England, and in the great crusade against the "Social Evil",

---

1   Michael J. F. McCarthy, *Priests and People in Ireland* (1902) pp.492-3. It is, of course, well-known that this man was a noted anti-Catholic. The facts presented in the above quotation, however, are undisputed; and his restrained comment – particularly in the light of recent evidence regarding both Industrial Schools and Magdalen Asylums - reveals not only his courage and sagacity, but the extent to which he was in advance of public opinion. There can surely be no-one a century after he wrote these words, who would disagree with his sentiments.

2   E. Downey, *Illustrated Guide to Waterford* (1915) p.51.

Magdalen Asylums, Refuges and Penitentiaries were established and even duplicated, in all important towns.

A more detailed account of the Home's origins is contained in Rev. Patrick Power's *History of Waterford and Lismore* published in 1937. This man was Chaplain to the Good Shepherd Monastery for many years, and since his report closely resembles that contained in the Convent's Annals, it is safe to regard these as his source. The same material (slightly embellished) appears both in A. M. Clarke's 1895 biography of Mother St. Euphrasia, and in the 1933 Life of the Foundress, written "by a Religious of the Congregation" and referred to above. Both works discuss the origins of each of the Irish Houses, details of which had clearly been made available for the purpose. The Waterford Good Shepherd Annals then, are the basis, directly or indirectly, of all the above.

These records began in 1858 when, at the invitation of Rev. John Crotty a Waterford priest, the nuns took over the city's existing Magdalen Home. The background and purpose of this early Refuge are confirmed by its Founder and Guardian, Rev. Timothy Dowley, who, in January 1848, published an unusually sympathetic account of the Home and its inmates in a Circular in the *Chronicle and Munster Advertiser* :

> "For many years all classes of the community felt and admitted the necessity of an asylum [for] those erring beings, whose lives have been a profession of sin, but who sincerely desire to abandon the evil of their ways ... Many of these helpless victims of crime and despair have fallen an easy prey to the wiles of the heartless seducer, who first corrupted and then abandoned [them] to the nameless horrors of a career of vice. It is no less certain that poverty is one, perhaps the greatest cause of the degradation of these daughters of misfortune ... we resolved six years ago to attempt the establishment of an institution [for their reception] ..."

The Circular noted that of the 59 women admitted since the Home's foundation in June 1842, only six had relapsed into sin. Two had died in "a fervour of penitence" in the institution, others had emigrated or been restored to respectable society, and 28 were still in the House "happy and contented", cheerfully washing to augment their own support. In addition they prayed constantly for those whose charity provided them with shelter.

According to the paper's editorial, there was no more charitable institution than this Asylum for repentant sinners; for where else could these "daughters of St. Mary Magdalen" be raised from the "depths of their debasement?" Where, but in such an institution, could they repair by a future good life the "scandals of the past"; since in the world, these repentant sinners would find "only coldness and contempt and rejection as outcasts."[3]

It is noted in Chapter 7 that reports of this kind were a constant feature of Rescue literature, from its beginnings in the mid eighteenth century, until well after the First World War. Throughout this period hundreds of Homes relied on the good will - if not the funds - of a dubious public, a situation which accounts in part for the material's sometimes misleading, often optimistic, but always sanctimonious tone. "Successes" are highlighted, failures glossed over and deaths in the institutions portrayed in a romantic, unrealistic light. Anxious to forestall, on the one hand, accusations that such Homes "rewarded vice",[4] and on the other, charges of ill usage and exploitation, most Annual Reports and Circulars are, by their very nature unconvincing and contradictory. Thus inmates, though "cheerful and contented", are consumed with remorse. They pay dearly for their sins, but if allowed to remain at large, corrupting present and future generations, the cost to society would be even greater.

Rev. Dowley's appeal - balanced and kindly, citing seduction and poverty as contributory, if not determining factors in the women's downfall - is in marked contrast to the language and imagery used by Cork priest Rev. Maguire, for example, some of whose violent outbursts to the 1871 Royal Commission are included in Chapter 7. It is part of a significant body of evidence indicating that as the Rescue Movement gathered momentum in Ireland, and was relinquished to enclosed Orders of nuns, its original character was altered, and its purpose undermined. No longer concerned in the rescue of such women, society became as removed from their fate and experience, as they were from it. Normal attitudes and influences, such as had been applied to the

---

3   *Chronicle and Munster Advertiser*, 22 January 1848.
4   As late as 1922, for example, the *Eighty-sixth Report of the Female Aid Society - (Sixty-fourth Annual Report of the Female Mission to the Fallen)* noted that the Bishop of Kensington "recently took great pains to prove that the common excuse for withholding support to rescue work, viz., that it condoned vice, was groundless". p.3.

work in its early years, were no longer brought to bear; and out of reach and out of sight, the Movement became more inhumane and developed along more stringent lines. This is indicated in the Limerick Home, but is particularly noticeable in the response over the period, to prostitution in Waterford. It is apparent too, in the general structure of the Irish Good Shepherd system, which, by the turn of the century was adopting harsher methods and more intolerant attitudes than even the Foundress had proscribed. Further, as the institutions themselves became larger, more efficient and more impersonal; and as local admissions diminished in proportion to cases from further afield, this austerity became more fixed. The same process occurred with Refuges taken over by other Orders, some of which were not enclosed.

Early rescue efforts in Waterford were hampered by the limited accommodation available in Father Dowley's Refuge, and it was feared that applicants who were refused admission had returned to a life of shame. The Governors of the Home (Rev. Dr. Foran, Chief Patron; Rev. T. Dowley, Guardian; Rev. Dr. Cooke, Chaplain; and Thomas Meagher, M.P., Treasurer) were anxious to extend the work, and the above Circular appealed for funds to support and enlarge the Asylum. It was claimed that not only was the terraced house in Barrack Street too small (it could accommodate only 20 women at that time); it was unhealthy, and badly adapted for its use. The dormitory and the rooms for washing, mangling, drying and ironing, for example, were all under one roof, and (most inconveniently for a laundry) there was no water supply. Equally unsatisfactory was its location on a busy main street, and within yards of the Infantry Barracks.

The Appeal resulted in more women being housed, but possibly under worse, rather than improved conditions. Managed by two lay Matrons and under the direction of its founder and another Waterford priest - Rev. John Crotty, referred to above - the Asylum continued unaltered for a further ten years. With Fr. Dowley's removal from Waterford in 1849, however,[5] Rev. Crotty became solely responsible for the women in the Home.

Daunted by the work's increasing difficulties, and impressed by reports of their activities in Hammersmith and Limerick, the priest eventually decided to invite the Sisters of the Good

---

5   He was appointed parish Priest of Rathcormac in Co. Waterford.

Shepherd to take over the Refuge, and wrote to the Mother General in Angers. According to the Waterford Annals:[6]

"On 29th February 1858 Mother Mary of St. Aloysius de Baligand received an urgent letter from Mother Provincial Hammersmith, London, desiring her to meet and welcome a Colony of five Sisters who were being sent by our Very Reverend Mother General, Mother Mary of St. Euphrasia Pelletier, at the request of Father Crotty."

Early in April the five Foundresses of Ireland's second Good Shepherd Asylum arrived in Waterford from Angers. Though they had trained in the French Mother House the new Sisters were all Irish. The Superioress of the new Foundation, Mother Mary of St. Magdalen Crilly,[7] who was to govern the Waterford Monastery for the next forty years, was accompanied by Sister Mary of St. Constantine Cregan, Assistant; Sister Mary of St. Thomas of Aquino Crilly, Mistress of Penitents; Sister Mary of St. Luke Mullen and Sister Mary of St. Appolinaire Fagen. They were welcomed by Mother Louis de Baligand, Prioress of the Limerick Home.[8]

Various writers, including Rev. Power the most reliable, note that 32 penitents were in the small Waterford lay Refuge when the Sisters arrived; a figure confirmed in, and presumably taken from, the Order's Annals.[9] The Sisters' Register of Penitents,[*] however, a source not made available before the present study was begun, lists only 21 inmates when the nuns first took up the work.

This contradictory evidence probably results from the hasty departure of approximately one third of the penitents, following their exposure to the nuns. It seems likely (as was to be the case with many of Rev. Shinkwin's enthusiasts in Cork eighteen years later (see pages 180-82) that eleven of the women fled the

---

6   Properly titled, Annals of the Convent of Our Lady of Charity of the Good Shepherd of Angers at Waterford.

7   This woman's younger sister, Sister Mary of the Immaculate Conception Crilly, was also in the Order; and had recently joined the Limerick Convent from Angers. Typescript of Limerick Annals *op. cit.*, p.5.

8   *Ibid.*, p.6.

9   To add to the confusion, the Annals note at another point, that "30 inmates" were in the House.

*   Properly titled "List of the Names of Penitents Admitted into this Asylum and their Discharge".

Refuge before the Sisters could register them - the very formality of such proceedings, coupled with the nuns' forbidding presence and hints of impending change - no doubt increasing their alarm. From various records (their source undoubtedly the Waterford Annals) it appears that at the time of the Sisters' arrival the women were not only self-supporting, but largely self-governing, in a fairly relaxed regime. By the late 1850s, the two lay Matrons of the earlier period had apparently gone, and Father Crotty superintended the laundry himself. The Annals record that in these early years there was no van, for example; and the penitents collected and returned the customers' washing themselves. Since inevitably, they attended some public place of worship too, there was no question at this time, of their complete confinement to the Home.

Only one glimpse of the Refuge survives - repeated with some amusement in later sources as evidence of how unsatisfactory the existing system was. The Annals record that one very wet Monday, a penitent who had been out collecting the laundry returned with a heavy pack on her shoulders. As she counted out each family's clothes - as usual, in the presence of the priest - it was found she had forgotten a cobbler's shirt. To spare the woman, who was wet and exhausted, Fr. Crotty went for it himself.[10] Though trivial, the incident suggests a kindly, almost normal operation compared with the harsh and unnatural structure, soon afterwards imposed.

A. M. Clarke's 1895 account of the take-over provides further details of the system in place when the nuns arrived:

> "The Sisters had much to contend with. The young girls had been accustomed to fetch the linen, take it home, purchase whatever they deemed necessary for the household, and, in short, dispose as they pleased of their earnings. It will be readily imagined how all but impossible it appeared to put an end to this state of things, and establish the order and regularity necessary in a duly organised convent." [11]

It would seem from this description that in spite of their communal and avowed existence as "penitents" - clear evidence of their remorse and desire to reform - the women were leading semi-normal lives. Treated as adults, and not wholly

---

10 Waterford Annals.
11 A. M. Clarke, *op. cit.*, p.303.

institutionalised, their transition back into society (the professed purpose of their rescue) might well have been achieved. As it was however, of the 21 inmates who in 1858 came under the French Order's control, only 5 were to leave the system alive. It was shown in the previous Chapter, that a similar pattern emerged in the re-structured Limerick Home.

The virtual imprisonment and total isolation of penitents already committed to reform is extraordinary, and was clearly determined by the nuns' Rule of strict Enclosure, rather than any aspect of the women's lives. The desirability of absolute confinement, and the necessity for such a measure, was not questioned. Instead, women successfully demonstrating their willingness to make amends were wholly removed from society, becoming, as their detention lengthened, and their vulnerability increased, easy prey to those who, purged of their own sexuality, were obsessed with others' "sin".

It is worth noting that most of these inmates, contrary to the misleading description above, were not, in fact, "young girls", but rather in their late 30s when the nuns arrived, the most junior of them being 31 years old. Mary Kenneely, for example, from Waterford, was 22 when the Home first opened under Rev. Dowley; and 38 when the Sisters took control. She died in the Asylum in 1882, her conduct being "very good". Also admitted in 1842 was 26 year old Honora Power from Lismore. She was 42 when the Refuge changed hands, and died in the Institution in 1886, aged 70. Mary Power from Waterford was 32 when the nuns took over; Joanna Gleeson, who died in the Home in 1891 was 33; and Mary Daly, who died 7 years after the take-over was 31 when the Sisters arrived.[12]

In contrast to the extreme youth of some of the Good Shepherd penitents later admitted to the Waterford Asylum, the youngest girl to enter Rev. Dowley's Refuge had been 17 year old Julia Curran from Waterford, recommended to the Home by Fr. Crotty in 1845.[13] Her conduct with the Sisters was

---

12 Waterford Register of Penitents, 22 July and 8 December 1842, 8 May 1844 and 28 August 1845.

13 *Ibid.*, 24 July 1845. Rev. Crotty continued to interest himself in Rescue Work even after his appointment as parish Priest of Powerstown, Clonmel. In August, 1869, for example, he recommended 24 year old Bridget Walsh, of Waterford, to the New Ross Magdalen Asylum. She left the Home three months' later. See New Ross Register of Penitents, 2 August 1869.

later reported as "very good"; and since she entered the Province's new class of "Magdalens" in December 1872 (see below) she clearly remained in the institution for life. Margaret Reid from Cork, who was aged 22 when admitted to the original Asylum in 1848, entered the Order's Magdalen Class in 1873; and Margaret Walsh from Co. Tipperary (aged 28 when admitted in 1855) was another pre-Good Shepherd penitent who progressed to the Order's austere Magdalen Rule.[14] An unusually high proportion of this group (16 of the 21 inmates who came under the charge of the nuns) remained in the institution until they died, with 13 of them continuing in the penitents' section, and the three women referred to above, becoming Magdalens. Even a lifetime's atonement did not guarantee the nuns' approval, so desperately yearned for in that unnatural setting, but so begrudgingly bestowed. Bridget Barry, for example, from Waterford, had been admitted in 1845 when she was 24 years old; and was 37 when the nuns took over. She died in the Asylum in 1906, when she was aged 85. After 61 years' remorse, confinement and virtual servitude, her conduct was described as "sometimes good".[15] Another early inmate, Abbey Hunt from Kilmacthomas, Co. Waterford, was commented on in the same way following her death in 1908. However protracted her early "sin", her penance lasted almost sixty years.[16]

It is clear from Rev. Dowley's early appeals for funds, that even as a lay Refuge, the Barrack Street house had been inadequate. As a Convent Asylum, however, it was quite impossible, and the nuns began looking for new accommodation immediately after their arrival in 1858. With the help of Mother de Baligand who remained in Waterford for two weeks, and Fr. John Crotty who came to be regarded as the Asylum's Founder and first benefactor, the Sisters acquired the lease of a disused Convent in nearby Hennessey's Road.[17] Extensive repairs and alterations

---

14 Waterford Register of Penitents, 9 October 1848 and 11 August 1855.

15 *Ibid.*, 28 June 1845.

16 *Ibid.*, 8 May 1849.

17 This Convent had been built for the Presentation Sisters in the first decade of the nineteenth century. Following their removal in May 1848 to their Pugin-designed premises in Lisduggan (then on the outskirts of Waterford) a healthier as well as exquisite set of buildings, the Hennessey's Road property had been acquired by the Poor Law Commissioners for use as an auxiliary workhouse. *Waterford's Presentation Community, A Bicentenary Record, 1798-1998*, pp.12-22.

were required; but in spite of a builders' strike,[18] work progressed
so rapidly under Fr. Crotty's supervision, that the small
Community of 26 penitents and 5 Sisters was able to move into
the renovated Convent on 2nd August 1858. Almost immediately
typhus broke out amongst the inmates, though all recovered from
the disease. With the continued expansion of the Community,
additional building took place, including a laundry and a modest
new Chapel, completed in 1864

During its years as a Magdalen Asylum (1858-1894)
approximately 500 women and girls were admitted to the
Hennessey's Road Enclosure, some of them remaining for life. It
was not until the end of this period however (by which time the
construction of the Order's vast new premises on the Manor was
already underway) that the public was told how unhealthy, and
how inappropriate for its purpose, the institution had always
been. Such an extraordinary admission, published twenty or even
thirty years earlier, would have made little difference to the
history of the Home. Already the public had become distanced
from the matter, enabled to disassociate itself from what was
going on. The Enclosure walls - symbolic, as much as physical
barriers - were as effective in keeping society out, as they were
instrumental in locking penitents in. These women were in the
hands of the Religious, and it was not for ordinary citizens, or
even governments, to interfere. If, as was rumoured, conditions
weren't quite as they should be - the "fallen" deserved no better,
and in any case, were accustomed to worse.

In May 1892 the Foundation Stone of the Order's new
Convent and Asylum was laid by the Bishop, Rev. Dr. Sheehan -
the public's lack of attendance on this important and
well-advertised occasion being attributed to unfavourable
weather. In his address the Bishop deplored the Order's existing
accommodation in Hennessey's Road - accommodation which
the Community, pending the completion of the new buildings,
was to occupy for a further two years. His description, therefore,

---

18 "We understand that what is commonly termed a "strike" has taken place amongst
the men employed in repairing the above Convent for the reception of the Sisters of
the "Good Shepherd". The sum for which the men originally agreed to work, was
18s. per week. On turning out for higher wages, the Rev. John Crotty agreed to their
terms; but no sooner had he done so, than they again struck. The Rev. Gentleman was
then obliged to proceed to Clonmel and Limerick, and engage men to complete the
work." *Waterford Chronicle*, 17 April 1858.

concerns most of the period covered in this study and can be appropriately included at this point:

"The Sisters of the Good Shepherd, no-one can say, have entered on this work too soon. For many and many a year they have borne discomforts, and such as only a few know. They seek no comforts in their life of self-denial ... But to say that the Convent which they have so long occupied was comfortless and cheerless is only describing imperfectly its condition. The House heretofore occupied by the Magdalens, was perhaps of all charitable institutions in the Kingdom the most completely unsuited for its purpose. Its rooms were small and gloomy, its passages were narrow and tortuous. There was very little of pure air in it, and in every way the house was completely unfit as a place for the reception of penitents. No one would say that for them money should be lavished ... But I believe it was absolutely necessary that the work of the Good Shepherds should be continued and if it was to be done with any degree of efficiency, I believe it was absolutely necessary that they should seek another house for their penitents."[19]

It was noted above that 26 penitents and 5 Sisters had moved into the Hennessey's Road Convent in 1858. In the following decades numbers increased steadily, and by the 1901 Census, there were 105 penitents (15 of them "Magdalens") and 38 Nuns in the Community's new premises in the Manor.[20]

Throughout this period the Waterford Magdalen Asylum admitted the same wide range of inmates as the Order's other Homes. In each of the establishments very young, probably hopeful cases, for example, were mixed with severely institutionalised, or more depraved older women. One such adolescent was 14 year old Mary Russell from Waterford, who was recommended by the Home's Chaplain in 1864, but left three years later and was "sometimes very bold". She returned to the Institution in 1870.[21] Kate Noonan, from Waterford, was also 14 when she entered "voluntarily". Although she was "very good" she left within a month.[22] Another 14 year old was Bridget Dorky from

19 *The Waterford News*, 4 June 1892.
20 1901 Census.
21 Waterford Register of Penitents, 30 October 1864.
22 *Ibid.*, 12 April 1878.

nearby Carrick-on-Suir in County Tipperary. She had entered voluntarily in 1880, but was taken out by her mother three months later. Her conduct too, was described as "very good".[23] Fourteen year old Mary Baker from Waterford was brought by her aunt Mrs. Lalor in November 1886; but within a fortnight, she left at her aunt's request.[24] It is possible that some of these placements were intended as warnings, or carried out for the girls' protection. Annie Jelly, for example, a 13 year old, was put in the Asylum by her aunt and a Dr. Phelan in 1891. No further information about her is recorded, except that she came from Clonmel.[25] Another 13 year old, Mary Murphy, from Ballytruckle in Waterford, was brought to the Home in February 1888 by her mother, who took her out exactly two years later.[26] Three young girls were placed in the Asylum by their mothers in 1895 (by which time the new building was occupied) only to be taken out shortly afterwards by the same women. Sarah Sullivan aged 14, from Green's Lane in Waterford was admitted in February for a stay lasting nine months and was "very good"; Katie Kenny from Tramore, also 14 and "very good" stayed for three months; and Mary Sanders aged 19, was removed by her mother after a stay of less than four weeks.[27] In the same year another 14 year old, Mary Griffin from Waterford, was brought to the Home by a policeman, but no further information is recorded.[28]

In 1897 two very young sisters, Mary and Ellie Doyle from Thomastown, Co. Kilkenny were admitted to the Asylum. The first, aged 14, was brought by her father and mother in August; and her sister aged 13 was brought by her father and brother in the following month. This girl, described in the Register as "idiotic", left at her own request, though no date for her departure is given.[29] A few days after she was admitted another 13 year old, Christina Smith from Wexford, was placed in the Home by a Mrs. Kelly. She too was "partly idiotic", and left after only ten days.[30] Mary Anne Fitzgerald, also aged only 13 on

---

23 *Ibid.*, 20 September 1880.
24 *Ibid.*, 27 November 1886.
25 *Ibid.*, No date, July 1891.
26 *Ibid.*, 22 February 1888.
27 *Ibid.*, 12 February, and 24 and 3 May 1895.
28 *Ibid.*, 3 September 1895.
29 *Ibid.*, 2 August and 3 September 1897.
30 *Ibid.*, 7 September 1897.

admission, was one of several penitents in this period recommended to the institution by the Mercy Nuns in Wexford. Most of their cases were unsatisfactory. Through their influence two 15 year olds, Stasia Purcell and Mary Berry, for example, were admitted in October 1897. The former, "a quiet child", was taken out by her parents six months later; and the latter - "sullen, deep and vindictive" was removed by her brother after three months.[31] Maggie Scallion, aged 23 and admitted in May 1898, was "half idiot"; and 36 year old Maria Flynn, registered in the following month on the recommendation of the Wexford nuns, was described in the Register as "a real discontented tramp".[32]

Minnie Morrisey from Post Office Lane, Tramore was 14 when she first entered the Home, having been sent by a priest. She must have left shortly afterwards as she was re-admitted a few months later, only to leave again "half mad".[33] The youngest admission to the Waterford Home was Mary McCabe from Drogheda Row, Monasterevan, Co. Kildare. She was sent by the local Mercy nuns in November 1899 when she was only 12 years old; and died in the Asylum 14 years later, aged 26.[34] Meanwhile the Mercy nuns sent two more penitents from Monasterevan in the last weeks of 1899 - 16 year old Annie Brennan (also from Drogheda Row) a "quiet child" who left the Home eighteen months later; and 20 year old Rose Ryan, from Whellans Row, Monasterevan. She too was "quiet" but "unsettled", and she left after six months. [35]

Some of the women, of course, were much older when they entered the Asylum, their advanced years making the gruelling regime ahead of them a nightmare. A local woman Anne Walsh, for example, was aged 50 when she entered voluntarily in September 1898. Ten months later she died of rheumatism.[36] For women in poor health or elderly, even the climb to the dormitories must have been daunting. The stairs in the Waterford Home were unusually steep – an additional discomfort to women worn out with drudgery and prayer. Various of the women were even older than Anne Walsh when they entered the Asylum - an

---

31 *Ibid.*, 23 May 1898, 15 September and 2 October 1897.
32 *Ibid.*, 21 May and 21 June 1898.
33 *Ibid.*, 24 September 1898 and 12 February 1899.
34 *Ibid.*, 10 November 1899.
35 *Ibid.*, 29 November and 9 December 1899.
36 *Ibid.*, 24 September 1898.

indication of their hopeless state. One, for example, was aged 57 at the time she was registered, one was 58 and another was 59 years old. The vast majority of inmates, however, were aged between 17 and 30 on admission, with a third of the overall total being 17 to 20 year olds. This wide range of inmates, so harmful to adolescents in need of protection rather than punishment, would not have been tolerated in English Protestant Homes.

In common with the penitents in Limerick, those in the Waterford Home can rarely be categorised into groups such as prostitutes, "first-fall" cases, victims of incest, etc., because of lack of information on the women's previous history. Observations on their character and mental state are unusually harsh in the Waterford Register, with comments such as "idiotic", "half insane", "dissipated" and "sly", occurring with greater frequency than is the case elsewhere. Such descriptions (less charitable, perhaps, than the nuns' vocations required) refer, of course, to behaviour in the Home and are not necessarily an indication of the women's pasts.

In common with the Asylums in New Ross and Cork, the only women who can positively be identified as prostitutes during the period (though clearly, there were others) are those recommended by Miss Farrell, the Matron, between 1870 and 1886, of the country's two "Certified" Hospitals set up under the Contagious Diseases Acts. In addition, various other women were recommended to the Homes by Rev. Reed of Cork; who, as discussed in Chapter 6, was Chaplain to the city's Government Lock Hospital, and gave evidence to the Select Committee of Enquiry into the Contagious Diseases Acts in 1881.

The first of these admissions to the Waterford Asylum occurred in December 1871, when 21 year old Caroline Salbert from Dublin was recommended by "Miss Farrell, Matron of Lock Hospital, Kildare". The girl was described as "very quite" [sic]; and "died happily", though no date was given.[37] A few weeks later (by which time the Matron had moved to the Hospital in Cork) two of Miss Farrell's cases were admitted on the same day. Eighteen year old Bessy Murphy from Cork stayed in the Asylum for only four months and was described as "very bold"; and 30 year old Mary Walsh, also from Cork, left at her own request eight

---

37 *Ibid.*, 8 December 1871.

months later, and was considered "very hasty". Another prostitute recommended by Miss Farrell was 38 year old Eliza Holmes, whose address was not known. She was allowed to leave after only two weeks in the Home.[38]

Thirty year old Alice Holden, originally from Kilkenny, was recommended to the Asylum by Miss Farrell ("Matron of Lock Hospital, Cork") in November 1872. Although her behaviour was described as "sometimes satisfactory", she left after 18 months for "bad conduct".[39] A Dublin woman, 34 year old Lizzie Anderson was possibly one of those much-publicised prostitutes allegedly discharged from Certified Hospitals before being properly cured. In February, 1873, just ten weeks after being admitted to the Waterford Good Shepherd from Miss Farrell's institution, she had to be sent to the Fever Hospital. Although she did not return to the Asylum, her conduct had been "very good".[40]

In the same month 26 year old Julia Manaly of Cork was recommended to the Refuge by Fr. Reede [sic], at this time Chaplain to the Government Lock Hospital in that city. Part of his duties under the amended Contagious Diseases legislation was the attempted reform of prostitutes detained for the treatment of venereal disease, and their placement, if possible, in suitable Rescue Homes. This woman - not one of his successful cases - is an indication of how unreliable his evidence to the Government Select Committee was. Far from remaining in the Home in which "Divine Providence" had placed her, she was "very unsettled" and left after only 6 days.[41] A few days later another of Miss Farrell's Lock Hospital converts, 19 year old Mary Kelly, originally from Clonmel, was admitted to the Waterford Home. Eighteen months after her arrival she left at her own request, but returned after nine months, only to leave again in August 1875. She was described as "very bold".[42] Meanwhile, in March 1873 Miss Farrell sent 40 year old Margaret McGuire to the Sisters in Waterford. Although this woman had undergone compulsory treatment in the prison-like Hospital in Cork, after

---

38 *Ibid.*, 23 January and 22 June 1872.
39 *Ibid.*, 12 March 1872.
40 *Ibid.*, 29 November 1872.
41 *Ibid.*, 20 February 1873.
42 *Ibid.*, 6 March 1873.

which she served two full years as a penitent - the most that was required, and even permitted, in the vast majority of Homes - she was described as "very hasty" when she left in 1875.[43]

By July 1873 Miss Farrell was once more stationed in the Certified Hospital in Kildare. In the middle of that month 18 year old Elizabeth Kavanagh was admitted to the Waterford Good Shepherd on the Matron's recommendation. She stayed in the Asylum for eleven days.[44] Meanwhile in the Cork Lock Hospital, Fr. Reed persuaded 24 year old prostitute Ellen McCarthy to enter the Waterford Home. Another of his failed conversions, she stayed only two weeks, and was "disobedient".[45] He was slightly more successful with Margaret Hopkins, originally from Limerick and aged 26. She stayed in the Home for six months, but her conduct was "very bold".[46] Fr. Reed next recommended 38 year old Eliza Keily of Cork, another of those Lock Hospital patients who may well have been prematurely discharged as cured. Within ten days of her arrival she left for hospital because of "ill health". [47]

In his evidence to the Select Committee in 1881 the Hospital Chaplain claimed that the vast majority of his cases were successful. He was confident of this because he did not "lose sight" of the women, and had any of them left the institutions in which they had been placed, he would have been informed.[48] If Rev. Reed had followed up his conversions more thoroughly before giving evidence (or alternatively, had he not been misinformed regarding their behaviour in the Homes and their actual length of stay) his faith in the Acts' tendency to reclaim these women by means of the Penitentiary System would have been shaken. His evidence might well have been different - and certainly, it would have been more to the point. As it is, with such a record of failure behind him, his insistence on the legislation's reclamatory influence is remarkable. If, for example, he had followed the progress of another of his converts, 22 year old Cork prostitute Ellen McCarthy, he would have known that she was

---

43 *Ibid.*, 16 March 1873.
44 *Ibid.*, 18 July 1873.
45 *Ibid.*, 14 August 1873.
46 *Ibid.*, 3 February 1874.
47 *Ibid.*, 8 April 1874.
48 See pages 169-70.

"very idle"; and that she left the Waterford Asylum in July 1874, just nine days after she arrived.[49]

His referrals to the Limerick Good Shepherd were equally discouraging. In October 1875, Ellen Donovan, for example, 18 years old and a former penitent of the Order's Cork Refuge, was recommended to the Limerick Home following her treatment for venereal disease. She "escaped from the Asylum" after nine days but was brought back by the police, only to be sent out on the following day. Shortly afterwards another Cork prostitute, 22 year old Ellen Vaughan was referred to the Provincial House by the Hospital Chaplain. "Insubordination" ensured that she too, was "sent away". Also "sent out for insubordination" was forty year old Mary McGuire, another of Rev. Reed's converts who spent only a few days in the Limerick Home. Before being detained for treatment in the Government Lock Hospital, she had been a penitent in both Waterford and Cork.[50]

Another Waterford penitent who was clearly a registered prostitute before entering the Home was 23 year old Kate Collen, originally from Wexford. Recommended by Miss Farrell at the Kildare Lock Hospital in December 1874, she left after eight months for "bad conduct". Also admitted from the Lock Hospital in the period were 48 year old Bridget Brennon, from Carrick-on-Suir (she stayed for two days); 24 year old Elizabeth Perry from England (no date is given for her departure) and 20 year old Kate Ryan from Dublin. This girl, who in 1880 stayed in the Home for only four months, was a more hopeful case and left for a situation.[51] Twenty-five year old Lizzie Walsh, on the other hand, was one of the few women of this "state registered" category, to remain in the Home for life - though in her case it was a penance lasting only four years. Admitted from the Kildare Lock Hospital in May 1880, she died in the Asylum in May 1884.[52]

More typical was the behaviour of 40 year old Mary Clark from Belfast, who "received the name of Winefred" and left in February 1881, only three weeks after being admitted. In common with

---

49 Waterford Register of Penitents, 20 July 1874.
50 Limerick Register of Penitents, 31 March and late April 1875; and 7 October 1876.
51 Waterford Register of Penitents, 30 December 1874, 19 February 1876, and 2 October and 14 December 1879.
52 *Ibid.*, no date May 1880.

several other cases sent by Miss Farrell, she was "very idle".[53] Mary Filey from Kildare was another 40 year old who came straight from the Lock Hospital. She was registered in the Asylum in February 1881, but her date of departure is not known. [54]

It has been noted that the Contagious Diseases Acts were suspended in 1883, and repealed in 1886. This makes 29 year old Anne Mulbrooney's referral to the Waterford Home something of a mystery, since she was recommended by "Miss Farrell, Lock Hospital", in September 1886. The woman, who was from Borrisoleigh, Co. Tipperary, stayed in the Waterford penitentiary for ten months but was "very troublesome". She was Miss Farrell's last case.[55]

Several of the above women, as well as others who were not Lock Hospital referrals, were recommended to the Waterford Home from Cork, a city with extensive Magdalen provision of its own. It was clearly thought desirable that some women should be sent to Homes far removed from old associations, where no-one knew them, and where "awakened memories" were less likely to intrude.[56] Such transfers began with the opening of the Waterford Asylum; and while the New Ross Mission only marginally extended the process, it was most evident following the foundation of the Home in Cork. As well as these "internal" transfers, women were sometimes referred to the Irish Monasteries by Superiors from the English Province; and occasionally, an inmate from another Order's Asylum was sent to

---

53 *Ibid.*, 6 February 1881. Curiously, the previous entry in the Register was also for a 40 year old Mary Clark (29 October 1880). She, however, was originally from Dublin, had been sent from the Hammersmith Home, had "received the name of Benedict" and was "very good". Admissions at this time were unusually infrequent, with only 7 inmates being registered in 1881. Between October 1880 and June 1885, only 28 penitents were received - an average of 5.5 per year over the four year period.

54 *Ibid.*, 7 February 1881.

55 *Ibid.*, 28 September 1886.

56 This practice occurred in English Homes too. An 18 year old prostitute Margaret Elizabeth Madden, for example, was admitted to the Lincoln Asylum for Female Penitents in November 1901. She had spent her childhood in an Industrial School in Hull before going into domestic service in Bradford. She then worked in a factory, "lived a bad life", and was imprisoned for 12 days. Her conduct in the Home (where she met past associates) was so bad that she was transferred to the Salvation Army Refuge in Leeds. (Ladies Minute Books, 1901-2.)

As mentioned in Chapter 3 and illustrated above, another manifestation of this attempt to break with the past, was the Good Shepherd practice of assigning new names to penitents, though in the process a woman's identity, as well as her background, might well be suppressed.

a Good Shepherd Home. There is little evidence of reciprocal referrals taking place. It was not only the case that few penitents were recommended to rival institutions. Few were sent to the Order's own, non-Irish Homes.[57]

Thus 39 year old Bridget Kane, for example "left our Convent of Hammersmith for entering here" [Waterford] in November 1876; and three years later, 40 year old Elizabeth Gregory, was admitted from Dalbreth, the Order's Asylum in Glasgow.[58] In October 1880 a Dublin woman, 40 year old Mary Clark, who received the name of Benedict "came [to Waterford] from Hammersmith"; and in May 1887, 19 year old Kate Connelly from Naas was admitted from the Gloucester Street Home in Dublin. She was dismissed and re-admitted several times over the next few months and was "very boisterous and idle".[59] In the following year Ellen O'Neil aged 32, from Ballybricken Waterford, was received direct from the Good Shepherd Asylum, Cardiff, but was "very discontented"; and in December 1891, 19 year old Maria Santo, from Aberdeen, Scotland, was sent to the Waterford Home by the Mother Prioress of Dalbreth, Glasgow. She left three months later because of ill health, but her conduct was satisfactory.[60] Shortly afterwards Ellen Dwyer aged 19, though brought by her mother, was recommended by the Order's Prioress in New Ross, the girl's home town. In April 1894, 16 year old Kate McMahon from Limerick was sent by the Mother Provincial in that city (she left after only two months); and in the following year, 18 year old Mary Cooney, admitted direct from the Limerick Monastery, remained for just over a year.[61] Another Limerick woman recommended to Waterford by the Mother Provincial was 40 year old Mary Anne Shea, who stayed for 7 months in 1896. Also in this period a Belfast woman Kate Bryd was transferred from the Limerick to the Waterford Home, but was "very violent"; and in the same month (September 1896) a Co. Tipperary woman Katie Burke, aged 20, made the same

---

57 This occasionally occurred. In 1880, for example, Johanna Cokely left the Cork Good Shepherd for the Peacock Lane Asylum (run by the Sisters of Charity) - though whether she was "recommended" to do so, is doubtful. Seventeen year old Ann Frost, on the other hand, admitted to the Cork Good Shepherd in 1885, was actually "taken" to the Peacock Lane premises in the following year.

58 Waterford Register of Penitents, 27 November 1876 and 27 July 1879.

59 *Ibid.*, 29 October 1880 and 18 May 1887.

60 *Ibid.*, March/April, 1888, and 9 December 1891.

61 *Ibid.*, 19 April 1892, April 1894 and 28 August 1895.

move. She left the Waterford Home shortly afterwards (twice) and was "disobedient". Three years later she was in and out of the Home on two further occasions, but had now become "very troublesome and quarrelsome".[62]

A final example of such transfers is the history of Fanny Forty, a Waterford girl whose father put her in the institution in July 1884 when she was 20 years old. Thirty-one years later she "left for our class in New Ross". She returned soon afterwards, and died in the Waterford Asylum in April, 1937, at which time she was 73 years old and had been a penitent for more than half a century. Her conduct in the Home was not described.[63]

Difficult cases were sometimes transferred in the hope that they would do better elsewhere - evidence of the nuns' unwillingness to relinquish these "lost sheep". Twenty-two year old Jilly Troy, from Youghal, Co. Cork, for example, was sent from the Waterford Home to the New Ross Asylum in August 1899, being subject to that evil tendency - "full of particular friendships". Bridget Whelan, on the other hand, a Kilkenny woman recommended by a priest, had been "expelled" for this behaviour, only two years before.[64] Jane Sexton, originally from Kilrush, was another girl transferred from the Limerick to the Waterford Home. Soon after her arrival in January 1899, however, she was found to be "half lunatic", and left of her own choice. Within a few days of her departure she returned, only to be sent away shortly afterwards and again described as "half lunatic".[65]

It is noted in the following Chapter that the recognition by the New Ross Sisters that their Magdalen Home would never be financially viable, resulted in their immediate "petition" for an Industrial School, following the introduction of the system to Ireland, in 1868. The Community was fortunate in having a generous benefactor in Richard Devereux; and a substantial permanent premises for the purpose (without which, "certification" could not properly be granted) was immediately built.

---

62 *Ibid.*, 20 January and 2 and 27 September 1896.
63 *Ibid.*, 2 July 1884.
64 *Ibid.*, 24 August 1899 and 27 May 1897.
65 *Ibid.*, 13 January 1899.
66 For an account of similar conditions in other Industrial Schools, see *Suffer the Little Children, op. cit.*

The other Irish Houses were less fortunate. The Order's temporary Industrial School in Cork, for example, was thrown up with such indecent haste that the insanitary and overcrowded premises endangered the children's health (see page 171); and in Waterford, while the original accommodation may have been marginally better, a similar situation prevailed.[66]

The Annals record that the Convent in Hennessey's Road was small and bare, with many "privations"; and the Bishop's comments when funds for the new premises were called for, confirm this report. Further, the Annals note that for several years the place lacked suitable grounds. In spite of these drawbacks - or probably because of them, since they could only be remedied by a large influx of funds - in 1870 a preservation class of children was commenced in a "small house" adjoining the Convent.

Shortly afterwards, application was made to have this institution "Certified" under the new regulations. In April 1871 Sir John Lentaigne, then Inspector of Industrial Schools in Ireland visited the Community; and despite its cramped conditions and lack of grounds, the small house next to the Convent was approved as a suitable premises for over 100 children.[67] Not surprisingly, it soon proved to be both unhealthy and inadequate.

The Community (presumably on the strength of the profits the Industrial School now secured them) next purchased the semi-derelict St. John's College nearby, together with its adjoining lands. On the site of this premises, and with remarkable speed, the building of St. Dominic's, the Congregation's impressive new Industrial School, began. Fears that disease might break out in the severely overcrowded children's quarters no doubt hastened the project, and were not without foundation. Only six years previously the Order's Industrial children in Cork had been so imprudently housed in makeshift accommodation that an outbreak of opthalmia, lasting five months, occurred. Even more alarming, typhus fever had recently devastated the still temporary institution. Though only one girl died, fifty-six children and one of the Sisters caught the disease. According to the Cork Annals, this had been brought into the school by a child

---

67 Notes of Waterford Annals.

"barely recovered"; whose father, mother, two sisters and a brother had all died within the past week. Yet "none of the magistrates knew anything of this when the child was admitted."![68]

As well as buying St. John's College the Sisters gradually acquired the fields between it and the leased Convent in Hennessey's Road. The two properties, now separated only by Convent Hill Road, were linked by a tunnel built under this street, to ensure the complete isolation of the whole Community. This extraordinary arrangement, so revealing of the Order's mentality throughout the period, remained in operation until 1960 when the Sisters "ceded" the fields to Waterford Corporation as a site for a housing estate.[69]

Early in 1878 the new Industrial School was completed. It remains a magnificent structure, architecturally the most pleasing of the Order's Irish schools, and vaguely reminiscent of George Wilkinson's design for Ireland's thirty or so post-famine workhouses. None the less, its proximity to a Magdalen Asylum provoked Michael McCarthy's comments which introduced this Chapter.*

The opening of the Waterford Monastery's new Industrial School financed and co-incided with other changes in the eighteen-seventies. The increased numbers of children who could now be accommodated - together with a rising penitent population, the expansion of the laundry, and the establishment of the segregated "Magdalen" Class (see below) - all stimulated the demand for additional Sisters to run what was becoming a large, complex and lucrative enterprise. Since the old Convent in Hennessey's Road could scarcely house the existing Congregation, and the penitents' quarters were overcrowded and unfit, it was clear that new accommodation was urgently required. The land adjoining the large Industrial School was now leased and became the site for extensive development, with, as

---

68   Cork Annals, 1875. It is hard to believe that such a catastrophe - necessitating the child's admission to the Industrial School in the first place - would not have been known, both by the authorities and the Sisters themselves.
69   Named Rice Park, after Edmund Rice, founder of the Christian Brothers.
*   The shocking exposures concerning the Order's Magdalen Asylum and adjoining Industrial School in Limerick, entirely justify Michael J. McCarthy's apprehensions - though even he could hardly have envisaged the dangers inherent in such a system.

noted above, the foundation stone of the new Convent, Penitentiary and Laundry being laid by the Bishop, Dr. Sheehan, in May 1892.

In his address the Bishop stressed that the public was not expected to contribute to the cost of the "modest dwelling" intended for the nuns. They were prepared to pay for their Convent out of their own slender resources. Funds for the Magdalen Asylum and Laundry, however, "for perhaps the most miserable and abandoned class in the entire community" were required, and the generosity of Waterford's citizens was appealed to.[70]

It will be shown in Chapter 7 that whereas in 1870, the enormous sum of £7,000 had been collected in a single night for the foundation of the Order's new Magdalen Asylum in Cork, the public's response to an appeal on behalf of the same institution some thirty years later was disappointing. It may well be that the largest Female Penitentiary in that city was, after a quarter of a century, less popular than its founders had foreseen. A similar tendency is discernible in Waterford, and perhaps this was inevitable. It can hardly have gone un-noticed that the Homes had developed along very different lines from those originally envisaged. As "short-term" Refuges, designed to rehabilitate and train fallen women for future employment (the stated intention of their founders) the Homes were peculiarly unsuccessful. The rescue of many women was curiously protracted and, to judge from the state of those emerging from the institutions, achieved at dubious cost. Further, it was clear that many such departures were resisted rather than supported by the nuns; and despite their lengthy "training" remarkably few of the women (in fact, only 4 per cent of the overall total for the period analysed) were placed in situations straight from the Homes.

Yet there were few, if any, complaints. In contrast to the furious response to the Contagious Diseases legislation, there was no organised opposition to the Magdalen system, no agitation for the closure of the Homes, and no shortage of women being "voluntarily" reformed. Most survivors of the system preferred to deny their experience, especially if embarking on a more

---

70 *Waterford News*, 4 June 1892.

"respectable" life; and in this they were supported and encouraged by the priests.

Nevertheless, rumour was inevitable, and some of the women must have talked, particularly those who left shortly after admission. Hasty departures and dismissals could be justified both by damning accounts of the system, and frightening descriptions of long-term inmates, who, after years of toil and atonement, were no longer quite "all there".

Included in Chapter 6 is part of the testimony of Cork priest Rev. Maguire, who in 1871 (two decades before Bishop Sheehan's appeal for funds for the new Asylum in Waterford) was called to give evidence before the Royal Commission on the Contagious Diseases Acts. This witness was adamant that women who "fell" in country districts in Ireland could never return to their homes:

> "Any woman who commits herself in the country can never go back to it. There is a sense of propriety in the country where no man ever thinks to receive his child back after she has fallen ... wherever a woman makes a slip, she must fly, so if by chance a woman yields to passion on promise of marriage, she knows there is no chance of remaining there ... they would shun her..."

According to this priest even emigration and the prospect of joining relatives was limited, for in America too, a man's standing rested on the character of his family, whether there or back at home. For the purpose of concealment and punishment, then, Magdalen Asylums were the answer - the resort of relatives, as much as the unmarried mother herself.* This rural intolerance may well have been resented by those living in the shadow of such institutions, less, perhaps, for its hypocrisy than its expense. It may well have been considered that those making use of the Asylums, as well as the local urban community, should be appealed to or targeted for funds. This was a particularly sensitive issue in Waterford, which supported more than its share of

---

* This situation remained virtually unaltered (though the Mother and Baby Home replaced the workhouse as a place of confinement) until the mid-twentieth century. See, for example, the tragic evidence of Christina Mulcahy, who was forced into the Galway Magdalen Asylum in the 1940s by her father, after she tried to return home following the birth of her child. *Sex in a Cold Climate, op. cit.*

"sacerdotal institutions" - all of which, according to McCarthy, flourished, while the city and the lay Catholics decayed.[71]

By October 1894 the new Good Shepherd buildings were ready for occupation. The Convent, a "citadel of Piety" whose accommodation has been referred to in the previous Chapter, turned out to be rather less "modest" than expected; while the whole institution, hailed as one of the chief architectural adornments of a city rich in such charitable works, was said to be second to none of its kind in the world. Its situation and grounds were excellent, and from the upper floors of the Convent and Magdalen Asylum (though in the latter the glass in the windows was obscured) there were magnificent views:

> "The work [convent] when it leaves the Contractor's hands, will have cost fully twenty thousand pounds, and this immense sum of money is being provided for out of the resources of the Community alone - a fact which speaks eloquently for the self-denial and earnestness of the Sisterhood.[72]

The immense sum demonstrates too, the huge amount of money the local Order had so rapidly acquired.

Waterford's new Magdalen Asylum was the last to be built in Ireland. From a sanitary viewpoint it was admirable - the late Victorian obsession with through-ventilation and lofty, airy rooms being evident. As a place of lifelong, or even short-term confinement, however, it was a forbidding structure. The penitents' refectory, 52 feet long and 34 feet wide was approached and used in silence. Their workroom, of the same dimensions, was also their place of recreation and here too, the women were often forbidden to talk. A packing room connected with the vast laundry section at the rear of the building, housing washing, drying, ironing and starching rooms; in each of which again, for most of the time the women worked in silence or were obliged to sing hymns or chant prayers. There was also a penitents' airing ground or enclosure. The upper floor of the penitentiary contained an infirmary, a pharmacy and a convalescent ward, plus two large dormitories which housed

---

71 "Every variety of religious institution is to be found in Waterford, and they are all flourishing. It is only the town itself and the lay Catholics that are decaying". McCarthy, *op. cit.*, p.492. Also, "Waterford is, next to Dublin, the most priest-infested territory in Ireland. How shall I count up the lists of male and female religious in this diocese, where priests accumulate and men decay?" p.488.

72 *Waterford News*, October 1894.

more than a hundred women. We have seen that here particularly, the Rules of Silence and Surveillance were always enforced. This was the extent of the penitents' world, except for the cloister, which following its completion in 1903, led to the new Chapel.

Attached to the penitentiary, but entirely cut off from it, were the quarters of the Province's "Magdalens" - former penitents, now so consumed with remorse that they practiced strict self-denial and lived out their mortified lives in silence, solitude and prayer.* Engaged in lace-making, needlework and making altar wafers, they were isolated not only from the world, but from the Monastery itself. A small refectory and workroom, an infirmary and a dormitory were reserved for their use, as was a tiny private garden.

Shortly after the completion of these buildings the public was asked to contribute to the third phase of the Waterford Enclosure - the new Chapel. The Bishop's appeal occasioned a further opportunity for the Madonna/Mary Magdalen contrast, in which the nuns were elevated to extraordinary heights:

> "Round about that alter will ascend daily to heaven the co-mingled prayer of the consecrated virgin and the penitent girl that no blight of sin or sorrow may ever rest upon you or your children. My brethren, will it not remind you of that last, most touching scene of the life of our Divine Lord, when Mary the sinful but repentant Magdalen, and Mary His Immaculate Virgin Mother, stood beneath His cross." [73]

The Chapel is a superb and costly example of late Victorian Gothic, its use of high screens and separate cloistered entrances ensuring the complete segregation of the Classes. To the left of the altar a small room secluded the Magdalens, whose access to their quarters was via a private covered way.

A total of 703 women were registered in the Waterford Good Shepherd Asylum between 1842 and 1900, some of them being re-admitted several times. The youngest girls were aged 12 (one) and 13 (five) when admitted, and the oldest woman (one) was aged 59. Table 9 gives the age distribution of entrants over the period.

---

*   Until the mid-twentieth century the Order always referred to these women as Magdalens, and collectively, they were known as the Magdalen Class.
   In 1969 these women (now known as Sisters Magdalens) were removed to Belfast - at which time there were approximately 2,600 of them world-wide, but a mere handful in the Irish Province. They are now called the "Contemplative" Community.
73   *Waterford News*, 1 May 1903.

Table 9
Age on Admission: Waterford Good Shepherd 1842–1900

Years	Total 703	Percent
12–19	191	27
20–29	314	45
30–39	134	19
40–49	35	5
50–59	11	1.5
Not Given	18	2.5

Table 10 shows that almost half of the women in this Asylum were described in the Register as having "entered voluntarily". Most of the remainder were referred to the institution by priests, the Superiors of other Good Shepherd Convents and various other nuns.

Table 10
By Whom Recommended: Waterford Gd Shep.
1842–1900

	Total 703	Percent
Entered Voluntarily	348	49.5
Priests	189	27
Nuns	28	4
Ladies	23	3
Female Relatives	23	3
Other Good Shepherds	21	3
Miss Farrell	18	2.5
Prison	7	1
Hospital	4	0.5
Other	36	5
Not Given	6	1

Table 11 lists how inmates left the Home. For 137 individuals (approximately 20 percent of the overall total) this information was not recorded. Of the 566 penitents for whom this evidence exists, almost two thirds left at their own request. Yet although 348 women entered the Home voluntarily (almost 50 percent of the overall total) and 357 left "of their own accord", the extent to which voluntary admissions and departures are linked, is less than these figures would suggest. Only 166 women (approximately one third of the inmates for whom both types of information is listed) were classed as both entering and leaving the Asylum at their own request.

Table 11
Reasons for Leaving: Waterford Good Shepherd
1842–1900

	Total 566	Percent
Own Request	357	63
Expelled	51	9
Died in Home	48	8
Left for Family/Friends	45	8
Hospital	27	5
"Magdalen" Class	16	3
Left for Situation	5	0.9
America	5	0.9
Other Good Shepherds	4	0.7
Escaped	4	0.7
Other	4	0.7

Inmates' length of stay in the Waterford Asylum is given in Table 12. There is no discernible pattern or change over the period analysed, i.e. 1842 when the lay Refuge opened, to the 1940s, when the last of the penitents admitted in the period under review, died. The average length of stay for the 404 women for whom this information is recorded was 4.6 years. More than half the inmates, however, remained for less than nine months in the Home.

Table 13 shows that with only 40 percent of inmates coming from the city and county of Waterford, the Home might well have been viewed as catering for non-local needs - a factor which, as mentioned above, possibly contributed to its declining popularity by the end of the period. The public, though having little information on the origin of inmates, would certainly have been aware that many women coming in and out of the Asylum, were not from their own community. They are still remembered as being "not local, but coming from outside". It is significant that in spite of the Order's Asylum in nearby New Ross, the county of Wexford accounted for 12 percent of admissions to the Waterford Home.

Table 12
Length of Stay in Waterford Good Shepherd:
From 1842

	Total 404	Percent
Under 1 week	19	4.7
1-2 weeks	11	2.7
2-4 weeks	34	8.4
1-2 months	39	9.7
2-6 months	71	17.6
6-12 months	44	10.9
1-2 years	83	20.5
2-5 years	46	11.4
5-10 years	15	3.7
10-15 years	6	1.5
15-20 years	4	1.0
20-30 years	10	2.5
30-40 years	8	2.0
40-50 years	7	1.7
50 years +	7	1.7

Table 13
Birthplace of Waterford Penitents: 1842-1900

	Total 703	Percent
Waterford City	220	31
Co. Wexford	87	12
Co. Tipperary	78	11
Co. Waterford	64	9
Co. Kilkenny	50	7
Co. Cork	38	5.5
Other	124	18
Not Given	42	6

Apart from 2 Protestants and one inmate whose religion was not recorded, all were listed as Catholics in this source. Eight of the women were married.

The 1901 Census reveals that at the end of the period, there were 38 Sisters in the Waterford Good Shepherd Convent. The Forms for the Religious were completed by the Mother Superior, Sister Mary Raphael O'Loughlin, who, at that time was 45 years of age, and had been Superioress for five years. The Magdalen section contained 105 inmates, classed as "Reformed females employed in laundry of Good Shepherd Convent". For 90 of these women, their Rank, Profession or Occupation is described as "Penitent", after which, on each Form, are the words "All laundresses in Good Shepherd Convent". The other 15 inmates, appearing together on one form, are classed as "Magdalens"; and were members of the Province's austere contemplative Class, referred to above.

Table 14 gives the age distribution of all these women in 1901. The youngest nun at the time of the Census was 27 years of age, and the oldest was 75. The youngest penitent was aged 15 and the oldest was 82. The youngest Magdalen was 25 and the oldest was 71.

Table 14
Ages of Nuns, Penitents and "Magdalens" in the Waterford Good Shepherd: 1901 Census

Years	Nuns Number	Total 38 Percent	Pen. Number	Total 90 Percent	"Mags" Number	Total 15 Percent
15-19	–	–	11	12	–	–
20-29	4	11	37	41	1	7
30-39	6	16	13	14	4	27
40-49	11	29	15	17	2	13
50-59	4	11	7	8	5	33
60-69	10	26	2	2	2	13
70-79	3	8	3	3	1	7
80-89	–	–	2	2	–	–

Like the Sisters, all the Magdalens were described as able to read and write. For the penitents however, it was a different story, with only 16 (18 percent of the total) being literate. A further 53 inmates (59 percent) could read only and 21 of the women (23 percent of the total) were completely illiterate. This information approximates with that recorded for the New Ross and Cork Asylums; and indicates that the Limerick figures (showing a 93 percent literacy level) should be viewed with caution.

Some of the women recorded as illiterate or able to read only, had been in the Waterford Asylum for years. Mary Power, aged 82, for example (unable to read or write) had been admitted to the Refuge fourteen years prior to the nuns' arrival, and by 1901 had already been confined for well over half a century.[74] Bridget Barry, aged 77 at the time of the census, was unable to read after 56 years in the Home; and Mary Ann Barrett, who at the age of 40 was still illiterate, had been in the Waterford Asylum for approximately 22 years.[75] Maggie Hastings from Co. Dublin was another 40 year old whose lengthy stay in the Refuge had done little to improve her literacy; and even much younger women, such as 25 year old Maggie Duggan from Wexford were illiterate after several years' confinement in the Home.[76] As noted earlier, this reflects to some extent the situation for the general population (particularly the poor) as well as the fact that some of the women were probably of the "feeble-minded" class.

The birthplace of all 38 nuns and 15 Magdalens included on the Census was recorded as Waterford City - clearly an error on the Superior's part. Of the 90 ordinary penitents listed in the new Asylum, on the other hand, only 44 percent came from either the city or county of Waterford, and could be classed as "local". While 32 were from adjoining counties, others came from as far afield as Dublin, Belfast, Clare, Limerick, Kildare, Carlow and Galway.

---

74 Waterford Register of Penitents, 8 May 1844.
75 *Ibid.*, 28 June 1845. Mary Ann Barrett, who came from the nearby industrial village of Portlaw, left and re-entered the Home several times. 23 December 1879.
76 *Ibid.*, 27 November 1886 and 24 June 1895.

It was noted earlier in this Chapter that the number of penitents in Waterford steadily increased over the period. At the time of the Census there were 105 women in the institution, and by 1904, according to the Annals, there were 130 inmates in the Home. In the reactionary climate of the 1920s and 30s, the Irish Magdalen Movement experienced something of a revival, and ambitions for expanding and consolidating the system soared. In that period of dire poverty, a magnificent Chapel was built for the Community in Limerick; and in Waterford (where hopes for the new Asylum sheltering "at least 300 refugees" were never to be realised) confidence in a glorious future was restored. Extensions to provide accommodation for 160 inmates were carried out in this bleak period, and the Irish Magdalen system, appalling in concept and practice, was given a further lease of life.

In July 1928, in an appeal against the Valuation for Rates on the Laundry, Magdalen Asylum, Convent and lands of the Waterford Good Shepherd Community, some interesting facts emerged. Counsel for the appellants stated that some 190 women now worked under the direction of the nuns. Money received from Laundry work done for the public went into the common fund; and the produce of the farm was used in the institution. The nuns' dowries were invested and could only be withdrawn in the event of a Sister leaving the Community. In addition to the interest on these sums, further income was received from the State-supported Industrial children, as well as from donations, subscriptions and bequests. Yet it was claimed there was a deficit of over £3,000, and they sought exemption from a valuation of £567.[77]

The nuns continued to plead poverty. According to an advertisement in 1931, a daily increase of penitents made their support impossible without the aid of generous benefactors. The large Laundry had lately been remodelled, the latest new machinery had been installed and the most up-to-date methods were used in every department. As well as laundry work, hair mattresses were

---

77 *Waterford News*, 27 July 1928.

made and re-made, plain and fancy needlework was offered, shirt making was a speciality, hand embroidered ladies' trousseaux could be made to order and mortuary habits were kept in stock.[78]

But endless washing, starching and ironing was the mainstay of the community and continued to be so for the next half century. By the late nineteen seventies, however, the widespread use of the domestic washing machine (rather than any reforming legislation, public concern or liberal debate) heralded the end of the Magdalen system. No longer profitable, the Laundry was closed in 1982, and it was decided at provincial level that admissions to the Penitentiary (or "Home" as it was now being studiously called) should no longer take place.

In 1994 the Waterford Good Shepherd Asylum closed, and its Convent, Chapel, Penitentiary, former Magdalen Section and Laundry buildings were sold to the Regional Technical College - now the Waterford Institute of Technology. There are few reminders of its dark past in what is now the School of Humanities.

The former occupants of the penitentiary are now, like the nuns, housed in new accommodation a few yards from their old premises. The "Orphanage"* is now used as an Adult Education Centre.

---

78   The Fold of the Good Shepherd, op. cit.

*   The persistent and widespread misconception that Industrial Schools were "orphanages" has been challenged by the author of this study for at least twenty years. The recent publication of *Suffer the Little Children* (*op. cit.,*) allows for no further prevarication on this point:
     "The second important myth is that these institutions were "orphanages", and that the children behind their walls were orphans [whereas most] children's institutions were specially defined as industrial schools, established and funded for the industrial training of the children within them. Most of the children within the system had either one or both parents still living, and so could not in any sense be described as orphans ... Had there been a proper understanding of the true nature of the system, it is likely that it would not have survived for so long. Public concern would most probably have been voiced at a much earlier stage (as in Britain) about the inappropriate nature of such institutions for child care. In Ireland, the State's policy of removing children from their families and funding religious orders to care for them remained unchanged until 1970. The 'orphan' myth essentially meant that the obviously preferable option of giving that same funding to families to allow them to keep their children at home was never publicly debated.
     This misconception was so pervasive that even many of those who grew up within the system were not aware that they had actually been in an industrial school". pp.12-13. More inexcusable is the fact that some of these children - taught to regard themselves as "orphans" - were unaware that their parents were alive, or, as has since been reported, were actually informed that they were dead.

5

The Good Shepherd Magdalen Asylum, New Ross

"There is a Magdalen Asylum at New Ross, in which there were 45 selected fallen women in 1901, whose histories I should like to inquire into."[1]

In May 1860 five Good Shepherd Sisters set out for Ireland from the French Mother House - their mission to establish a Foundation in the small Co. Wexford town of New Ross.[2] The nuns were all Irish - Sister Mary of St. Stanislaus Keghan, Superioress; Sister Mary of St. Ignatious Doyle, Assistant; Sister Mary of St. Ursula Rabbitt, Sister Mary of St. John Evangelist Hurley, and Sister Mary of St. Blandrine Smith.

Their first impressions were discouraging. Their "Convent", the dilapidated corn-store of a disused brewery in Irishtown, was described in the Annals as scarcely habitable; while a loft, reached by a rickety ladder, represented the future Magdalen Home.[3] The poverty of the neighbourhood may be judged from the fact that the makeshift Chapel (once the brewery owner's dwelling house) was shared with the public, and soon proved a "godsend" to those of the labouring classes, who, "from feeble health or the want of decent clothing" could not attend the nearby parish church.[4]

In response to an urgent request from the new Prioress, the Superior at Limerick sent two trusted penitents to help train the

---

1   McCarthy, *op. cit.*, p.470.
2   The population of New Ross in 1860 was only about 8,000 – probably a contributory factor in the Home's early lack of success. The Order's other Irish Foundations were established in much larger centres. The Limerick Mother House, for example, began in a city with a population of about 53,000. Waterford had a population of approximately 24,000 in 1858, and in Cork in 1870 the population was almost 80,000.
3   Annals of the New Ross Magdalen Asylum, 1860.
4   *Ibid.*

"uncultivated" women expected to arrive. Admitted on 21st of August, these helpers were the first inmates to be registered in the Home. One of them, 32 year old Ellen Moor, left at her own request four years later.[5] The other, 28 year old Margaret Williamson, originally from Co. Cork, spent the next forty-one years in the Institution.[6] She had been a penitent before the Good Shepherds came to Ireland, having entered the original Limerick lay Refuge in 1846, when she was just 15 years old. She was re-named "Magdalen", following the nuns' arrival in 1848; and fifty years later in New Ross, she became the first Irish penitent to celebrate her "Golden Jubilee" - the Sisters dating her conversion not from when it actually occurred, but from their arrival in the country. The 1901 Census records that at 70 years of age, she was the oldest woman in the Refuge. In common with 42 other inmates listed, she was described in the Returns as a "laundress", while two others were classed as "seamstresses".[7] Following her death a few months later, however, her actual status was revealed. She was buried in the communal penitents' plot, in an otherwise unmarked grave in the neighbouring public cemetery.[8]

As well as training new arrivals in laundry work, the two auxiliaries taught the women to respect the nuns, to sew, and to make underclothing. According to the Annals, their good behaviour and industry had far-reaching, beneficial effects on the Class. It was noted in Chapter 3, that unlike the Limerick and Waterford Foundations, which owed their origins to earlier attempts at Rescue Work, the New Ross Mission was entirely begun by the Order. Consequently, it was believed by the local Sisters that their penitents were the best in the Province - having fallen directly into Good Shepherd hands.[9]

---

5   New Ross Register of Penitents, 21 August 1860.
6   *Ibid.*, and Limerick Register of Penitents - ("Names of the Penitents who were in the Magdalen Asylum Before the Sisters of the Good Shepherd Took up the Charge"). 1846, No. 241.
7   1901 Census.
8   For a discussion regarding the burial of penitents, see pages 155-6.
     Though both the New Ross Register of Penitents, and the 1901 Census give this woman's name as Williamson, the Limerick Register (which notes she was "sent to our Convent, New Ross") lists her as Margaret Williams.
9   Sister Mary Coppinger, Mistress of Penitents at Cork however, apparently differed from this view. Her testimony, read to the Select Committee in 1882, stated that women previously registered under the Acts (i.e. those former Cork prostitutes who had been detained in hospital and subjected to moral influence as well as medical treatment) were less vicious and more amenable to reform than penitents in the Order's other Houses.

The appalling difficulties encountered by the new Foundation became legendary, and arose chiefly from its location and lack of support. It was noted in Chapter 1 that well before the 1860s, various Irish towns with a "Social Evil" problem had responded by setting up Homes. The absence of such measures in New Ross suggests that local prostitution was not a major issue; and a Female Penitentiary may well have been unpopular as well as unnecessary in the town. Clearly, the Order's Magdalen Asylum in Waterford, only fifteen miles away and already claiming women from further afield must have added to the new Home's problems - overshadowing its beginnings, and jeopardising its future prospects of success. The Waterford Asylum continued to draw women from Co. Wexford throughout the period (as late as the turn of the century they accounted for one quarter of penitents in the Home) lending weight to McCarthy's contention that such an institution was not needed in New Ross; and contributing to the Home's chronic shortage of inmates, and closure in 1967.

It was noted in Chapter 3 that in compliance with directives from Rome, the Institute, rapidly expanding and under pressure for more regional autonomy, was divided into Provinces in 1855. Any country with three or more Foundations acquired Provincial status, and, equally important, its own Novitiate so that Sisters could be trained at home. With the opening of the Waterford Home in 1858 there were two Irish Monasteries under the Provincial House at Hammersmith, and unless a third Foundation could be made, these would remain attached to England. It was the urgency of this requirement that prompted the new Mission, but why such an unfavourable location was agreed to, is unclear.[10] Apart from a few interested clergy who gave daily Mass free of charge,[11] the Community's early presence in the town went almost unnoticed, and its desperate situation was apparently ignored.

It was probably believed that the nuns exaggerated their poverty to solicit sympathy and funds. Who, after all, would have

---

10 According to Patrick Donovan (*The Christian Brothers in New Ross*, 1849-1949, p.143) the Sisters were invited to the town by Bishop Furlong. Possibly he was prompted to make this gesture, which, though politically expedient, was, from a practical viewpoint, remarkably ill-conceived.

11 Their only remuneration was the retention of the Sunday collection, but in view of the poverty of the Irishtown community using the Chapel, it is doubtful if this amounted to much.

credited the Mother House, let alone the Irish Foundations, with allowing such hardship to exist? By this time the Order was well enough established to assist new Missions; and to informed outsiders it must have seemed irresponsible to expose the Sisters - to say nothing of their charges - to such unnecessary risk. It was the Foundress' practice, however, to send out her daughters and let them fend for themselves. In their many troubles, she poured out letters of sympathy, invoked Saints' intercessions and called on Communities for prayers. But no matter how desperate their situation, a return to the Mother House was unthinkable, and whatever their circumstances, she seldom advanced them funds. Only very rarely were Sisters withdrawn, and seldom for financial reasons. In 1837, for example, there had been an aborted Foundation at Bordeaux. The nuns were recalled by Mother Pelletier, but only because the local Bishop's interference had undermined the purpose and the practice of their Rule.[12]

Three years later a further attempted Foundation - again undertaken rashly and with little consideration for the Sisters - proved unsuccessful. In May 1840, Mother Mary of the Angels Levoyer, Superior of the House at Lille, together with another Sister, was sent to England, accompanied by a priest. The journey was undertaken solely on the strength of a German prelate's wish to see the Good Shepherds established in London. No arrangements had been made, there was no House to receive them, and within a fortnight of their arrival, their companion returned to France:

> "But the daughters of Mother St. Euphrasia were not so easily discouraged. She had infused into them her own courage, and absolute dependence upon Providence.* Besides, she did not recall them, and so they remained, in virtue of holy obedience, ready to endure poverty and humiliation."[13]

Their situation eventually became so critical that Mgr. Paysant,

---

12 *Blessed Mary of Saint Euphrasia, op. cit.*, p.161.
*   This "Trusting to Providence" is a recurring theme in the literature. See particularly Chapter 7. The Mother Foundress, for example, had often "had recourse to the blessed Virgin for assistance, and many a time did her gracious Patroness intervene in the most unmistakable manner to enable her to pay the debts incurred by the Community." A. M. Clarke, *op. cit.*, pp.161-2.
13 *Ibid.*, pp.231-233.

Bishop of Angers intervened, ordering the aggrieved Mother General to recall them "on account of the large outlay which must inevitably be made". Even so, the coveted Mission (England, "steeped in heresy" had long been the object of the Foundress' prayers) was not given up. Six months later, in response to an offer of a house and land in St. Leonards-on-Sea, Mother Pelletier sent out two more of her daughters. They were accompanied by an English postulant acting as interpreter, and escorted by an elderly, eccentric priest. Apprehensions for their safety in what was clearly regarded as a perilous venture, may be judged from the fact that all four religious resorted to secular dress. In spite of anticipated hazards the two Sisters, "absolutely ignorant" of the English language, were provided with only forty pounds to start the new Foundation. Not surprisingly, St. Leonards-on-Sea "offered no scope for the Institute", and that particular project had to be shelved.[14] The Sisters, however, were not recalled, and for some months were forced to rely on the generosity of the Benedictine Nuns in Hammersmith. Meanwhile the Congregations at Angers and Lille redoubled their prayers - the Memorare and office of the Immaculate Conception being daily recited for a year to obtain the success of the new Mission.[15]

Even in times of crisis such as the 1848 revolutionary period, when Houses on the Continent were attacked and closed down by anti-clerical mobs, the Mother General was intractable. The withdrawal of a Foundation was resisted or delayed to the very last moment, with a callous indifference to the safety of the nuns. When penitents were dispersed by angry rabbles, and terrified Sisters driven from their Convents - as happened in Bourg, Macon, Dole and Genoa, for example - she circularised Superiors of other Houses with instructions on how to avert such disasters themselves. If the religious habit was "obnoxious to the populace" the nuns were to put on secular dress and remain quietly in their enclosures. They should conduct themselves as

---

14 A small Protestant Refuge, St. Monica's Home (Hastings) was eventually established at St. Leonards-on-Sea. Founded in 1889, it had accommodation for ten inmates under 30 years of age; and specialised in temporary Rescue and Preventative cases - *The Classified List of Child-Saving Institutions* .... *Including Homes and Institutions for Women and Inebriate Retreats.* Reformatory and Refuge Union, 1935, pp.110-11.

15 A. M. Clarke, *op. cit.*, pp.236-8; and *Blessed Mary of Saint Euphrasia*, *op. cit.*, pp.195-201.

much as possible "like ordinary persons", and "earn their bread by the labour of their hands". Whatever the cost, however, they must not give up their Houses.[16]

Given such recent tradition, it is hardly surprising that a new Foundation's poverty - in a land long characterised by destitution, but renowned for its devotion to the Church - should be so steadfastly ignored. Assistance from the Mother House, or the Irish Foundations, would not merely squander existing resources, needed elsewhere. By discouraging local benevolence it would endanger future income too. Equally important, since the establishment of a Province was at stake, the new Mission could not be abandoned, nor its Community withdrawn.

In spite of the Order's expansion, therefore, the New Ross Congregation continued in absolute want, as is testified in its own Annals, those of the Asylum at Cork, and in the biographies of the Foundress. Father Kenny, a local parish priest who often visited the Convent during this early period, was shocked that the nuns were allowed to continue without food, without funds, and so completely lacking in support.[17]

After two years' extreme privation the situation was critical, with the nuns' hapless dependence on the penitents to generate an income being evident. By this time it was widely felt that the Foundation should be abandoned, since it was obvious that the insufficient work occupying the few inmates then in the Home, could not support the Community. Still determined to avoid such a measure the Mother General recalled the Superior to Angers, and appointed Sister Mary of Joseph of the Cross Mullen from Limerick to take charge of the "sinking boat". The Annals record that even after this decisive step, the Mission continued in the balance for a further two years.[18]

At the close of 1864, there were still only twelve penitents in the institution, and several of these were shortly afterwards to leave. By any standards, the enterprise was a disaster, with only 31

16 The last instruction was not always possible. In February 1848 the Convent of Bourg was wrecked and the entire Community driven out. Popular hatred of the Order was such that the House was never re-opened and was eventually sold. In Genoa the Convent was sacked and its inmates dispersed. It took nine years for the nuns to re-establish themselves in the city, at which time they were forced to buy another premises. A. M. Clarke, *op. cit.*, pp.287-89.
17 Annals of the New Ross Magdalen Asylum, 1860-64.
18 *Ibid.*, 1864-66.

admissions in its first four years. Few, even of these, were "satisfactory" cases, and only one woman left the Asylum to take up a situation. If these penitents were the best in the Province, then the Order's success rate, as is demonstrated by a summary of the Home's early intake, was depressingly low. Statistics of length of stay in the different Houses, however (see Table 26) indicate that the reputation of the penitents in New Ross was based on this all important characteristic. It was in this Home that inmates stayed longest, and were most likely to remain for life.

Following the arrival of the two Limerick helpers, the first woman to be registered was 35 year old Mary Slatterey, sent by the Superioress at Waterford. For some reason, the clothing of early penitents was listed, this one owning a petticoat, a chemise, and an old shawl. She not only absconded by "going over the wall", but helped herself to some of the other inmates' clothes.[19] Four days later, 17 year old Alice Edwards, from New Ross was brought in by a priest; and in the following week, 27 year old Ellen Madigan, from Co. Limerick, entered of her own free will. One year later she was dismissed "for bad conduct", her departure too, being marked by the disappearance of various items.[20]

Three other women admitted at this time all left to join their parents; and twenty-four year old Margaret Toomey, from Cork was expelled for robbery.[21] Of the seven others registered in 1860, three left within a short time at their own request; one was sent out for "bad conduct"; one left for hospital, and two (one of them aged 13) seem to have stayed in the institution.[22]

Only five women were admitted in 1861. One of these, twenty-nine year old Margaret Roche, of Co. Wexford, was the first long-term inmate at New Ross. She spent the next thirty years in the Asylum, and died in the Home in 1892. Three others left after a brief stay, and one, having spent four years in the Refuge, was sent to a situation in Co. Cork.[23]

The record for the following year was even less hopeful, with only two penitents being registered - one of whom was "expelled for boldness" nine months later, and the other remaining for ten

---

19 New Ross Register of Penitents, September 1860.
20 *Ibid.*, 10 September 1860.
21 *Ibid.*, 4 October 1860.
22 *Ibid.*, 1860.
23 *Ibid.*, 1861.

years.[24] In 1863, only four women were admitted, three of them on the same day. One of these stayed in the Home for ten years; and the other two, "placed here by Rev. Synnott", were sent out for bad conduct. The fourth woman, 22 year old Mary Gibson of Gorey, spent the next 72 years in the institution, her life-long penance being a record for the whole Province in the period. She was the second "laundress" listed in the 1901 Census, and died in the Home in 1936, aged 95.[25] Finally, seven women entered the Asylum in 1864. Two inmates left of their own accord shortly after entering; two were sent out for bad conduct; one left for hospital; and one was expelled for dishonesty and "throwing Public clothes over the enclosure wall".[26]

Discouraging though many of these cases were, the period was, in fact, a turning point both for the Irish Order and the Home itself. By virtue of its three Foundations, the Irish Institute was now detached from England and acquired Provincial status; enabling, as described in Chapter 3, Irish women to make their Novitiate in the Provincial House in Limerick, rather than in Hammersmith or France.

Also in 1863 three nieces of Mr. Richard Devereux (later regarded as the Home's founder, since he provided for the purchase of the house and eleven acres of land) paid their first, momentous visit to the nuns.[27] One of these ladies, Miss Teresa Devereux decided to join the Order and immediately entered the new Novitiate in Limerick. Her large dowry was assigned to the impoverished New Ross Convent, and from about this time, at least one of the young ladies began recommending women to the Home.[28]

Shortly afterwards Mother St. Euphrasia, having retained the right to appoint Superiors to each of the Order's Convents, named Sister Mary of the Compassionate Bartley, then in Limerick, and only twenty-seven years old, as the new Prioress of

---

24 *Ibid.* Both these women were admitted on 16 October, 1862.

25 *Ibid.*, 25 April and 15 December 1863.

26 *Ibid.*, 1864.

27 *Ibid.* For an analysis of the influence and philanthropy of Richard Devereux (1795-1883), see Jarlath Glynn, *The Catholic Church in Wexford Town*, 1800-1858. A Mr. Howlett of New Ross also bequeathed a large sum to the Convent - see Annals.

28 Kate Clarke was admitted in August 1865, for example, and Mary Connors in April 1866. Both were aged 22, were from Wexford, and were recommended by Miss Devereux of that town. Mary Connors died in the Home in 1879. New Ross Register of Penitents.

the Home.[29] From this period Richard Devereux was a constant benefactor, donating statues, pictures, furniture, and even cows. Yet in spite of these gifts, which may have lessened some aspects of the Mission's poverty, conditions worsened rather than improved, as the buildings rapidly deteriorated, and the number of inmates slowly increased. Though the laundry was remodelled, it was soon described as inadequate, and the dilapidated Convent was both unhealthy and unsound. A Bazaar, "the like of which the people of New Ross had never seen" was held in the following year, but the results were disappointing. The £700 raised, was sufficient only for temporary repairs.[30]

No sooner had Sister Mary of St. Teresa Devereux made her vows in Limerick, than her older sister, Miss Devereux, asked to be received direct into the New Ross Home. Special permission was granted by the Mother General, and the young woman entered the Convent in September 1867.[31] This concession was expensively bought.

In the following year the Order's Foundress, Mother St. Euphrasia Pelletier, died in Angers. Provinces were required to supply the statistics of their individual Congregations; and from these, it was calculated that at the time of the Mother General's death, 110 Good Shepherd Convents had been founded world-wide. There were now more than 3,000 Good Shepherd Sisters; 960 "Magdalens" or contemplative penitents; and over 6,000 "children" (i.e. women and girls) of the ordinary penitent class. In addition to these Magdalen or Penitentiary sections, there were attached to the institutions, some 14,000 "Industrial" children, female prisoners, "reformatory" and "preservation" girls.[32]

While it was occasionally the case that girls and women in Ireland were committed to Convent Magdalen Asylums by the Courts (The Kennedy Report notes, for example, that this was taking place in the 1960s[33]); and apparently, women found guilty of infanticide were typically sent to these institutions rather than to prison, it has already been noted that the vast majority of Irish penitents either "entered voluntarily", or were "brought" or

29 New Ross Annals, 1864.
30 *Ibid.*, 1866-68.
31 *Ibid.*, 1868.
32 Bernoville, *op. cit.*, p.172.
33 Kennedy Report, *op. cit.* p.39-40.

"recommended" to the Asylums, by priests, the staff of other institutions, relatives or friends. Few, if any, of the inmates could be held against their will - legally, at least - and there was no category of segregated female prisoners employed by the Good Shepherds in Ireland.[34]

Nevertheless, for more than a century, this Order, though virtually enclosed, had complete mastery over the lives of many women; and further, its controlling influence extended to thousands of "vagrant" children's lives. This extraordinary situation arose partly from the voluntary nature of Rescue Work, which, in the absence of Government funding, precluded the possibility of State intervention, regulation, or control. The fact that unpaid women could be so conveniently confined and worked in a system accountable to no-one, advanced an operation which, so long as it was profitable, continued to exist.

The Managers of Industrial Schools, on the other hand (technically at least) were answerable to the Government, from which they received a substantial grant for the children in their care. The Industrial School system was extended from England to Ireland in 1868; and since Local Authorities were reputedly reluctant to undertake the work, the Religious Orders attained a virtual monopoly over the lives of children of the neglected, orphaned and abandoned class. By the turn of the century, 71 Industrial Schools, catering for approximately 8,000 children, had been certified in Ireland. Four of these institutions, housing a total of approximately 600 girls, were run by the Good Shepherd Sisters; and though administered separately, they were attached to, and inevitably associated with, the Order's Magdalen Homes.

The Provincial House in Limerick, for example, continued solely as a Magdalen Asylum only up to January 1859, when, as noted in Chapter 3, "St. Joseph's", a Reformatory School for the reception of youthful (female) offenders committed by the Courts, was opened. It was under the inspection of the Government, and by 1901, it contained 42 girls - for each of whom it received £24.

---

34 As was the case in "Nazareth", outside Angers, for example. From 1852, large detachments of female prisoners were committed by the Government to the care of the Order, and worked on this "Industrial Farm" - the produce of which was supplied to the Mother House. A. M. Clarke, *op. cit.*, pp.307-10.

10s. 2p. a year.[35] In 1869 the Limerick Congregation expanded still further, with the opening of "St. George's", the first of the Irish Order's Industrial Schools. At the end of the century, with a total of 109 "derelict" girls, the institution was receiving an annual Government grant of £1,637.[36]

Within a decade of its opening, it was clear that the penitents' Class in New Ross would never be large, and that consequently, the Community's income - dependant on laundry profits - would always be small. With this in mind it was decided to opt for that other source of funding so profitable to Religious Orders in the period; and in 1868 the Congregation "petitioned" the Government for an Industrial School Certificate, which would ensure public funding for each of the children maintained in the Home.[37]

Since a condition of the award was the provision of suitable premises, a new, purpose-built Industrial School, "St. Aidan's", was immediately commissioned, with Mr. Devereux footing the bill. His niece Sister Mary of St. Teresa Devereux was transferred from the Limerick Mother House to be Mistress in Charge of the new Institution - though a few months later, as described in Chapter 6, she was appointed Superioress of the new Foundation in Cork. As well as financing the Industrial School, Richard Devereux bought a small house adjoining the Convent, and converted it to a parlour for the reception of visitors. He also presented the nuns with a fully rigged-out ship, which they sensibly sold. As a mark of its gratitude, the Community hung a portrait of their benefactor in the penitents' class.

As discussed in the previous Chapter, in 1871 the Order's Industrial School in Waterford was also certified - albeit in a temporary building until the new premises was completed in 1878. By 1901 this institution contained 176 children, and

---

35 1901 Census, and McCarthy, *op. cit.*, p.540. By 1969 the number of inmates in the Reformatory had dwindled to only 7. (See Kennedy Report, *op. cit.*, p.2.)
36 McCarthy, *op. cit.*, p.540.
37 Although this financial motive and the fact of the petition is clearly stated in the Convent's Annals, a later account (provided by the New Ross Sisters themselves) states: "In 1867 the Sisters were asked to accept charge of an In-school". *The Fold of the Good Shepherd, op. cit.*, p.26. The date too, is incorrect, since the Industrial School system was not applied to Ireland until 1868, and St. Aidan's was not opened until November 1869.

received an annual grant of £3,173.[38] Only the Order's Foundation in Belfast, established in 1867, continued exclusively as a Magdalen Asylum throughout the whole period – certification for a girls' Industrial School in that city having been acquired by the Sisters of Mercy in 1869.[39]

The unusual circumstances leading to the foundation of the Good Shepherd in Cork in 1870, have already been referred to. In contrast to the other Irish Houses, funding for a permanent Magdalen Asylum was immediately available, and the reception of inmates was postponed until July 1872 when the extensive penitentiary and laundry section was completed. Well before this, however, the scramble for "certification" was already underway. Consequently, though the Cork Asylum was more officially linked to prostitution than any other Magdalen Home in Ireland, its immediate intake was not fallen women, but destitute, abandoned and vagrant girls. As has been shown, the speed with which their temporary accommodation was assembled and stocked in 1870 endangered the Industrial children's health. More sanitary and substantial premises were opened four years later; and by 1901 this Institution, with 196 "vagrant" girls, was drawing from the State the substantial sum of £3,157 per year.[40]

The wisdom of consigning "Industrial" children to the sole care of untrained, rarely supervised and virtually unaccountable nuns is questionable, particularly if such women belonged to Orders that were enclosed. The suggestion that no-one else was prepared to undertake the work is not convincing. By being allowed to almost monopolise the area, the Religious Orders deprived lay people of the opportunity to carry out, or train for, what was, in many respects, a rewarding career.[*] There is clear

---

38 McCarthy, *op. cit.*, pp.492-3.
39 Their premises in Crumlin Road, founded shortly after the extension of the Industrial Schools Act to Ireland, could accommodate 90 girls aged between 7-14 years. By the turn of the century, with 88 children in their institution, the Mercy Sisters were receiving a Government Grant of £1,450 per year. They opened a second Industrial School in the city - attached to their Convent at Abbeyville, in 1896. This could accommodate 120 girls, and in 1901, with 95 inmates, was awarded a Government Grant of £1,558. McCarthy, *op. cit.*, p.57.
40 *Ibid.*, pp. 511-12.
*   "..... at a fair estimate, there are 2,000 religious in the single county of Cork, engaged in crippling the intellects of the youth, extracting money from the adults, depriving laymen and laywomen of honourable employment ...... The priests' organisation in county Cork draws £20,377. per annum for the maintenance of young vagrants! Every year sees a contingent of helpless young male and female vagrants discharged upon the laity to swell the ranks of the incompetents." McCarthy, *op. cit.*, pp.514-15.

evidence, that far from being "invited" to undertake the role, and accepting it with diffidence, the Good Shepherds, for example, eagerly "petitioned", for what they regarded as a lucrative side-line to their real life's work. It is to be feared that, obsessed as they were with "sin", they extended this dark side of their vocation to the children; but such was not the purpose of "Industrial" Schools, nor should it have been assumed that abandoned, orphaned, or even illegitimate juveniles, were necessarily of the "evil" class.

If this entrusting of "Industrial" youngsters to the sole care of celibates, male or female, whose only qualification was a "vocation", and whose powers over their charges were virtually unchecked - if such a policy can be seen in retrospect, and in the light of recent exposures of brutality and neglect in Irish Industrial Schools, to have been a grotesque abrogation of official responsibility, with disastrous, far reaching consequences - how much more undesirable was the submission of such children (the most vulnerable in the State) to enclosures containing Magdalen Asylums, and to an Order preoccupied with penance and sin?

We have seen that the Foundress expressly forbade any form of communication between the different Sections, and this applied particularly to the Industrial and Penitent Class. Even in church the two groups were strictly segregated, with total isolation at all times being strictly enforced. In spite of these precautions, however, it was clearly undesirable that schools containing orphaned, abandoned, and particularly illegitimate children, should be so closely associated with Magdalen Asylums; and it was patently improper that two such institutions should co-exist under virtually the same roof.

It was, after all, the case that the unmarried mother entering a Magdalen Asylum, had first to dispose of her child. How many such infants, disowned by their fathers, and rejected by the families of the women, were conveniently placed in adjoining Industrial Schools? Further, many children reared in the system, and notoriously ill-equipped to cope with life outside, found themselves " in trouble" after leaving the Homes. How many girls, like the following cases, progressed with only brief interruption, from the "Industrial" or "Reformatory" Sections, to the Order's "Penitent" Class?

Bridget Shea, for example, was an orphan reared in the Waterford Industrial School, and later admitted to the adjoining Magdalen Asylum. In 1900, by which time she was 26, she entered the Order's New Ross Home - only to leave shortly afterwards, for hospital.[41] Similarly Johanna Cokely from Dungarvan, Co. Waterford, progressed from "St. Joseph's", the Reformatory School in Limerick, to "St. Mary's", the Magdalen Asylum in Waterford, where she stayed for almost three years. She left on 6 March 1880 and on the following day was admitted to the Cork Good Shepherd. She then left for the Sisters of Charity Magdalen Asylum, in Peacock Lane. She was re-admitted to the Good Shepherd a few days later, and left in the following year when she was allegedly still only nineteen years old.[42] Twenty-three year old Ellie O'Shea, from Tralee, was transferred from the Cork Good Shepherd, in 1876, to the Limerick Home - though nine months later, the Mother Provincial returned her to the Cork Asylum. This girl too, was a past inmate of St. Joseph's Reformatory.[43] Mary Boman of Kilrush, Co. Clare, was admitted to the Limerick Magdalen Asylum in June 1877. Aged twenty-four she was described as an "incorrigible" child, and was expelled ("not to be taken back") for bad conduct. She had previously been in the Reformatory attached to the Home.[44] Similarly, 23 year old Catherine Hickey, referred to the Cork Good Shepherd in March 1877 by the Chaplain of the County goal, left the Home two months later in a "bad disposition". The Register records that she was "six years in our reformatory in Limerick."[45] A final example is Mary Buckley, another product of St. Joseph's Reformatory. At the age of 21 she became an inmate of the adjacent Magdalen Asylum, and in 1880 after three years' penance, she joined her sister in America.[46]

Tradition has it that even up to the mid-twentieth century, such re-cycling within the system was not unusual. It is claimed by local Limerick residents, for example, that it was

---

41 New Ross Register of Penitents, 9 February 1900. Mary Dunne, who entered the New Ross Home in August 1895 had also been in the Waterford Industrial School.
42 Waterford Register of Penitents, 18 July 1877 and Cork Register of Penitents, 7 March 1880.
43 Cork Register of Penitents, 12 May 1876.
44 Limerick Register of Penitents, 6 June 1877.
45 Cork Register of Penitents, 11 March 1877.
46 Limerick Register of Penitents, 10 September 1877.

commonplace for adolescent girls from both "St. Joseph's" Reformatory, and "St. George's" Industrial School, to be sent out to farmers, either as servants or to work in the fields. Some, would return shortly afterwards, pregnant, their ultimate destination the Order's Magdalen Home. Meanwhile, the Industrial Schools absorbed more unwanted infants - some of whom, like their mothers before them, would remain in the system for life.*

Allegations such as these are confirmed in the Kennedy Report on *Reformatory and Industrial Schools Systems*, published as late as 1970; and already referred to in Chapter 2. Detailed comments from the appropriate sections demonstrate that after a full century the system was still in operation, with little fundamental change having taken place. The Report noted that certain types of girl offenders (particularly those with recurring sexual offenses) were not welcome in the country's two girls' reformatories - though this was partly the purpose of these Homes. Such cases were sometimes placed on probation or on remand from the courts, in one of the several Convent Magdalen Homes willing to accept them. Others, considered by parents, relatives, social workers, Welfare Officers, Clergy or the police to be in moral danger, were also accepted in these convents on a voluntary basis. The Committee estimated that at least 70 young girls aged between 13 and 19 years were currently confined in this way, in the company of older, more experienced and more depraved women who were likely to have a corrupting influence. A major concern was that in most cases:

> "the nuns running these institutions have neither the training nor the resources to enable them to rehabilitate these girls and to deal with the problem ... There are generally no proper facilities for the education of these girls many of whom are thought to be retarded."

---

* Even more disturbing are suggestions that within living memory justification for such re-cycling could be completely by-passed, with girls being transferred direct from Industrial Schools into the Magdalen Homes. The conduct of those who had been segregated from men since infancy, of course, could hardly have qualified them as penitents - though recent allegations of sexual abuse in Industrial Schools by priests, may well have necessitated such a move. "Protective" action too, might result in such a transfer, particularly if a girl was pretty or considered "wilful" – to prevent her "falling away".

Fig.1

Mother Mary of St. Euphrasia Pelletier (1796-1868), Foundress of the Generalate of the Congregation of our Lady of Charity of the Good Shepherds of Angers.

Fig.2

Le Bon Pasteur — a nineteenth-century engraving of the Good Shepherd
saving a lost sheep. A much favoured image of Rescue Work, this picture
was formerly in the Waterford Good Shepherd Convent.

Fig.3

A painting of Mother Mary of St. Joseph Regaudiat, Superior of the first
Good Shepherd foundation in England (Hammersmith, established in
1841). The secular dress thought advisable for the initial undertaking
proved an unnecessary precaution, and she here wears the familiar habit
of the Order. The three women are Consecrates — penitents who took an
annual vow to remain in the Asylum, and each wears the black dress, silver cross and white bonnet of this particularly fervent class.

Fig.4

The London Female Penitentiary, established in 1807 for the
rescue, reclamation and protection of betrayed and fallen women.

Fig.5

The Laundry in one of the larger Magdalen Asylums in England in the early years of the twentieth century.

Fig. 6

Arthur J. S. Maddison, Secretary of the Reformatory and Refuge Union and author of the influential *Hints on Rescue Work*, published in 1898. This and the following photograph was taken at the Conference of Managers and Superintendents of Reformatory and Industrial Institutions - an annual gathering of Rescue Workers which in 1911 took place in Edinburgh.

Fig. 7

Miss Jane Paterson, Superintendent of the Edinburgh Magdalen Asylum, established in 1797. In 1935 the institution had accommodation for 92 girls willing to reform, and who were prepared to remain in the Asylum for two years.

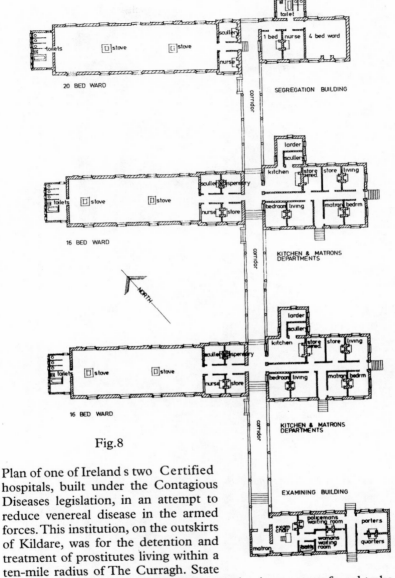

Fig. 8

Plan of one of Ireland's two Certified hospitals, built under the Contagious Diseases legislation, in an attempt to reduce venereal disease in the armed forces. This institution, on the outskirts of Kildare, was for the detention and treatment of prostitutes living within a ten-mile radius of The Curragh. State registered, and subject to fortnightly examination, women found to be diseased were dispatched straight from the examining room to the hospital wards. Efforts were made to place patients in Magdalen Asylums at the end of their treatment, and each of the Good Shepherd Penitentiaries in this study admitted women from this source. The hospital was opened in 1869 and closed after the suspension of the Acts in 1883.

Fig.9

An unidentified Magdalen Laundry in Ireland. The primitive equipment, the extreme youth of two of the girls and the shaven head of the older woman are precisely the conditions that the Factory and Workshop legislation — had it been extended to Magdalen Laundries — would have ended.

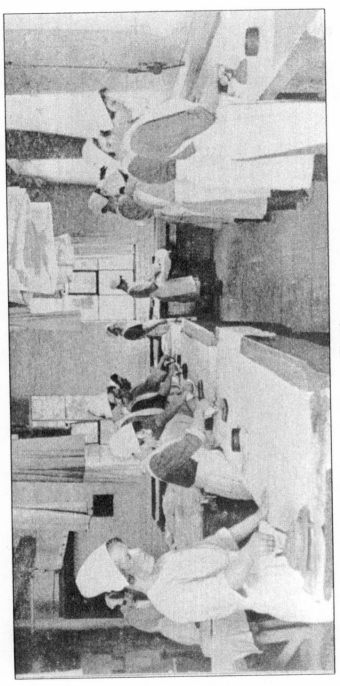

Fig.10

The Laundry, in 1934, of the Clifton Home for Girls - formerly the York Penitentiary. This Refuge for fallen women was established in 1822 and inmates (like Isabella Corkhill) received a two-year training to equip them for a more respectable life. At the time of this photograph, 30 girls were in the Home and the President of the Society was Quaker, B. Seebohm Rowntree, whose book *Poverty a Study of Town Life* was one of the most influential investigations of its time.

Fig.11

Penitents working in the Sewing Room of the Good Shepherd Magdalen Asylum, Strasbourg, 1932. At the back of the room a nun is reading, flanked by two Consecrates. These bonneted auxilliaries are also placed halfway down the class. Penitents were forbidden to speak while working, but prayed and sang hymns.

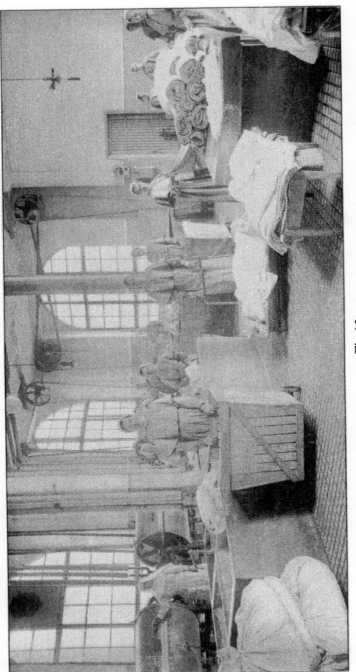

Fig.12

The Laundry, the Good Shepherd Magdalen Asylum, Strasbourg, 1932. In contrast to Fig. 9, this is a well-ordered and well-equipped operation. The same penitents' uniform, or something like it, was still being worn in Ireland in the 1950s. Former inmates from that period describe caps and shoulder capes

Fig.13

Statue of Our Lady of the Dolours, formerly in the Limerick Mother House. This sorrowing figure was of particular significance to Consecrates, who, having attained the silver cross, were given the title of the Dolours . Thus the last two women referred to in this book — each of whom spent 56 years in the Good Shepherd penitentiary in Cork - were re-named Magdalen and Mary of the Dolours.

Fig 14

Front view of Antonio Canova s Penitent Magdalen (1796) - see
Frontispiece. In the original of the statue (Palazzo Bianco Genoa) the
saint is holding a large crucifix across her knees. This copy, formerly in
the Limerick Good Shepherd Convent, reflects the nineteenth century
passion for reclaiming prostitutes and other fallen women.

Fig.15

Magdalens from the Gloucester Street Refuge, Dublin, in a Corpus Christi Procession, 1950s. Trusted girls were allowed to join these parades down Sean McDermot Street. The institution from which these women came was closed in 1996, and was the last of Ireland s Convent Magdalen Laundries.

Fig. 16

Dr. O Shaughnessy, an early benefactor of the Good Shepherd Asylum in Limerick, the Order s Irish Mother House. This painting, sold at the auction of the Convent s contents in September 1994, is now in the possession of the author.

Fig. 17

Richard Devereux

Many Catholic institutions - particularly in Co. Wexford - benefited from this wealthy merchant shipowner s pious generosity. He was a leading benefactor of the Good Shepherd Sisters, contributing large sums to their Monasteries in New Ross (where his portrait was hung in the Penitents Class) Cork and Belfast. Three of his nieces became Superiors in the Order. He also donated funds to Artane and various other Industrial Schools run by the Christian Brothers.

Significantly, the Report doubted the legal validity of the "voluntary" placements, noting that:

> "girls admitted in this irregular way and not being aware of their rights may remain for long periods and become, in the process, unfit for re-emergence into society. In the past many girls have been taken into these convents and remained there all their lives ... As no State grants are made ... there is, consequently, no State control or right of inspection of these institutions."[47]

Even for non-voluntary cases (those girls committed to Magdalen Asylums by the Courts, and Government-funded at seven shillings a day) State protection was illusory or inadequate. Only one Inspector was appointed, and according to the Kennedy Report, the statuary annual visit (hardly an adequate safeguard) was but rarely discharged.[48] Since the Report further noted that owing to lack of aftercare and training in Reformatories and Industrial Schools, some former pupils became involved in prostitution - the principal reason for admission to Magdalen Asylums - it is clear that as late as the nineteen-sixties females graduated from one type of institution to the other, with both the State and the public confining children and women in this way.

In November 1887 further statistics were required for the Order's Mother House, and the Irish Province, supplying information on all its Foundations, noted that since the commencement of the Waterford "Magdalen" Class in March 1872, forty women had entered, of whom five had since died.[49] Throughout the fifteen year period, not one of these women had come from the Home in New Ross.

---

47 Kennedy Report, *op. cit.*, p.39.
48 This situation is reminiscent of early Factory Legislation, under the terms of which children working in cotton mills were to be protected by law. However, since it was not until 1833 that a mere four Factory Inspectors were appointed for the whole of Britain, the exploitation of the juvenile workforce continued almost unaltered.
49 Statistics of the Province of Ireland Previous to and Since the Death of the Foundress. There were thus 35 Magdalens then in the Class. These figures were clearly not maintained, since it was noted in Chapter 4 that at the 1901 Census the Province's "Magdalens" numbered only 15. In the 1960s the Sisters Magdalens - now re-named the "Contemplative Community" - were moved to Belfast. A description of such women (in the French Mother House) occurs for 1950. It illustrates that by the mid-twentieth century, very little with regard to the perceived sin of female sexuality had changed. "I saw the Sisters Magdalens in their convent. They were at recreation when we arrived. While I looked with respectful emotion at these brown-clad figures, I felt that I had never seen so striking a picture of monastic poverty and mortification ....

The elite of the penitents were always the "Magdalens" - the especial joy of the Order, and the jewel in the Foundress' crown. Originally women with such a vocation - those "victims of reparation, burning torches of repentance and self-oblation"[50] - had been sent to the Magdalen Class in the Hammersmith Convent, the Mother House of the English Province, to which, as has been noted, Ireland initially belonged. With the establishment of the special Magdalen Class in Waterford, however, such a removal was no longer necessary, though it still occasionally occurred. Former prostitute Jane Barry, for example, one of Rev. Reed's early converts, and the first woman to be registered in the new Cork Asylum, was sent to Hammersmith "to become a Magdalen", as late as 1879 - by which time, a comparable Class in Waterford had existed for seven years.[51]

"Magdalens" rarely reverted to their penitent status, though a comment in the Limerick Register suggests that this might occasionally occur. Twenty-five year old Bridget Tully of Galway left the Asylum at the Mother House in October 1875 because "she could not agree with others". She had been in the Home twice before, "and with the Magdalenes at Waterford"[52]

The Asylum at New Ross continued without Magdalen vocations throughout the whole of the nineteenth century; though in the same period, each of the other Irish Houses produced women of this contemplative class. Their absence in a Home containing so few inmates, is not surprising. Just as the penitent's life was repellent to most women, so the austere Magdalen existence inspired most penitents with reverence and fear. Less understandable, is the relative scarcity of "Consecrates" in the New Ross Refuge, where thirteen years were to pass before the first of the penitents "took the black dress". This was in marked contrast to the Cork Foundation, for

---

Their faces bear the unmistakable stamp of strict self-denial. Some are very old, their faces worn, their sight weakened. They had travelled far in the way of grace. And now they are safe in the brightness which prefigures eternal light, pure with a new-found and newly-won purity, loving the only object worth loving, silent but mutely eloquent; more than merely saved, they are the agents of the Redemption of others." - Bernoville, *op. cit.*, p.178.

50 Bernoville, *op. cit.*, p.90.
51 See Cork Register of Penitents 29 July 1872, and Rev. Henry Reed's evidence to the Select Committee on the Contagious Diseases Acts, 27 June 1881.
52 Limerick Register of Penitents, 14 October 1875.

example, where within a year of the Home's opening, twelve of the penitents became Children of Mary, and several of these were later to become Consecrates.[53]

It has already been noted that Consecrated Penitents were used by the Order to help the Religious, and to ensure the smooth running, discipline and productivity of the Class. The New Ross Foundresses had called for assistants immediately on arrival (though those sent appear to have been "trusted" penitents rather than "consecrates") - so vital were they in the management of the Homes. Within four years, however, one of the two women provided by the Provincial Mother House left the new Foundation, and it was not until July 1873, that the first of the Community's own Consecrates emerged. Until then, and for some time afterwards, their virtual absence in the Home must have hampered the New Ross Sisters and minimised classification - to the detriment of those more hopeful, younger cases in the Class. Also, from a missionary point of view, this want of special ardour was discouraging, casting doubt on the claim that New Ross converts were the most pious of their kind.

Consecrated penitents were inmates who, without wishing to become Magdalens, had no desire to return to the world. They had an "apostolic spirit", and were those "dependable children" who assisted the nuns, were their trusted surveillants and helped maintain the silence so rigorously imposed. According to "A Religious of the Congregation" whose biography of the Foundress was published in 1933, Consecrated children were powerful allies to the First Mistress. They were given charge of new-comers to be initiated in local customs, and were in effect "what good non-commissioned officers are in a regiment."[54] Intermediaries between the ordinary penitents (which they had formerly been) and the nuns (to whose ranks they could never aspire) they were both monitors, and useful instruments in the hierarchy of control. In practice, no doubt, they could be vindictive to one group and ingratiating to the other - the system encouraging abuses, and fostering the tyrannies of limited power.

Like the Sisters (who wore white habits) and the Magdalens (whose brown robes were adapted from the Carmelite Rule) the

---

53 Cork Annals, 1873.
54 *Blessed Mary of Saint Euphrasia, op. cit.*, p.146.

Consecrates' dress was distinctive. Their uniform was of black serge, with belt, girdle and rosary. They also wore little shoulder shawls and white bonnets which, in the late nineteen-fifties, were replaced by small veils. Consecrates recited daily the Little Office of Our Lady of Seven Dolours, a Servite devotion.[55]

The Sodality of Consecrated Penitents was instituted in the French Mother House in 1835, shortly after the Order's Generalate was formed. The women had exhibited extraordinary religious fervour – some begging to wear hair-shirts, chains of iron and to fast on bread and water. In the beds of others were discovered bundles of nettles, branches of thorns and pillows filled with stones;[56] while in the Limerick Asylum, according to the Annals, they had mixed soot or soap with drinking water to punish themselves for past intemperance. In the East Finchley Home, Consecrates reputedly were scourging themselves as late as the 1950s. Though some of these tendencies were discouraged, the episodes indicate how disturbed were some of the most "successful" cases of reform.

Consecrated status took several years to achieve. Good conduct and evidence of remorse could enable a penitent first, to become a "Child of Mary" and after two years' probation, to "take the black dress." Consecrates made a formal promise to remain in the House for twelve months. This engagement, read at the alter-rails in the presence of the Chaplain, the Superior, the First Mistress and the ordinary penitents, was a highly emotional occasion. It was proof of the heights to which all sinners could aspire, and a dramatic episode in the women's otherwise dreary lives. It was renewed each year, usually at the close of a feverishly-charged annual retreat. Those who persevered in their good purpose wore a silver cross as a mark of their perpetual consecration.

A formula to promote the sanctification of Consecrates, had been composed by the Foundress in 1835. Consisting of "wishes" to be addressed to these women by the entire Congregation, it is a revelation of pressure and control.

"Penitent souls, who dwell in solitude and in forgetfulness of the world, fortunate sheep whom the Good Shepherd has sought

---

55 *Ibid.*, p.145.
56 A. M. Clarke, *op. cit.*, pp.157-8.

after with the utmost solicitude ... may you never wander from the safe and tranquil path into which Providence has directed your steps! Continue, by your constant observance of the Rule laid down for you, to walk in the way that leads to the heavenly country, which is the object of your hopes."[57]

The first of the New Ross Consecrates were so affected by their vows, that two of the three spent the rest of their days in the institution, each of them dying a "most holy" death. The joy of their Consecration, however, was marred by an unfortunate incident. The Annual Retreat was conducted by a Redemptorist Priest, and on the closing day, a poor man suddenly "lost his mind" and cut his throat a few yards from the hall door.[58]

In 1876, Mother Mary of the Compassion Bartley, who had been Superior at New Ross for 13 years, was named Provincial and left for the Mother House in Limerick. She was replaced by Mother Mary of St. Magdalen of Jesus Devereux (another member of that pious Wexford family) who had been Assistant in Waterford, and was to remain in charge of the New Ross Monastery until her death in 1906.[59]

Although by 1879 there were still only 18 penitents in the Asylum, a new premises, with accommodation for fifty women, was built. By this time the dilapidated state of the old Convent too, was causing concern and endangering the health of the nuns. In the wake of the havoc wrought by tuberculosis amongst the Sisters (see below) the doctor recommended a new building, and work began in 1884. Another Bazaar raised £1,000 of the £7,000 required and in 1886 the Sisters were installed. Increasing numbers in both Community and classes meant that a new Chapel was now required - for the interior, or Convent part of which, William Howlett bequeathed £2,000. An exterior or public wing with an entrance in Irishtown was added for the "necessity" and convenience of the people. It was paid for by Dean Kavanagh.[60] The Chapel was opened in 1895, and three

---

57 *Ibid.*, 158.
58 New Ross Annals, July 1873.
59 *Ibid.*, 1876.
60 New Ross Annals, and Donovan, *op. cit.*, p.143.
    The public continued to use this Chapel for several years after the Good Shepherd Sisters had left New Ross in 1967. In the 1990s after almost a century of use it was eventually closed as a place of worship and converted to living accommodation.

years later - the parish clergy having other "pressing duties" to perform - Rev. Fr. McCormack, a "zealous young priest" was appointed Chaplain to the Community[61]

Thus, by the turn of the century the appalling living conditions which had characterised the New Ross Community for almost forty years, had largely disappeared. Further improvements were gradually carried out - though it was not until 1907 that the penitents' "class room" was extended, and their sleeping quarters enlarged. The single dormitory to which all the women had been consigned for nearly half a century was inadequate for the increase in numbers, and a second was provided over the ironing room. Also at this time, a badly needed refectory was built; and the Annals mention an important addition - a new infirmary.

Most large Homes such as the Good Shepherds and the London Female Penitentiary, for example, had their own infirmaries for the care of sick inmates; and the majority of women could be treated in the Asylums if they were ill. Few Refuges, however, could run the risk of contagion, and "fever" cases were generally dispatched to local fever hospitals or workhouse infirmaries, from which they seldom returned. As early as 1814, the first *Annual Report* of the Dublin Female Penitentiary, for example, noted that even in its temporary accommodation in Eccles Street, a hospital room had been established in each ward, to prevent sending out patients "except in cases of fever".

Few Refuges were willing to admit applicants with venereal disease - such cases being regarded as less hopeful from a rescue point of view, difficult or distasteful to nurse, and damaging to the reputation (particularly with regard to laundry work) of the Homes. The Good Shepherds were unusually charitable in caring for such women; but as is shown in Chapter 6, even they made use of the Government Lock Hospitals (improperly, from a legal standpoint) while the Contagious Diseases legislation was in place. To refrain from doing so, could be disastrous, and a shocking case occurred in Cork. In November 1881, twenty-five year old Mary Ann Donaghan from Waterford was recommended to the Cork Good Shepherd Asylum by a priest. Her disease must have been advanced, and the severity of her condition unrecognised. She left

61 New Ross Annals, 1898.

for the Government Lock Hospital about ten weeks later - and died on the day she was admitted.[62]

The London Female Penitentiary too, was prepared to take on such cases, noting in its 5th *Annual Report*:

> "Females who apply in a diseased condition are not on that account rejected, provided in other respects they appear to be suitable objects of charity."[63]

Nevertheless, however well-intentioned, Homes relying on income from their laundries were forced to take public concern on the matter into account. Thus the Cork Annals for 1899 record that a small sanatorium for the isolation of infectious cases had been built for the Industrial School. This was to avoid sending fever patients to hospital, since "the rumour of Contagious Diseases might severely injure our Laundry."[64]

Consumptive cases on the other hand, were often retained in the Homes, endangering those nursing them and putting other inmates' health at risk. The Irish Registers contain numerous examples of women who died soon after being admitted; but to what extent previous ill health, rather than present circumstances brought about their deaths, will never be known. The evidence suggests that certainly for some inmates, an "awareness of guilt", carefully nurtured, provoked rapid decline; while for others, tragic memories, no less than a chilling future, diminished the will to survive. Sixteen year old Anne Finley, for example, from Waterford, was "placed in the [New Ross] Asylum by her parents" in August 1880. She died in the Home six months' later.[65] In 1886 nineteen year old Bridget Cotton from New Ross, was brought to the Asylum by her father and step-mother. She died within three years, having given "great edification during her illness".[66] Ill health stalked the Rescue Homes, and in the Limerick Refuge, for example, where, as we have seen, penitents' daytime accommodation was in a basement beneath the Chapel, tuberculosis was particularly evident during the 1860s when harrowing deaths occurred. The unwholesome

---

62 Cork Register of Penitents, 29 November, 1881.
63 *London Female Penitentiary, 5th Annual Report*, 1812.
64 Cork Annals, 1899.
65 New Ross Register of Penitents, 8 August 1880.
66 *Ibid.*, 23 January 1886.

confinement of the women (many of whom were sickly in the first place) to quarters that were overcrowded and unfit; coupled with their constant occupation in damp, unhealthy and unregulated laundries, made contagion inevitable. Added to these factors were the morbid purpose of the institutions, and the system's constant emphasis on sin. To work and sleep alongside elderly drudges who might once have been normal, was to be reminded of one's future in a Home. Such a prospect disturbed not only the penitents but Mother St. Euphrasia, who urged the Mistresses to treat aged persons "whatever defects they may have" with kindness and forbearance, particularly if they had spent many years in the house:

> "They may have rendered great services in their younger days and it is only just that we do all in our power to make supportable a life which in many ways must be very painful at their advanced years. If the young penitents see the ancient ones unhappy they will not attach themselves to the house, on the contrary, they will be anxious to leave while yet young. If we should be kind to the young in order to encourage them we are still more obliged to be kind to the aged, taking into account their infirmities, not over working them, procuring them little comforts and not reprimanding them before their young companions unless for a public fault which our silence would seem to excuse too much."[67]

For grieving mothers and those filled with longing or remorse, such a prospect, in such a setting, was appalling. For some it led inevitably, to depression, decline and death. Cases of suicide in the Homes – if such occurred – are not referred to in the Records.

Even in short-term Homes women were broken, as haunted by, or yearning for the past, they were urged to repent. Such was the history of Mary Handcock, for example, who "died suddenly" in 1834, three months after being admitted to the Limerick Refuge – at that time still a lay-run institution.[68] The betrayed, post-natal servant, forced to relinquish the symbol of her shame before entering a Magdalen Asylum, or dying a remorseful, workhouse death, has been dismissed by feminist historians as a sentimental stereotype, an outmoded tale of female passivity, a simplistic view of womanhood oppressed. This research reveals that in Ireland

---

67 *Rules for the Direction of the Classes*, pp.201-2.
68 Limerick Register of Penitents, 1834.

particularly, she was a familiar figure, becoming more, rather than less common, as the nineteenth century progressed. The following history is unusual only in its detail, and the fact that it exists through a Home's surviving correspondence. It illustrates, incidentally, the emotional blackmail wielded to keep women in the institutions - in this case, an English Protestant Home.

In December 1885 the Committee of the York Female Penitentiary, a small Refuge catering exclusively for young penitents, received a letter from the Female Aid Society in the Isle of Man. It concerned Isabella Corkhill who was thirty-one years old, "honest, sober and hard working, but not moral in her conduct." She had, in fact, recently borne a child which was to be "properly provided for" in the Isle of Man:

> "[Her] age is the difficulty, so few Homes take them over 25 ... of course, the Committee would send a donation if this poor woman could be admitted. She has worked as a servant, and bears a very good character except in this one respect."

The Managers of the York Refuge decided to accept her, provided she was amenable to discipline, prepared to work, considerate to the younger inmates, not liable to outbursts of temper, really desirous of reform, and undertook to remain in the institution for the full two years demanded by the Rules.

A few weeks later a letter from Rev. Savage, Vicar of Douglas, assured the Committee that the woman had promised "unreservedly" all that was required. Within a few months of her arrival, however, she was desperate to leave, and the Ladies reported that her violent temper and bad language were "very injurious to the younger girls". Rev. Savage responded:

> "I thank you for writing about Lizzie Corkhill, but I am distressed to find she is behaving so badly. I send a letter to her enclosed in this, which you can read. She is a foolish girl to throw away her chance now, and what she will do with herself I don't know. I think it will be best to use her care for her child as a hold over her for good. I am paying for it at present, but I shall decline to do so if she leaves your institution."

Subdued by this threat she stayed on in the Refuge, but her health was soon broken, and the doctor advised her immediate return to the Isle of Man. Her parents were too poor to receive her; and

Rev. Savage's suggestion that the Douglas House of Industry might admit her, came too late. By the time it arrived she was in the York union hospital, too ill to be moved.

For the Rescue Worker gripped in a moral crusade, the anguish and remorse this woman suffered were incomplete. Her humiliation and sacrifice - the loss of the baby she so clearly mourned, her submission to a Magdalen Asylum and even her approaching workhouse death - were not enough. Never doubting that her "fall" rather than her "rescue" had destroyed her, Rev. Savage pursued her to the last:

> "Will you kindly remember me to her, and say how I would urge her to repentance for her sin against God; this is, I always think, the point such people miss. They see they have sinned against their own family, but as to sin against God, there seems to be no idea of it."[69]

In the following month she died in the workhouse, the York Union Register listing Phthisis as the cause of death.[70] Rev. Savage offered to settle the "full extent" of the funeral costs, but in fact, her burial was paid for by the Vicar and Wardens of Marygold, her homeplace in the Isle of Man. There was no further mention of her baby, and throughout the correspondence not a single reference was made to the father of her child.

Particularly in Convent Homes, the Sisters too, of course, were subject to tuberculosis, their close confinement, and the fact that there was little awareness of the need for segregation once illness occurred, adding to the risk. Unlike the penitents, however, the nuns at least had the advantage of sleeping in single cells; and with the exception of the Laundry Mistress and her Assistants, labour in the steam-filled wash and ironing rooms was not their daily lot.

Several tragic cases occurred of nuns who were dying of consumption being returned to Ireland, particularly from the Angers Mother House. Hopes that their "native air" would restore them to health have an unconvincing ring, and the journey alone must have aggravated their condition. These women, who had made their novitiates and trained in the Angers Mother House before Ireland's Provincial status, had spent their working-lives in France. Doubtless they were homesick, but only

69 Correspondence, York Female Penitentiary, 1885-87.
70 York Union Register of Deaths, April, 1887.

when incurably ill were they returned. Such removal can hardly have been to their advantage, since they now exchanged familiar scenes and faces for those they had never known. And however beneficial the properties of "native air" were claimed to be, it is doubtful if much of this illusive vapour penetrated Enclosure sickrooms. The return of these invalids convenienced the Mother House rather than the Homes they were dispatched to, sometimes – as occurred in the New Ross Monastery towards the end of the century – with such disastrous results.

In 1879 Sister Mary of St. Colmon O'Donnell had been sent to the New Ross Convent from Angers, her health already "broken". The vain hope that her native air would restore her (she was buried in the Sisters' little cemetery within the year) was succeeded by anxiety. The Annals record:

> "Dying of consumption as she did, we have good reason to fear that the germ of the malady was sown in the community, notwithstanding that every precaution was taken against it."[71]

The first victim was one of the penitents who died shortly afterwards in the new infirmary; and a few months later, in 1881, Sister Mary of St. Appolinaire Fagen, for many years Mistress of Penitents, succumbed to an illness which had lasted two years.[72]

In 1882 Sister Mary Teresa Neville died of consumption, the Annals reporting that regardless of all precautions taken, the "dread malady made great havoc in the Community for years after".[73] Thus, in spite of the services of a doctor, consumption carried off Sister Mary of St. Francis Bargis O'Connor, in 1883, Sister Mary of Black Mullally (a young nun) in November 1884, and another Sister in 1886.[74] Ten years previously, when the first of the New Ross Sisters (Mary of St. Alphonsus) had died in the institution, a cemetery for the Religious had been made in the corner of the garden. By the turn of the century this was so filled with graves that it, and its occupants, were moved further from the Convent. As an added precaution, a new infirmary was built three years later.[75] In the meantime, Margaret Dempsey, a 22 year old penitent, was taken out by her mother in 1902. She was "very

---

71 New Ross Annals, 1880.
72 *Ibid.*, 1880 and 1881.
73 *Ibid.*, 1882.
74 *Ibid.*, 1883, 1884 and 1886.
75 *Ibid.*, 1904 and 1907.

sick in consumption", having been in the Asylum for eighteen months.[76]

A year after Sister Mary O'Donnell's fatal removal to New Ross, the Mother General arranged the transfer of another dying Irish Sister - this time from Avingnon. The Cork Annals for 1881 record:

> "Our dear Sr. Mary of the Alphonsus Corbett died on 28th January of consumption. She was many years suffering from this disease and was sent by the very honoured Mother General from Avingnon to this mission, hoping her native air might restore her, but when our dear Mother saw her arrive she was so alarmed at her delicate appearance she sent for the doctor, and after a good examination, he pronounced her in the last stages of consumption, that she would not live more than a few months."[77]

Thirteen years later a similar death occurred - though this patient, Sister Mary of St. Irene, again from the Mother House, had been returned to Ireland in the early stages of her disease:

> "in the hope that her native air would help, but [she grew] weaker and weaker every day and at last succumbed to the fatal disease consumption."[78]

There is no doubt that the health of the Sisters as well as the penitents, was sometimes neglected. Mother Teresa Devereux, for example, died young as a result of rheumatic fever (see Chapter 6) and though her sister, who succeeded her as Prioress at Cork, lived to be almost ninety, a third member of that extraordinary family - Sister Mary of Teresa, their niece - also suffered from ill health. She visited the Cork Convent in 1902, having stayed in the Limerick Mother House to receive Postulants for the Mission. The Annals record that eight years in India had "completely broken her health", and she was "unrecognisable".[79] The nuns' early convent in Belfast was so unwholesome that typhus fever broke out in the 1870s, killing two of the Sisters and necessitating the removal of the Community to a healthier part of the city.[80]

In 1902 at the end of our period Michael McCarthy - solitary critic of the Order's dual role in Magdalen Asylums and

---

76 *Ibid.*, 8 June 1900.
77 Cork Annals 1881.
78 *Ibid.*, 1894.
79 *Ibid.*, 1902 and 1904.
80 *Holy Rosary Parish Golden Jubilee Souvenir, 1898-1948*, pp.15-16.

Industrial Schools - made the following observation, already quoted at the beginning of this Chapter:

"There is a Magdalen Asylum at New Ross, in which there were 45 selected fallen women in 1901, whose histories I should like to inquire into."[81]

McCarthy did not have access to the records, but almost a century after the publication of his *Priests and People in Ireland*, such enquiries can be made. Listed on the 1901 Census are the 45 women he refers to; and by tracing them back to their original entries in the Penitents' Register, a little of their histories, and even what happened to them in later years, can be learned. All but three of the inmates enumerated on Census night (31 March) can be matched in the Convent's records. The remainder were either not registered when first admitted (at best improbable and at worst sinister) or their details differ to such an extent in the two sources that positive identification is impossible.

Unlike the Cork Annals, which provide such a valuable background for the following Chapters, those for New Ross contain little supplementary material on individual penitents. There are practically no details in these records, for example, of women's histories, conversions, or unusually harrowing deaths. But the Convent's Register of Penitents contains enough information to indicate that McCarthy was right in his conjecture, hinted at above, that some of the women were not, in fact, proper subjects for a Magdalen Home.[82]

---

81 McCarthy, *op. cit.*, p.470.
82 "Not a fit subject for a Magdalen Home" was the description applied to three admissions to the Cork Good Shepherd in the period, each of whom was withdrawn or sent away - numbers 308, 595, and 792. Whether this meant that their remorse was inadequate, or alternatively, that they were not of the "fallen" class, is difficult to determine. In view of their age, the latter seems more probable, though as we have seen, very young victims of incest (and perhaps rape) though innocent, were expected to atone; and there is evidence that this was occurring into the 1950s. Girls entirely free from "sin" on the other hand (such as those referred to above who were transferred direct from Industrial Schools run by the Order) were, nevertheless, accepted into Magdalen Homes. The three girls in question in the Cork context were Bridget Tobin, aged 19 from Mallow, who was sent out after a few days in December 1877 "as she said she was not a subject for a Penitents' Class"; Mary May, a 30 year old from Cork who left after two weeks in May 1881 "not being a subject for a Magdalen Asylum" and 18 year old Annie Higgins, who was sent back to Youghal after two months in April 1882, for the same reason. The first two women had entered the Home "of their own accord" while Annie Higgins had been brought by a former penitent Annie Higgins - "Monica".

As we have seen, penitent numbers in the Asylum were always low - a factor which contributed to the Home's early closure in 1967. Throughout its history, as well as rescuing the "fallen" on its doorstep, the New Ross Refuge was forced to draw in women from much further afield - a development hardly popular with the local community, and proof that the location of the Home was both unnecessary and unsound. More significant, the institution admitted an unusually wide range of penitents - both very young girls and older women - who continued unsegregated, regardless of their category of "sin". The following examples from the 45 women appearing on the 1901 Census, illustrate these points.

It was noted in Chapter 2 that in 1871 twelve year old Mary Connolly of New Ross (given the name Philomena) was brought to the Magdalen Asylum "for protection", by a local priest. She spent the next 70 years in the Asylum, dying a "holy and happy death" in 1941.[83] Though resident in the Home in 1901, she can hardly have warranted the title "fallen", and her history would undoubtedly have interested McCarthy. Another casualty of the Rescue Movement was Anne Rellis, admitted in 1873 when she was only 13 years of age. She too, was brought by a parish priest and left six years later with her step-father. She was re-admitted in 1893, and ten years later she left the Institution for Enniscorthy workhouse.[84] Also included in the Census was Elizabeth Macgrath from Enniscorthy, who was 14 when admitted to the Home on the recommendation of a priest in 1883. She left and re-entered several times, eventually quitting the institution in May 1901.[85]

The history of Margaret Williamson, the "trusted" helper from Limerick, has already been described. At the time of the Census she was over 70, and since she had been a penitent for some 55 years, for her too, the title "fallen" was surely undeserved. The same is true of Mary Gibson, who, as has been noted, was to spend 73 years in the institution, having entered the Home in 1863 at the age of 22.[86] Another woman recommended by a

---

83 New Ross Register of Penitents, 5 March 1871.
84 *Ibid.*, 15 May 1873.
85 *Ibid.*, 14 February 1883.
86 *Ibid.*, 21 August 1860 and 15 December 1863.

priest (in 1873) was 18 year old Ellen Dwyer. After spending 65 years in the Home, she was buried in the communal penitents' grave in 1938.[87]

There were other inmates who were probably not of the "fallen" class even when admitted; but for whom the term was surely inappropriate by 1901. They were also not from the region. Winifred McCarthy, from Clare, for example, was registered in 1875 when she was twenty-four years old. She died in the Home half a century later in 1925. She was deaf and dumb.[88] The case of 37 year old Margaret Mullery, from Co. Wicklow was similar, though she spent only two years in the institution, leaving shortly after having been included on the Census. She had been brought by her father, and she too, was deaf and dumb.[89]

Ann Gillis, on the other hand, was from New Ross. She entered the Home in 1875 when she was 25 years old; left two years later, returned after a few months, and died in the institution in January 1904.[90] Ann Lawler, also from New Ross, was 41 at the time of the Census. The Penitents' Register, however, records that she was only 16 when admitted in 1877. She left the Home twice at the turn of the century, each time to take up a situation, but returned in 1903 "of her own free will". She died in the institution in 1931.[91] Similarly, Mary Cleary, from Co. Wexford was aged 43 when enumerated in 1901. She had been admitted, however, in 1878. Her remorse dragged out for 45 years and she died in the Home in 1923.[92]

Other life-long inmates were Ellen Murphy, aged 28 when admitted in 1879, and almost 70 when she died in the Home in 1916;[93] and Elizabeth Howlett from New Ross. Aged only 17 when registered in 1879, this woman was still doing penance 64 years later. She died in the Institution in 1943.[94] Annie Roy from Wexford, had an almost identical history. She had been admitted in 1881 when she was a young girl of 19. After 63 years' penance,

---

87 *Ibid.*, 4 December 1873.
88 *Ibid.*, 12 June 1875.
89 *Ibid.*, 13 June 1899.
90 *Ibid.*, no date, 1875.
91 *Ibid.*, 14 June 1877.
92 *Ibid.*, 15 August 1878.
93 *Ibid.*, 25 March 1879.
94 *Ibid.*, 19 September 1879.

she died in the Home in 1944, by which time she was in her eighties.[95]

It has already been noted that even Consecrates could suffer a fall. In 1893 Anastasia Flinn, a nineteen year old girl from Clonmel entered the Asylum of her "own accord", having previously been in the Order's Waterford Home. Although she "had the black dress" and was finally Consecrated, she was "very troublesome", and left in 1913 to return to the Asylum in Waterford.[96]

The fact that most Protestant Homes refused to re-admit penitents who left without approval or before their training was complete, has already been discussed. The history of Bridget Gantly from Nenagh Co. Tipperary, is an interesting example of how tolerant the Good Shepherd Sisters were, in this respect. From the evidence, it would appear that in contrast to most of the examples illustrated above, this woman probably did belong to that class for whom Magdalen Asylums were originally intended. She was first admitted in May 1898 when she was 25 years old, having previously been an inmate of the Limerick Magdalen Home. Four years later she left, but returned within 3 days, and remained for a further 4 years. She then left, and after 15 months, was re-admitted for two weeks. A year later, in June 1908, she returned for 6 months; and having left in January 1909, she was re-admitted a few weeks' later. She finally quitted the institution in December 1912.[97] Katie Burke from Clonmel, Co. Tipperary, who was registered in the New Ross Home in August 1900, was possibly of a similar category; since at the age of 28, she had already been an inmate of the Order's Asylums in Limerick, Waterford and Cork.[98] A further case of this type is nineteen year old Maggie Pierce "(or Tobin)", who had been a penitent in the Waterford Home for two years, before being admitted to New Ross in 1900. She left with her aunt in 1904, returned a week later, left in the following month, and returned after three years. Shortly afterwards, she left for hospital, and after an absence of almost four years, was re-admitted briefly, before leaving for hospital again.[99]

95 *Ibid.*, 19 May 1881.
96 *Ibid.*, 1 June 1893.
97 *Ibid.*, 21 May 1898.
98 *Ibid.*, 30 August 1900.
99 *Ibid.*, 30 November 1900.

Finally, the history of Mary Ann Barrett from Waterford is particularly grim. A previous inmate of the Waterford Asylum, she was 36 years old when admitted to the New Ross Home in 1898. She left after only 8 weeks but re-entered 6 months later. In 1905 she left again and returned within 2 days. After a few months, however, she "had to be sent to the workhouse" - and the Register notes that she died in the Lunatic Asylum, in Enniscorthy.[100]

The above cases illustrate the wide range of inmates classed as "fallen" at the time of the Census - some of whose histories and long-term confinements justify Michael McCarthy's qualms. By 1901, with 45 penitents listed, the place was filled almost to capacity with penitent women of every class.

Valuable as the Census is, it is a record of one day only - a snapshot at a particular point in time. Though it provides a clear picture of the overall composition of the Home at the turn of the century - a picture which could hardly be obtained elsewhere - it gives no indication of how long individuals had been in the institution; or how long they would remain. Further, of course, it tells us nothing of those many women who, over a forty year period, had been admitted but had already left the Home. A significant number of these may well have belonged to that class for whom the Asylum was intended. It would seem, however, that of all categories of "the fallen", prostitutes were least disposed to make a long-term stay. And as time went by, they were those least inclined to seek admission.

McCarthy hinted that for many cases in this Home, the term "fallen" was improperly applied, and that even by the Church's standards women were being unjustly and needlessly confined. There is little background information on the penitents, but even if known, a girl's history might be misleading. Contemporary observers such as Arthur J. S. Maddison, emphasised that generalisations based on age, for example, were dangerous; since very young girls were often more "steeped in vice" than their elders; and relative newcomers to prostitution could be even more depraved than those who had been on the streets for years:

"The classification by age, adopted by most of the Homes, is practically useless, for every experienced rescue worker knows

---

100 *Ibid.*, 26 May 1898.

that young girls are often more depraved than their elders. Nor can we recommend a hard and fast rule of placing together all who have not been on the streets. Sometimes a girl who has only once fallen, is worse in language and influence than one who has been on the streets for some time."[101]

It was noted in Chapter 3 that in the Limerick Asylum, for example, a very young penitent, Mary Pinder, was unusually disruptive. Aged only 13 when she was sent to the institution by the Loughrea Sisters of Mercy in June 1874, she was expelled in the following year, for beating up one of the penitents.[102] Four years previously, 14 year old Kate Quin, from Cashel, Co. Tipperary had been recommended by a Father Ryan to the Limerick Home. Eighteen months later she was expelled for bad conduct – the record stating (in red) that she is "never to be admitted again".[103] A final example of youthful depravity is two young sisters, Ellen and Bridget Donoher aged 17 and 18, who were recommended to the Waterford Asylum in July 1875 by Rev. Keating, a local parish priest. Both "left for bad conduct" five months later, each being described as "very dissipated and disobedient".[104]

Generally, however, it would seem reasonable to conclude that 12 and 13 year olds, brought to the Home by priests "for protection", were not so "thoroughly degraded", as those common prostitutes for whom such institutions were built. Similar reservations must surely apply too, to unfortunate women like Isabella Corkhill, who – on the Female Aid Society's own admission – was honest, hardworking and sober, and whose sole transgression had been the birth of her child.

In the New Ross Magdalen Asylum in common with the Cork and Waterford Homes, only referrals from the Government Hospitals can be definitely classed as prostitutes – those women who, while detained for treatment under the Contagious Diseases legislation were induced to reform. As noted earlier, this information contained in the Registers of Penitents, establishes conclusively that both extremes of the "fallen" were accepted and

---

101 Maddison, *op. cit.*, pp.106-7.
102 Limerick Register of Penitents, 11 June 1874.
103 *Ibid.*, 6 October 1871.
104 Waterford Register of Penitents, 2 July 1875.

confined. In New Ross, however, regardless of their histories or present states of mind, they were admitted to an institution which for most of the period contained only one dormitory, and insufficient "auxiliaries" to segregate and supervise the Class.

In October 1872, eighteen months after the start of 12 year old Mary Connolly's long confinement in the Home, the first of several women registered as prostitutes under the new Acts, arrived. This was 17 year old Johanne Scanlan from Kildare, who was recommended by Miss Farrell, Matron of the Government Lock Hospital. After 14 months she left the Asylum to look after her sick mother, but returned shortly afterwards, in March 1874. Thirteen years later she went out as Under Laundress to Lady Kildare - her restoration to society, albeit delayed, being unusual evidence of successful reform via exposure to the Acts. The fact that the Penitents' Register records her "happy" death in 1929, however, is ominous; and coupled with the improbability of her still being employed at the age of 74, indicates her post-censual return to the Home.[105]

In the month following her initial registration, another former prostitute from the Curragh who had been detained for treatment in the Kildare Lock Hospital - Elizabeth Warren from Clare - was recommended by Miss Farrell. She stayed for only 2 months and left "of her own accord" in January 1873.[106] Meanwhile, two more patients from the Government Hospital had been admitted to the Home. Eliza Nolan from Newbridge left after 6 months, with "E.H."; and Mary McKelvy, from Drogheda left after only 4 weeks.[107] By 1873, Miss Farrell had apparently been transferred to the Lock Hospital in Cork, and various patients from that institution were now sent to the Asylum in New Ross. In April that year 28 year old Mary Connell from Cork, for example, was admitted on the Matron's recommendation. She died in the Home seven years later.[108] In October 1874, Mary Hogan aged 27, was also admitted on the recommendation of Miss Farrell. She may have been one of those patients who, as discussed in the following Chapter, were discharged prematurely; since less than

---

105 New Ross Register of Penitents, 2 October 1872.
106 *Ibid.*, 9 November 1872.
107 *Ibid.*, 4 and 11 January, 1873.
108 *Ibid.*, 4 April 1873.

two years later, she had to be sent to hospital.[109] Twenty-five year old Eliza Cullen from Carlow was a more hopeful case, and in 1874 she left the Home after only five months to take up a situation.[110] Miss Farrell recommended two women in 1876 - 32 year old Mary Melia from Portlaw, Co. Waterford; and 24 year old Bridget Kane from Queen's County. Both left the Asylum within a few weeks.[111]

Twenty-six year old Anne Shea, from Clonmel was another of Miss Farrell's converts; but after only 12 days in the institution in December 1876, she was sent out for "bad conduct".[112] Jane Lucas ("or Kate Collins") a forty year old prostitute from Co. Tipperary, was also recommended by the Lock Hospital Matron at about this time; but she caused "much trouble" during her four year stay at the Home.[113] Another of the Matron's cases was 22 year old Bridget Keegan, from Dublin. She was admitted to the Asylum in May 1878, but was sent out within a few weeks "for bad conduct".[114]

A full discussion of the Contagious Diseases legislation is contained in the following Chapter, but it was noted earlier that the Acts were suspended in 1883. Thus the last woman to be recommended by Miss Farrell - who by this time had returned to the Lock Hospital in Kildare - was 26 year old Marion King from Thurles. Before being registered as a common prostitute in The Curragh, this woman had been an inmate of the Asylum in Limerick. Her latest conversion was short-lived and her penance lasted only two days.[115] Following the Repeal of the Acts in 1886 no further cases are recorded from Ireland's two "Certified" Hospitals - both of which were presumably closed down or converted to other use.

It has been suggested that while women of the prostitute class continued to enter Magdalen Asylums, they now did so with less frequency than had formerly been the case. Further, they were less likely - both than their predecessors and other penitents - to remain in such Homes. Nevertheless, in all the Irish Houses,

---

109 *Ibid.*, 18 October 1874.
110 *Ibid.*, 1 December 1873.
111 *Ibid.*, 11 January and 15 February 1876.
112 *Ibid.*, 30 November 1876.
113 *Ibid.*, 12 January 1877.
114 *Ibid.*, 11 May 1878.
115 *Ibid.*, 13 May 1884.

prostitutes inevitably associated, and were identified with, inmates not properly of the Magdalen Class.

We have seen in the Chapters on Limerick and Waterford, that as well as providing an overall picture of the Homes at the end of our period, the 1901 Census contains a category of information not available elsewhere - that relating to literacy. Under the column Education, the Head of Household (in the New Ross Asylum, Mother Mary of St. Magdalen Jesus Devereux) was required to state whether the inmates could "read and write", "read only", or "cannot read". Of the 45 women listed, a total of 30 were described as able to read and write. Eight could read but not write; and seven were illiterate. Of the last category, Ellen Murphy had been an inmate for 22 years at the time of the Census; Annie Roy had spent 20 years in the Home; Mary Moore had been admitted in 1886; and Mary Ann Walsh (from Wexford) in 1889. Both Anastasia Flinn and Mary Anne Walsh (from Cork) were relatively recent inmates, but both had previously been penitents at the Waterford Asylum.[116]

Allegations that the "feeble-minded" were forming an increasing proportion of penitents have already been referred to; and no doubt such women accounted for much of the deficiency recorded above. As well as this, even by the turn of the century, large sections of the poor and labouring classes were barely educated - a situation inevitably reflected in the Homes. Women in particular were vulnerable, and the fact that newly admitted inmates could neither read nor write, was an indictment, not of the Rescue Movement, but of society itself. Nevertheless, it is clear from the Annual Reports of other institutions, equally challenged, that efforts were being made to educate inmates - such Reports containing frequent reference to the teaching activities of Visiting Ladies as well as of resident staff. An increasing emphasis was placed on this aspect of training in the York Penitentiary, for example, from the 1860s; and in the Glasgow Magdalen Institution a conscious effort was made to keep standards in line with educational improvements in the population at large. To this end, the basic reading and writing lessons of the early period were extended by the end of the

116 *Ibid*, 25 March 1879, 19 May 1881, 10 May 1886, 7 January 1889, 1 June 1893 and 10 October 1897.

nineteenth century to include special classes in geography, arithmetic and music, and weekly lectures in "homely and interesting" subjects.[117]

For the Good Shepherd penitents, however, education was restricted to "religious instruction", "pious readings" and prayers. These alternated with the silences, and all were extended to the work. Depressing, rather than stimulating, and recognised even by the Foundress as tending to fatigue, such practices were nevertheless, regretfully urged:

> "We should not judge the children severely if sometimes they do not answer the prayers, particularly those said during work. Of course it is desirable that all should pray; by so doing they sanctify themselves and avoid vain and evil imaginations, but they are not obliged to pray often; they may be absorbed by their work, or without being wanting in true devotion, they may fear the fatigues of answering in a loud voice."[118]

At the same time Mother St. Euphrasia stressed the importance of the orphans and "preservation" children, being properly taught in reading, writing, and arithmetic, etc.; so that they could support themselves, and even their families after leaving the Homes. Those who had passed their childhood in the Order's Houses should not be "less advanced" in secular knowledge than others, as this might damage the reputation of the Homes.

Industrial Schools in Ireland were owned and managed almost exclusively by religious Orders, who received substantial Government maintenance for the children in their care. These children were required to receive a basic education, but standards generally in Industrial Schools were notoriously low, and aftercare was almost non-existent. The *Rules* - published thirty years after the opening of the Order's first Industrial School in Ireland – advise that:

> "In schools under Government where payment is given for the maintenance of the children, the regulations imposed by the authorities should be conscientiously carried out".

---

117 Finnegan, *op. cit.*, p.202; and Linda Mahood, *op. cit.*, p.84.
118 *Rules for the Direction of the Classes, op. cit.* These comments are an interesting indication of the physical and mental condition of the penitents. They are a chill reminder too, of the torpor of their daily lives.

However, Mother Euphrasia's personal insistence that Sacred History should take precedence over all other studies, and her closing remarks on the subject:

> "Above all, the salvation of their souls is the only real object in this life to which they should aim. Consequently more attention should be paid to their religious training than all else."[119]

make it unlikely that the Good Shepherd Industrial pupils were the exception to the rule. Given the nuns' own lack of training, and commitment to other goals, this is hardly surprising; and for almost a century the fate of these and other Industrial pupils was sealed. The deprivation and abuses occurring in Irish Homes - physical, sexual and psychological - are now seen to have existed on such a massive scale that the deficiencies of educational provision seem, by comparison, almost unimportant. Nevertheless, Industrial School regulations, however ineffectually complied with, were at least in place.

For penitents in Magdalen Asylums on the other hand - many of whom, it was hoped, would remain in the institutions for life - the need for even elementary education did not arise. These women were not only unwanted and undeserving, they were of the "fallen" class. Penance, not advancement, was the object of their stay. In any case, with every moment of their lives accounted for, there was neither time for education nor opportunity to profit from it, even had it been considered appropriate for women of that class.

Yet even the Foundress was compelled to recognise the inevitability of the departure of most inmates. With this prospect in mind she recommended additional chores, rather than education, to fit them for their lives:

> "As the greater number of our children are not called to remain all their life in the cloister, they should be formed so as to be able, on leaving the Good Shepherd, to earn an honest livelihood and one day take their place at the head of the family. They should be taught housework, some time of each month should be employed

---

119 *Ibid.*, p.221 and p.224.

teaching them to mend their clothes, and every means taken to train them in habits of order and cleanliness."[120]

Though convenient for the Community, such chores did not improve the women's minds. Deprived of basic education, external influence, wholesome pursuits and normal channels of development, the penitents (a significant proportion of whom had entered the Order's Homes in adolescence) were retarded rather than advanced. Irrespective of ability and regardless of age on admission (and girls like Mary Connolly and Ann Rellis, for example, were younger than many Industrial pupils*) the policy was uniform. Whatever the extent of feeble-mindedness - never, apparently, exceeding 30 percent of admissions - it is hardly to the credit of the Order that illiterate, long-term inmates were denied the opportunity to learn to read and write.

The total number of penitents admitted to the New Ross Magdalen Asylum between 1860 and 1900 was 321. Of these, 314 were single, 5 were married and 2 were widowed.

Ages on admission ranged from 12 years (one) to 57 years (one); with this Home containing a high proportion of very young inmates, almost one third of the total being aged under twenty. Age on admission was recorded for only 301 penitents.

Table 15
Age on Admission: New Ross Good Shepherd
1860-1900

Years	Total 301	Percent
12-19	96	32
20-29	147	49
30-39	39	13
40-49	14	5
50-57	5	2

---

120 *Ibid.*, p.68.

* Industrial pupils were not only provided with an education - in theory at least. They had the added advantage of being forced to leave the institutions when they reached the age of 16 - and the Government grant for their maintenance expired.

Fewer women went into the New Ross Home "voluntarily" than was the case with the Order's other Irish Asylums. Of those for whom this information was provided (291 out of a total 321) only 22 percent (compared with 43 percent for Limerick, 49 percent for Waterford and 47 percent for Cork) entered of their own accord. To a greater extent than was the case in the Order's other Irish Homes, priests were responsible for most of the referrals to New Ross; and while local prelates such as Fr. Aylward were particularly active, some, like Rev. Henry Reed, recommended women from as far away as Cork.

Table 16
By Whom Recommended: New Ross Gd Shepherd
1860-1900

	Total 291	Percent
Priests	147	51
Own Accord	65	22
Good Shepherds	19	7
Other Nuns	13	4
Female Relatives	13	4
Miss Farrell/Lock H.	13	4
Ladies	6	2
Other	15	5

Table 17 lists how inmates left the New Ross Asylum over the period - this information being recorded for 311 of the total 321 inmates. Once again, the very low proportion leaving to take up a situation is an indication of the failure of penitential Rescue Work. Women leaving to join family or friends (23 percent of the total for the whole period) might perhaps be regarded as "successful" cases; though a return to those responsible for their confinement in the first place - or at least tolerant of it - makes such a supposition unlikely.

In this Home, the percentage of women leaving "of their own accord" over the period (39 percent) was almost double that of those entering the Asylum voluntarily. Only 36 women out of the total, however (approximately 12 percent of those for whom this information is recorded) both entered and left the Home of their own free will.

Table 17
Reasons for Leaving New Ross Good Shepherd: 1860–1900

	Total 311	Percent
Left of Own Accord	120	39
Family/Friends	70	23
Died in Home	33	11
Expelled	28	9
Hospital	19	6
Left for Situation	15	5
Escaped	11	4
Other Good Shepherds	7	2
Other	8	3

For the 244 penitents in the New Ross Asylum whose date of departure as well as admission is recorded (76 percent of the total) it is possible to determine length of stay. It is clear from the Table below that this institution, as well as admitting younger girls than the other Irish Good Shepherds, detained them for longer, and was more likely to keep them for life. The average term of penance in this Home was 6.7 years; though approximately one half of the inmates left the Asylum within 18 months of arrival.

Table 18
Length of Stay in New Ross Good Shepherd: From 1860.

	Total 244	Percent
Under 1 week	12	4.9
1–2 weeks	1	0.4
2–4 weeks	16	6.6
1–2 months	21	8.6
2–6 months	26	10.7
6–12 months	23	9.4
1–2 years	38	15.6
2–5 years	37	15.2
5–10 years	27	11.1
10–15 years	15	6.1
15–20 years	5	2.0
20–30 years	8	3.3
30–40 years	4	1.6
40–50 years	3	1.2
50 years +	8	3.3

The New Ross Penitents' Register contains little information on the parents of inmates. Of the 321 women admitted over the forty year period, 28 were orphans, 21 were recorded as having both parents alive and 66 had one parent only. For two-thirds of the women, however, this information was not provided.

Table 19 gives inmates' place of birth. Fifty percent were born in County Wexford, most of them in the towns of New Ross (52), Wexford (45) and Enniscorthy (29). Neighbouring counties accounted for most of the other women - a pattern discernible in each of the Order's Houses.

Table 19
Birthplace of New Ross Penitents: 1860-1900

	Total 321	Percent
Wexford & County	159	50
Waterford & County	33	10
Co. Tipperary	19	6
Other nearby Counties	17	5
Dublin	16	5
England	7	2
Other	50	16

At the time of the Census all 45 inmates were Irish-born. Twenty-six of the total came from Co. Wexford (New Ross was not specified) and a further 8 from the neighbouring counties of Waterford, Kilkenny and Tipperary.

With the exception of 33 year old Elizabeth Mahony from Co. Cork, who was a widow, all the inmates were unmarried. And as noted above, two women were deaf and dumb - these being the only such infirmities listed.

As for the nuns, there were 26 Sisters recorded in the Home in 1901. The oldest of these was Mother Devereux, who was 74, and who, as we have seen, had been appointed Superior in 1876. She died in 1906, aged almost 80. The youngest Sister was Julia Furlong, aged 20.

The Good Shepherd Monastery in New Ross closed in 1967, when its inmates were transferred to the Order's other Magdalen Asylums, and its records deposited in the Limerick Mother House. But an awkward legacy remained. Almost opposite the

Enclosure, in St. Stephen's Cemetery, a large stone cross marked the communal burial plot of those penitents who, over the past century, had died in the neighbouring institution.

The original inscription on the monument no longer served its purpose, and was eventually erased in favour of the following:

"In loving memory of the Residents of the Good Shepherd Convent, New Ross. 1860-1967".

Far from honouring the memory of these women, this denial of their real status and experience adds to the injury done them. The word "Residents", so misleading and so belatedly applied, far from restoring these loved ones to society, absolves those responsible for their exclusion from it. In the process, a further injustice has been done, and for a second time these women's lives are lost.

Following the publication of this book in 2001, the above-mentioned monument was demolished - its replacement again describing unpaid workers confined to a female penitentiary as "residents" of St. Mary's Good Shepherd Convent. At least now, however, sixty-two of the women who died in the Home, and whose bodies lie in the communal grave, have been recorded - and given their proper names.

6

"Do Penance or Perish" Prostitution, The Contagious Diseases Acts and the Good Shepherd Magdalen Asylum, Cork

In 1809 a small Catholic Magdalen Asylum was founded in Peacock Lane, Cork, by a Mr. Terry. A Matron governed the institution under the direction of a committee of ladies; but so many difficulties were encountered that it was eventually decided to place the Home in the care of a religious community. The Irish Sisters of Charity were invited to undertake the work, and following extensive negotiations, and the completion of their new Convent, St. Vincent's, which was built on the Asylum's grounds, they finally took charge of the Home in June 1846.

In contrast to the nuns' accommodation, the nearby building inhabited by the penitents "partly from age and partly from defective construction" was in a derelict, even dangerous state. It could house only twenty inmates, lacked the equipment necessary for a Magdalen Asylum and was described by the incoming Sisters as being disorderly and without the means to set things right.[1]

Undaunted in spite of these difficulties, the nuns set about their task, and as happened in other lay Refuges taken over by Religious Orders, the existing penitents soon found the new regime intolerable. In this case, however, the Sisters were neither enclosed nor were they specifically devoted to the reform of fallen women. An account of what occurred appears in the nineteenth-century biography of Mary Aikenhead, the Foundress of the Irish Sisters of Charity.

"The poor penitents, thirteen in number, though at first they seemed delighted with the change, were so unaccustomed to order of any kind that they soon grew weary of restraint, and by

---

1   *Mary Aikenhead; Her Life, Her Work and Her Friends* (1879) pp.362-3.

157

degrees dismissed themselves. When the house was thus cleared of its ancient population, the sisters began to form the penitents newly received, to the duties of their state.[2]

Despite the onset of the famine, the total number of penitents in the new Asylum in its first two years never exceeded twenty.[3] Eventually, however, under the patronage of Rev. Dr. Delaney, the new Bishop, St. Mary Magdalen's Asylum (popularly known as St. Vincent's) could provide accommodation for about 70 inmates, who supported themselves by washing. Described in 1871 as a "rather severe" institution, it had limited appeal even for those most filled with remorse, since it offered no training for future employment, and women who entered, allegedly undertook to remain in the Refuge for life.[*] As has been demonstrated, the Good Shepherds' design on such women was similar, though less openly expressed.

In 1810 a second Cork Refuge, modelled on the London Female Penitentiary and similar establishments in Liverpool and Hull,[4] was founded in South Terrace. Supported and managed by Protestants, this Home accommodated about 25 women (mostly Catholics) who were admitted for a limited period only - their atonement and training not exceeding two years. In common with Rev. Fitzgibbon's early Refuge in Limerick, many of the penitents were admitted straight from the female prison.[5]

These institutions may well have reformed individuals (though the severity of one and religion of the other doubtless limited their influence) but their impact on the city was negligible. Far from diminishing, the numbers of Cork prostitutes increased; and by the middle of the century their presence and behaviour in the streets was causing increasing concern.

In 1848 William Logan, a Rescue Worker with considerable experience in Scotland and England spent several weeks in Cork, allegedly inspecting all the principal public institutions in the city,

---

2   *Ibid.*, pp.362-3.
3   *Ibid.*, *p.363.*
*   See below p. 168 and ft. 16.
4   *Fourth Annual Report of the London Female Penitentiary*, 1811, p.10.
5   By 1886 this "Refuge and Penitentiary for destitute Females" was listed in Sawmill Street (off South Terrace). Its Physician was Dr. J. G. Curtis, who, as a supporter of the C.D. Acts had given evidence to the Select Committee in June 1882 (see pages 183 and 185). The Chaplain to the institution was Rev. F. W. Ainley, and the Matron was Mrs. Shade. Francis Guy's *County and City of Cork Directory*, 1886, p.344.

and calling at the Magdalen Asylums referred to above. His report is curiously unconvincing and his whole visit lacks comment or personal description of any kind. He claimed, however, to have discussed the work of reclamation with one of the nuns - the most "intelligent lady" he had ever conversed with on the subject; and he also interviewed a "philanthropic gentleman ... more favourably situated for obtaining authentic information" on local prostitution than anyone in the county. This man had written a paper on the topic which Logan quoted at length in his subsequent book, *The Great Social Evil*, published in 1871 at the height of the Contagious Diseases Acts debate.[6]

According to this source, at the 1841 census - when the population of Cork was about 80,000 - the constabulary listed 85 "regular" brothels in the city, in which 356 public prostitutes were housed. In addition there were at least 100 prostitutes living in lodgings - women referred to locally as "privateers". In common with other localities, Cork prostitutes were recruited largely from the ranks of low dressmakers and servants - with manure collectors, "sent very young to the streets for the purpose" being another, less typical source of supply. It was claimed that there were many procuresses in the city who were well paid for their services, and that in many cases, prostitutes (sometimes sisters) supported their parents and families from the money they earned. Though poverty, vicious habits, idleness, and "love of dress",[7] were said to be the main reasons for taking part in the activity, seduction was almost invariably the initial cause, being followed by a term of "privateering" before turning to the streets. Women of this degraded class were not admitted to superior brothels, and any females in these establishments who began to street-walk were, apparently, instantly dismissed. Girls were received into such houses only on the recommendation of another prostitute; and it was claimed that brothel-keepers charged about eight shillings a week for board - the remainder of each girl's earnings being kept for herself. Logan's informant estimated that most prostitutes in the city were aged between sixteen and thirty, though some were much younger. And although most were "consigned to an early grave", it is clear that others survived into

---

6   Logan, *op. cit.*, pp.48-51.
7   For a case history of a local girl plunging into infamy through this failing, see below pp. 193-95.

old age, without, however, continuing in the activity. From the 1850s, Cork Union Workhouse contained specially segregated "foul" wards, in which at least a hundred elderly and "broken-down" prostitutes - often diseased - remained until death.[8]

According to other reports, immorality in Cork at this time was "indescribable". "Nests" of prostitutes terrorised the community, and after dusk "no proper man" could pass the ends of lanes without being insulted. "Open scenes of indecency" were commonplace, and half-naked women, drunken and blaspheming, attached themselves to passers by.[9] Both syphilis and gonorrhoea "prevailed very extensively" in the city, yet hospital accommodation for venereal patients was limited (apart from that provided in the workhouse) to a small ward in the Northern Infirmary. This contained only four or five beds, which were occupied by the "better class" of prostitutes. Other hospitals in the city did not admit such cases - openly at least.[10]

Cork's notoriety was not unique. By the early 1860s prostitution everywhere was causing alarm. It was regarded as an evil of such magnitude, that it could no longer be countered by voluntary effort alone. Refuges and Penitentiaries, though admirable in their rescue of individuals, left untouched that mass of "foul beings" who polluted all major cities, corrupting the minds and bodies of the country's vulnerable young men. Claims that there were up to 80,000 prostitutes at large in London alone, and at least 2,000 in cities such as Liverpool and Glasgow, gained credence both from frequent repetition, and the fact that they were urged by such undisputed authorities as Dr. William Acton, William Logan, and *The Lancet*. Medical opinion was extremely vocal on the subject, emphasising the crisis' alarming sanitary and economic implications. The armed forces were dangerously depleted and rendered inefficient through venereal disease; and existing Lock hospitals were no longer adequate for the treatment of the civilian population. In the absence of alternatives, state intervention to regulate and sanitise prostitution - at least in

---

8   Logan, *op. cit.*, pp. 48-50.
9   See particularly the evidence of Rev. Maguire, Roman Catholic Curate, *Royal Commission, op. cit.*, 6 May 1871; and Rev. Thomas O'Reilly, Chaplain to Cork Good Shepherd Magdalen Asylum, *Minutes of Evidence, Select Committee on Contagious Diseases Acts*, 21 June 1882.
10 Mr. James Curtis, senior Surgeon to the County and City of Cork General Hospital and South Infirmary. *Select Committee, op. cit.*, 21 June 1882. See also the evidence of the Catholic priests.

garrison districts - seemed the only remedy; and in July 1864, with very little publicity or debate, an Act "for the Prevention of Contagious Diseases at certain Naval and Military Stations", was passed.

According to the 1870 Royal Commission subsequently set up to enquire into the controversial legislation:

> "Without recognising incontinence as an unavoidable evil or prostitution as a consequent necessity, the peculiar conditions of the naval and military services, and the temptations to which the men were exposed, justified special precautions for the protection of their health, and their maintenance in a state of physical efficiency." [11]

Opponents of the legislation, on the other hand, regarded it as Parliament "protecting men from the baneful physical consequences of their own profligacy".

The 1864 Act applied to eleven seaport and garrison towns in England and Ireland, selected because of the virulence and extent of venereal disease in the armed forces stationed in them prior to the Act being passed. Special plain-clothed police were appointed to administer the Act, and empowered to pick up and bring before magistrates any prostitute thought to be diseased. The magistrates could order a surgical examination, and if necessary, the woman's detention in a Certified Hospital for a maximum period of three months. Prostitutes had the option of submitting voluntarily to examination and detention, thus avoiding an appearance at court; and the Act also contained penalties for brothel-keepers who knowingly harboured prostitutes who were diseased.

In 1866, a new Act - "for the better Prevention of Contagious Diseases at certain Naval and Military Stations" - provided important additions. In future, every woman in the proscribed districts suspected of being a common prostitute (rather than every common prostitute suspected of being diseased) was now compelled to attend for "periodical" examination. Those found to be infected could now be detained in a Certified Hospital for up to six months, solely on the authority of the surgeon's certificate - a magistrate's court hearing no longer being required.

---

11 *Royal Commission, op. cit.*, 1871.

The 1866 Act provided too, for the moral and religious instruction of women detained for treatment - an important clause, since its supporters could now point to the reclamatory nature of the legislation. The Act's opponents, however, claimed that this addition was an afterthought, inserted merely to undermine moral objections to the legislation. They regarded as particularly offensive, the Church's involvement in the state regulation of vice.

In the following year a Select Committee was appointed by the Commons, and its recommendations resulted in the Contagious Diseases Act of 1869. This enlarged and amended the earlier legislation, and provided particularly, for the more frequent and regular examination of prostitutes, whose period of hospital detention could, if necessary, now be increased from six months to nine.

Until these latest measures the subject had received little attention. Even the Act of 1869 initially provoked only limited opposition, and a year earlier the House of Lords' Select Committee on the legislation had reported that far from there being objections, many important towns now wished to be included in the new "reform". From late 1869, however, the full implications of the Acts could no longer be ignored. By this time, with hospital and police arrangements complete and in place, the full power of the State came into operation, and all prostitutes in the protected districts were being forced to appear for examination every fourteen days. Equally disturbing was the fact that a vocal body of influential opinion was in favour of extending the Acts still further, not merely to additional naval and garrison towns, but to the civilian population as a whole. Associations for this purpose were being formed in many large towns, particularly those with a "social evil" problem, and the implications of this progression caused increasing concern.

Opponents of the system were to claim that until the Acts became fully operational in late 1869, the public was unaware of what had taken place, such was the secrecy - or at least, the lack of debate - with which the legislation had been passed. It is more likely, however, that indifference and a general distaste for the topic, rather than ignorance, was the cause of this apathy. The public was not, in fact, as uninformed as the Acts' opponents maintained.

As early as 1862 the *Daily Mail* had carried articles by Harriet Martineau condemning the Regulation of Prostitution then being considered; and by 1868, mounting opposition had resulted in an increase of publicity and a Memorandum in protest against the Acts. Drawn up by Daniel Cooper, Secretary of the London Rescue Society, it was sent to every Member of Parliament, as well as to all leading Church of England clergymen and Nonconformist ministers. It met with little response. At the same time, many people were in favour of the legislation, and the fact that various large towns sought, "protected" status, and contained societies which vigorously promoted its extension, argues a considerable awareness both of the Acts and their intent.

Towards the end of 1869, however, effective opposition at last emerged, with the setting up of two groups determined to fight the principle, as well as demonstrate the futility of the state regulation of vice. In October, the National Association for the Repeal of the Contagious Diseases Acts, was formed; quickly followed by the Ladies' National Association for the same purpose, whose members published their manifesto in the *Daily News* on 31st December. This document, condemning the Acts on legal, as well as moral grounds, outraged supporters of the legislation, and scandalised others who believed it was a topic unsuitable for public debate - particularly by females. Undeterred, the Abolitionists set about organising (particularly in the subjected districts) opposition to the Acts, and petitioning parliament. Amid a storm of agitation, their leader Josephine Butler addressed over 90 public meetings in the first year of the campaign, attended 4 conferences and journeyed over 3,700 miles.[12]

By emphasising the class bias of the Acts (public women being overwhelmingly recruited from the ranks of the poor) the campaign gradually won the support of the newly enfranchised working man. At the same time, an increasingly conscious women's movement was inspired by, and contributed to, the Abolitionist cause, which could also rely on the support of the Quakers, the Wesleyan Methodists and the Congregationalists - together with a small, but influential body of legal and medical opinion. In October 1870, a stormy By-election at Colchester was

---

12 Josephine Butler, *Personal Reminiscences of a Great Crusade* (1896) and Millicent G. Fawcett and E. M. Turner, *Josephine Butler. Her Work and Principles and their Meaning for the Twentieth Century* (1927).

fought on the issue, resulting in the defeat of the Government's candidate, Sir Henry Storks who, as Governor of Malta, had recently enforced the Acts there. "Silence" on the question was now no longer possible, particularly since the Abolitionists' recently founded journal *The Shield*, continually sensationalised the worst aspects of the legislation, and was relentless in its demands for total Repeal.

In the face of growing agitation the Government appointed a Royal Commission in November 1870, to enquire into the operation and administration of the 1866-69 Acts, and to determine whether they should be amended, maintained, extended or repealed. The Report called for the immediate discontinuance of the compulsory medical examinations - the "very essence of the regulation system". However, it was not until April 1883 that the Acts were suspended, and another three years elapsed before the Repeal Bill received the Royal Assent and the whole episode was finally brought to an end.

The English military stations and garrisons designated as "protected" districts under the 1864 Act, were Portsmouth, Plymouth and Devonport, Woolwich, Chatham, Sheerness, Aldershot, Colchester and Shorncliffe and their respective limits. In Ireland the subjected districts were The Curragh (the certified hospital being built on the outskirts of Kildare) and Cork with Queenstown (Cobh) - together with their limits.* To this list, Windsor was added in 1866; and Canterbury, Dover, Maidstone, Gravesend, Winchester and Southampton in 1869. Initially, only prostitutes who were resident in these districts and their limits, or those living within a five mile radius but practising prostitution within the limits, were registered. From 1869, however, the radius was extended to ten miles; and to discourage non-resident women from visiting the limits for the purpose of prostitution, those doing so were also subject to the Act. Included too, were women remaining beyond the boundaries, but found in company for the purpose of prostitution, with men from the subjected stations.

These precautions were intended to prevent outside prostitutes (not under the sanitary influence of the legislation)

---

*   These limits were:

The Curragh: the limits of the parishes of Kilcullen, Kildare, Ballysax, Great Conwell and Morristown-beller.

Cork: the limits of the Borough of Cork for Municipal purposes. Queenstown: the limits of the town of Queenstown for the purposes of town improvement.

from endangering the "protected" districts. However, since regiments newly arrived from unprotected garrisons and naval stations were free to spread disease - as too were civilians, attracted to the stations by the prospect of "clean" women - it is unlikely that these measures had any great effect. Nevertheless, they demonstrate the ever-widening and more stringent application of the Acts; and for those demanding Repeal, they were proof of the progressive and sinister nature of the legislation.

Following the 1864 Act, prostitutes were initially sent to Lock Wards in existing hospitals - with new institutions, specially built for the purpose, being only gradually provided. Though a few of the latter were operational by 1866, the government Lock Hospitals at Kildare and Cork were not opened until the summer of 1869.★ By this time (if William Logan's figures for Cork in the 1840s are correct) the number of prostitutes in the city had almost doubled. Complying with the regulation to register all prostitutes within the Subjected District, the Cork police listed 600 such women in 1869, exclusive of "privateers" and clandestine women who were difficult to detect.

It was noted above that the new "Certified" or "Government" Lock Hospitals set up under the Acts were compelled to provide for the religious and moral instruction of the women detained. Although only specially appointed Chaplains could carry out this task, Rescue Workers were quick to see the possibilities for the Penitentiary System in general. Women normally outside the sway of priests and clergy could now be influenced to give up their evil ways, and in the remorseful atmosphere of ill-health and detention, might be induced, after their treatment, to enter a Refuge for training and reform. Thus, by belatedly providing for the moral and religious instruction of the patients, the Act claimed to contribute to Rescue Work; though a reduction in the number of prostitutes (rather than in the extent of their disease) was hardly what the architects of state regulation had in mind. The main purpose of the legislation was, after all, to enable healthy prostitutes to continue in their work without endangering

---

★   The authoritative supporter of the new legislation, Dr. William Acton, visited the Aldershot certified hospital early in that year. The institution, built for the accommodation of 90 patients, contained "comely looking girls appearing to great advantage in the hospital uniform." At the time of his inspection they were engaged in making "40 sets of clothing for the use of the Lock Hospital then about to opened in Cork." Acton, *op. cit.*, p.95.

the efficiency of the armed forces. In Cork the new legislation resulted in the establishment of the city's third and largest Refuge. This was the Good Shepherd Magdalen Asylum, at Sunday's Well.

Though anxious to avoid controversy (the national Campaign for the Repeal of the Acts was already well under way and attracting a measure of local support) the Bishop, Rev. Delaney, recognising the new legislation as a "legal fact", seized on the reformatory character of the latest amendment to press for a new Penitentiary. At a large public meeting in 1870, he exhorted the citizens of Cork to consolidate the efforts of the priests, whose statutory access to these women could now influence their reform. So great was the enthusiasm for the project that about seven thousand pounds was collected on the spot.

Evidence concerning the specific category of women for whom the Good Shepherd Asylum at Cork was originally intended, together with detailed information on how the Home came to be established in the city, appears in the Minutes of Evidence from the *Report of the Commission on the Administration of the Contagious Diseases Acts,* 1871. The testimony of Rev. Maguire, relating to the extent and type of prostitution in Cork at that time, and discussing the effects on the City of the recent application of the Acts, shows that at the time of the Government Enquiry (about a year after the fund-raising meeting) the Good Shepherd Sisters were already installed at Sunday's Well and running their Industrial School. The huge new Magdalen building was by that time almost complete, and Rev. Maguire told the Commission that it was shortly to open.

His evidence was quite specific as to the category of anticipated inmates and the limited time they would spend in the Home. Initially, it was intended that about 50 prostitutes claimed from the Lock Hospital would be accommodated - though according to this witness, the Bishop now hoped that about 200 of their number would eventually be housed. It was thus anticipated that the Order's Cork Asylum (its last Magdalen Foundation in Ireland) would be the largest in the Province. The proposed Home was clearly expected to be a place of temporary refuge only, and almost exclusively for women of the "abandoned" class. According to Rev. Maguire it would differ from the existing Magdalen Asylum, (that run by the Sisters of

Charity) whose rule was "rather severe", and whose penitents, entering for life, were not trained for later employment. In contrast, the money that had recently been collected, had been subscribed for:

> "The founding of an institution of a totally different character ... What we contemplate now is, under the care of the Good Shepherd nuns, the individual reform of the women, and then either to send them away to America or otherwise procure situations for them, and that has a much greater chance of being a success, than for the women to come in and then be immured in a convent".[13]

Rev. Maguire stated that even in the short period that had elapsed since the implementation of the Act, many women had already been sent from the Cork Lock Hospital to the Order's Mother House in Limerick; and that following their reform, they would be provided with openings in England and America. Questioned as to the difficulty of placing such women in employment, he stated that the Good Shepherd nuns:

> " ... keep them in the house a couple of years, and when they believe they are thoroughly reformed, either send them to America, or provide them with situations ... they have a great many of their community in America, and they send forward, especially from the parent house at Limerick, a great many whom they can trust."[14]

The priest's evidence at this point is hardly in accordance with the facts. The Limerick Register of Penitents shows that contrary to his assertions, very few women, between 1848 and 1871 (the year of the Enquiry) had been provided for in this way. Indeed, it has been shown in Table 2 that even by 1887 the figure was only 25, or 5 per cent of total admissions over the period.

Asked if there was "any indisposition in Ireland" to taking these women as servants, he replied:

> "Unfortunately there is, and any woman who falls in the city of Cork, with few exceptions, has no chance of getting a situation when she is known to come from a house of that kind. Sometimes

13 *Royal Commission, op. cit.,* 6 May 1871.
14 *Ibid.*

they do get situations. For instance, I know one who had been for 16 years in an asylum, I sent her there. She has come back, and is now with her family, and they never knew she was there, and now she is the best of women."[15]

Ten years later, a further Enquiry, the 1881/82 *Select Committee on the Contagious Diseases Acts*, provided information on the real nature of the Home. In marked contrast to its initial conception as a short-term Refuge, providing training and employment opportunities for the inmates temporarily committed to its care, the Home is revealed as a place intended for long-term or even life-time confinement. By 1882, it had been established for almost a decade. Over 600 penitents had been admitted, and approximately 160 were currently in the Home. It was already the case, however, that inmates' restitution was longer than had been anticipated, with three of the first four arrivals, for example, still continuing in the Cork Refuge, and the other inmate transferred to the "Magdalen" Class in the Hammersmith Home. They were all, in fact, to remain life-long penitents - their combined atonement totalling 130 years.

One of the witnesses giving evidence on the state and extent of prostitution in Cork at the 1882 Enquiry (the thirteenth year of the Act's full implementation) was Rev. Canon Hegarty. He continued to contrast the two Catholic Asylums in the city, emphasising the short-term nature of the Good Shepherd Magdalen Home, now ten years old:

"There is one Magdalen Asylum in Cork [run by the Sisters of Charity] and almost all that enter there remain all their lives; a great many remain until death ... The other, where they remain a short time, has only been in existence since 1870[*] ... it is a different Order, the Good Shepherd Nuns; and their rule is to provide for the girls, if they are sufficiently reformed, or to enable them to emigrate or rejoin their friends. In the other Order, the Sisters of Charity, they recommend them to consecrate themselves and remain in for ever."[16]

---

15 *Ibid.*
*   In fact the Magdalen Section was not ready for the reception of penitents until July 1872.
16 *Select Committee, op. cit.*, 20 June 1882.
     The Asylum run by the Sisters of Charity did not live up to its austere reputation. Life-long committals between 1846 and 1899 numbered only 119 – or less than ten percent of all admissions. See Luddy, *op. cit.*, Table 4.8, p.126.

A year previously the Committee had heard the testimony of Rev. H. Reed, who, from 1872 until 1881, had been Chaplain to the Certified Hospital in Cork. We have seen how in that capacity he was empowered to attempt the reform of all prostitutes detained there by the Government for treatment. During the nine year period of his Chaplaincy, 693 registered women had been admitted - some of them several times - bringing the total number of cases to 2,310. Rev. Reed estimated that since the opening of the Lock Hospital in 1869, a total of 184 of the women had gone straight into Asylums and Refuges, largely through his influence. Of these, 31 had left the Institutions and could not be accounted for - beyond stating that, since they were no longer on the C.D. Register, they had obviously not returned to prostitution in the city. Seventeen of the women had died in the Asylums "without relapse", and, to the best of his knowledge, 136 were still in the Homes:

> "With regard to the expression 'to the best of my knowledge', I have a remark to make. I have arranged with the superioresses of the convents to which I sent the women that they should state to me that these women have arrived and have been received, and that they will not be allowed to go out without my receiving an intimation of the fact; so that after hearing that they are there and going on well, and probably hearing again and going to visit them in the asylums, if I hear nothing to the contrary for six or eight months, or if they do not come under the Acts, I presume that they are there still."[17]

It has been demonstrated in previous Chapters that this was hardly the case. His evidence at this point was largely inaccurate, particularly with regard to those women he sent to the Good Shepherd Refuges in Limerick, Waterford, New Ross and Cork. It is probable that both priests' admiration for the Acts led them to exaggerate their reclamitory influence; and to lose sight of the original aim of the new Magdalen Asylum, which was to provide short-term training and shelter for prostitutes anxious to reform. Contrary to their testimony, it is clear that the restoration of these women to society was neither attempted nor achieved. Rev. Reed was examined further:

---

17 *Select Committee, op. cit.,* June 1881.

"Question: Comparing the state of things which you have described existing before the Acts, and the state of things existing now, you attribute the reformation of these women to the operation of the Acts? - Answer: The day on which the new Magdalen was opened I sent my first batch of penitents myself; that was nearly nine years ago, and out of that batch not one has left since; some one or two have died, and there is one at present at Hammersmith; she went on so well for eight years that she was sent there by the Sisters of the Good Shepherd to be amongst a higher class of penitents."[18]

The Penitents' Register shows that the Hospital Chaplain's evidence at this point too, was somewhat misleading. In the first place, although the Annals consistently record that six Penitents were admitted to the Home on its first day, only four women were actually registered.[*] It would appear that contrary to Rev. Reed's assertion that "not one has since left", two quitted the institution almost immediately. His remark that "some one or two [out of that 'batch' of six women] have died", is also incorrect, since they were all alive at the time of his statement. His further comment regarding those who had died in the Refuges, illustrates that sinister attitude referred to in Chapter 3:

"Those who are brought to the asylums, and die edifying deaths, are some of my best cases; we are secure of them to the last, as far as we can be, humanly."[19]

Canon Hegarty's evidence was similar:

Question: 'In your Magdalen Asylum ... Do you, on the average, keep them for a greater number of years than in other similar institutions?
Answer: We will keep them until their deaths if we can; but there is no compulsion at all."[20]

---

18 *Ibid.* This woman was 24 year old Jane Barry, who, on leaving the new Lock Hospital on 10th June had gone straight to the workhouse, where she was registered as a prostitute. Six weeks later, on the day of the opening of the Magdalen Asylum, she left the workhouse to become a lifelong penitent. Cork Union Register of Paupers. 10 June 1872. No.44901.
*   See below page 178.
19 *Select Committee, op. cit.*
20 *Ibid.*, 20 June 1882.

Early in 1870 Sister Mary of St. Teresa of Jesus Devereux was summoned from the Good Shepherd Convent in New Ross to the Order's Mother House in France. Here, she was appointed Mother Prioress of the new Cork Foundation; and in March she returned to Ireland accompanied by three other Irish nuns - Sister Mary of St Josephine Nolan (appointed Assistant); Sister Mary of St. Teresa of the Cross Holloran and Sister Mary of the Name of Mary Callaghan.[21]

Their arrival in Cork at the end of the month caused minor excitement in the city - an official welcoming party including the Lord Mayor, Mr. James Hegarty (the Convent's first benefactor) and several priests greeting them at the station and escorting them to the waiting Bishop and their temporary Home. Their Convent was a "closely lodged" cottage on three acres of land donated by Mr. Hegarty; and nearby a temporary Industrial school capable of accommodating 90 children was built in seven weeks. Almost immediately the nuns acquired a further five acres on which to build their intended Convent and Magdalen Asylum - the Foundation Stone being laid in October that year.

It has been noted that the unseemly haste with which the Industrial School was opened, in rapidly built, overcrowded and unhealthy accommodation, had unfortunate results. A "dreadful epidemic of sore eyes" (probably opthalmia) soon broke out amongst the children and lasted for over five months; and in the following year the Assistant fell ill with typhus and the Reverend Mother developed rheumatic fever. A major outbreak of typhus occurred early in 1875, and although only one case proved fatal, 56 of the children (still housed in their temporary quarters*) caught the disease, as did one of the Sisters. In the meantime the Reverend Mother's health had worsened and was causing increasing alarm.

This young woman belonged to a prominent Wexford family "highly esteemed" for its part in the Catholic Revival. Her uncle Richard Devereux, a wealthy merchant ship-owner, had endowed many schools and charitable institutions; and had been made Knight of the Order of St. Gregory, by Pope Pius IX. As noted in Chapter 5, it was his timely interest in the New Ross Mission that

---

21 Cork Annals, 1870. Sister Mary Callaghan died on 22 July 1876, and was the first of the Sisters (apart from the young Rev. Mother) to be buried in the nuns' graveyard.

* Shortly afterwards the children were moved to their permanent Industrial School - next to which was the recently completed Convent which separated the children's new premises from the huge Magdalen Asylum.

had helped secure its future; his generosity to that Foundation, as well as his liberal donations to the Cork and Belfast Houses, qualifying him as a principal benefactor of the Irish Good Shepherd nuns.

As described earlier, at a critical moment in its history, three of Richard Devereux's nieces had visited the impoverished Refuge in New Ross. One of these ladies, Miss Teresa Devereux, was so affected by the experience and drawn to the object of the Institute, that she joined the Order almost immediately. Her Novitiate and Profession were made in the Limerick Provincial House, and her large dowry was assigned to the Foundation in New Ross - till then in a hazardous state. In 1868 she made her final vows, and was shortly afterwards transferred from Limerick to the New Ross Convent. Here she was joined by her older sister, who had also decided to enter the Order. It has been noted that in her case a special dispensation was granted by the Mother General, and instead of being professed in Limerick, she was received direct into the New Ross Home. Her uncle immediately financed the building of a substantial Industrial School for the Community (thus ensuring the Sisters a vital income) and donated various other gifts.

His younger niece, Sister Teresa Devereux, was now appointed First Mistress of the new Industrial School. Though important, this position limited her authority and influence to the children's Section. The establishment of the huge Foundation in Cork shortly afterwards, however, resulted in the extraordinary selection of this young woman as its first Superior. She was given overall management of an entire Community - a crucial and difficult appointment in view of the Asylum's association with the Contagious Diseases Acts. She was less than thirty years old, and it was a surprising and inappropriate choice. According to the New Ross Annals, she was a "timid soul", and the shock of this appointment, as much as her subsequent ill health, hastened her early death.*

---

*   The Sisters may well have been aware of earlier similar cases. In 1835, for example, Mother St. Euphrasia had appointed a twenty-six year old nun Sister St. Basil "for whom she had the highest esteem" as Superior of the new Lille foundation. The young nun greatly dreaded her new post, and "it was a pious belief among her Sisters, that as soon as she learned the intention of her Superiors in regard to her, she had offered herself to God as a living holocaust" in order to promote the Order. Before the period fixed for her to leave Angers she was suddenly carried off by cholera "her agony was long and terrible, her sufferings being greatly aggravated by the absence of her beloved Mother General." A.M. Clarke, *op. cit.*, p.163.

Although the Cork Good Shepherd had been founded in March 1870, it was not until July 1872 that the large Magdalen Asylum was eventually opened; its earliest inmates, as described above, being Rev. Reed's first "batch" of penitents - registered prostitutes, "converted" while undergoing treatment for venereal disease. Amidst continuing admissions the Sisters moved into their imposing new Convent, in 1873, and late in the following year building work began on the adjoining Industrial School. By this time the Superior's condition was so precarious that the Mother Provincial hastened to Cork accompanied by the invalid's sister - Mary of St. Magdalen Devereux - only recently professed, but already First Mistress of the Limerick Industrial School. Within three weeks of their arrival the young Reverend Mother died, and her older sister was immediately appointed Superioress in her place.

This remarkable woman, henceforth known as Mother [Magdalen] Devereux was to dominate Rescue Work in the city for almost half a century. Brief accounts of her life appear in the Cork Good Shepherd Annals - at the time of her transfer from the Convent in 1912, and following her death in 1922, when one of the priests noted that even as a young girl in the world Miss Devereux had been "remarkable for her piety". He spoke of her work amongst the poor and suffering, and of "the care and devotion which she bestowed on the adornment of the altars of her parish church."[22]

That the Order was impressed by wealth and social status and mindful of financial gain is made clear both in the biographies of the Foundress and the Annals of the Irish Houses. Such considerations undoubtedly influenced the decision to promote the Devereux sisters so early in their Community lives, regardless of their limited experience and irrespective of their initial suitability for such roles. They may well have been better educated than many of the nuns, and no doubt their cultivated background and social contacts were particularly prized in such important administrative positions. Nevertheless, there must have been others in the Congregation with a better claim to

---

22 Cork Annals, 1922. In March 1868 just before she joined the New Ross Sisters she recommended 30 year old Mary O'Donnell from Wexford to the Waterford Asylum. The woman, who stayed in the Home for almost a year, was said to be "satisfactory".

preferment, having more knowledge of the Institute itself and of the Order's unusually demanding work.

Fundamental to Good Shepherd policy at this time was the memory of recent hostility to the religious; and a fear, amply justified by the events of 1848, that in spite of the rapid spread of the Institute (an extraordinary achievement in so short a time) new Foundations, even in France, were at risk. Popular hatred of the movement made exile a strong possibility, and the Order cultivated the protection of powerful families abroad. Strategic advancements and appointments ensured not only the support of those with influence, but a virtual guarantee of funds.

Also included in the Annals, is a newspaper tribute to the Reverend Mother which appeared at the time of her death in 1922. It reveals that even then her prestigious social contacts, as well as her personal ability, were standing the Community in good stead. Several years before, Countess Murphy of Cork had built a Convalescent Home for Catholic girls; and she later donated her own mansion at Clifton, Cork, to be used (after her death) as a Convent for the nuns in charge:

> "She did so almost entirely owing to her faith in the ability and zeal of her life-long friend Mother Mary of St. Magdalen, and it was her expressed will and desire that [she] should be the first Prioress of this Institution."[23]

The Annals confirm the extent to which the wishes of a wealthy benefactor could over-ride other considerations - in this case, the inclinations and advanced age of the former Mother Superior. In 1907 the Congregation had already suffered:

> "the heaviest cross that could be borne - the deposition of our beloved Mother Magdalen Devereux, who had guided the house with extraordinary wisdom and kindness for the long term of 33 years"

She was succeeded by a younger woman - Sister Mary Hickey - who had been her "devoted councillor", for many years; and who was now considered more suited to the task.[24] Five years later,

---

23 Newspaper tribute to Mother Mary of St. Magdalen Devereux, glued into Cork Annals, September 1922.
24 Cork Annals 1907. Sister Mary of St. Kieran Hickey died 17 July 1947.

however, in compliance with Countess Murphy's will; and at the insistence both of the Order's Mother General, Mother Mary of St. Domitilla and the fund-conscious Bishop, the former Superior was brought out of retirement, and appointed Prioress of the Clifton Home.

> "We had hoped that as Mother Magdalen was nearly eighty years of age, a younger sister would be selected and that our dear old mother would be left to us to the end. She took up the burden bravely - though feeling as if her heart would break at parting from this place which she had seen raised from the foundations, and from the community and classes which she had governed so long and so wisely."[25]

She remained at her new post until her death a decade later, by which time she was almost ninety years of age.

Apart from the early years of her sister's brief government, she directed the Foundation at Cork for much of the period of this study. Her influence guided the whole Community, with the Convent, the Magdalen Asylum and the Industrial School each being subject to her overall control. As has been noted, however, a total separation of the different Sections was required by the Institute's Rules. There was no communication whatsoever between the Classes, each of which came under the direct supervision of its own "First Mistress" or intermediary.

The office of First Mistress of Penitents was of supreme importance - the saving of these women being the original aim of the Institute, and remaining its first concern. This is emphasised in the Conferences and Instructions of the Foundress:

> "If you cannot establish several classes, you should give the preference to those for penitents and Magdalens. I have remarked that Houses which are satisfied with these two kinds of work always flourish. ... If you abandon them to take up other works you will forfeit the favours and blessings of God."

and again:

> "I must remind you that if the number of religious is limited and if there is not accommodation for more than one class, you

---

25 *Ibid.*, 1912.

should confine yourselves to receiving penitents only. Thus you will go straight to the end of your vocation." [26]

The longest Chapter in the *Rules for the Direction of the Classes* is devoted to the First Mistress of Penitents, her duties, and how these should be carried out. The task of selecting the right Sister for this most vital role was so formidable, that Mother St. Euphrasia directed Superiors to pray to the Good Shepherd himself, so that he, not they, could make the final choice.

Like the Devereux sisters, the First Mistress of Penitents at Cork came from an unusually distinguished family. In 1923 she celebrated the fiftieth anniversary of her appointment, and four years later she died[27] - both occasions providing information in the Annals on her background and history.

Sister Mary Coppinger was the orphaned daughter of "one of the oldest and most esteemed families in the South of Ireland". In 1870 her older sister had refused to let the young girl join the Order, but the near-drowning of their brother (a General in the American army) persuaded her that she was wrong to withhold her consent. The Annals record:

> "She was the first Postulate who entered here. She had casually heard that the nuns of the Good Shepherd had come to Cork with the object of bringing back lost sheep to the fold. Her heart was filled with pity for those erring ones, and an intense desire to follow in the Master's footsteps took possession of her. She presented herself for admission to Mother Mary of Teresa Devereux, the young and saintly Superior, who quickly discerned the admirable qualities of the postulant aspirant, who was sent to Limerick and warmly welcomed ... by Mother Provincial who had founded the Cork Convent a very short time before."[28]

---

26 *Conferences and Instructions*, op. cit., pp.48-50.
Because, rather than in spite of the Foundress' instructions on this matter, the Cork Sisters admitted Industrial children two years before penitents were received - Industrial Schools having proved so lucrative to other Orders in Ireland as well as to their own Congregations in Limerick, New Ross and Waterford. Vast funds were needed to build the huge penitentiary, the large Convent and beautiful Chapel, and by any standards, no expense was spared. The urgency with which the children were so unsuitably housed is an indication of the nuns' adherence to, rather than deviation from, their Rule. Recent claims that the nuns arrived in the city to educate and take care of needy children - are not only incorrect, but proof of how unpalatable has the Order's history become - even to itself.
27 Sister Mary of Our Lady of the Sacred Heart Coppinger died on 23 February 1927.
28 Cork Annals, 1927.

During her novitiate her conduct was so outstanding that the new Mother General, Mother Mary of St. Peter, then visiting Ireland from France, suggested the young novice as an ideal Mistress of Penitents for the Cork Foundation. As well as being selected so early in her Community life for this most crucial office, she was singled out, before leaving Limerick, to accompany the Mother Provincial to Angers for the Order's six-yearly elections. There is no doubt that her distinguished and wealthy background, as much as her personal ability, helped determine this important and most unusual choice.

Like Mother Devereux, Sister Mary Coppinger remained at her post well beyond the limits of the Victorian age, continuing without a break as First Mistress of Penitents for more than half a century. Venerated though they were, however, both women were inevitably locked in the past. They were fixed in another era, preserved in the decades of the discredited Contagious Diseases Acts, when, as young women they had quit the world. Virtually untouched from that time onwards by external change or progress, they nonetheless dictated the course of Irish Rescue Work - their influence extending far beyond their narrow enclosure and their own protracted lives.

Also closely concerned with the penitents was Sister Mary of St. Josephine Nolan, Assistant to the Superior and one of the three nuns who, with Mother Teresa Devereux, had founded the Community in Cork. Her influence on the treatment of the women was particularly significant, as she had strong links with the Order's Mother House, having spent her novitiate at Angers, and worked there in the Penitents' Class until named for Cork. She too continued in office into the twentieth century - dying in 1912 when ten of the penitents, hoping to "obtain her recovery", cut off their hair.[29]

Over the years various other nuns were assigned to Penitentiary duties - supervising the women in the laundry, the dormitories, the infirmary and at meals. A series of Chaplains looked after the Community's spiritual needs; and occasionally, a doctor or a workman might be summoned, or a party of visiting

---

29 *Ibid.*, 1912. Among the 38 priests who attended her Requiem Mass, 7 were former Chaplains of the Convent.

dignitaries allowed a glimpse of the women at work. Such intrusions, however, were rare, and for most of the time the world outside hardly existed. For all in the Community, life was virtually enclosed.[30]

We have seen that on July 29th (one week after the Feast-day of St. Mary Magdalen[31]) 1872, the new Asylum for repentant fallen women was opened in Cork. On the same day a number of prostitutes who had completed a course of treatment in the Government Lock Hospital were discharged as cured. Under Father Reed's influence, six of these women were dispatched direct to the newly opened Home (probably in "covered cars") but only four remained long enough to be entered in the new Register. These were the first penitents to be received, and there were no other admissions for a further eight days.[32]

Of the original four, Jane Barry, the first inmate to be registered in the Home, was 20 years old, a native of Cork, and an orphan. Seven years later she was, as Rev. Reed testified, transferred to the Hammersmith Good Shepherd Asylum in London. Here, she became "a professed Magdalen" - joining those contemplative penitents who chose a life of seclusion, austerity and prayer. She died at the Hammersmith Refuge in 1892, having spent 20 years atoning for her sins.[33]

The other three girls remained in the Cork Asylum for life. Mary McMahon aged 19 was another native of the city, and her parents too, were dead. Almost a quarter of a century after her admission she became a Consecrate, and spent almost sixty years in the Penitentiary before dying in 1928 at the age of 75.[34] Ellen McCarthy, aged 19, was from Ballinhassig near Cork. Her mother was alive but she had no father. She died in 1898 after a "lingering illness", and had been a "Child of Mary".[35]

The fourth woman received on that first day was 20 year old Nora Denchy from Tralee, given the name "Margaret of the

---

30 But not absolutely - for some of the nuns, at least. We have seen that each Mother Provincial was required to visit the Houses in her Province, and there was a certain amount of visiting between Convents - as noted, for example, above and on pages 173 and 232.

31 For a superb account of the symbolism, sensuality and ideal of penance attached to this saint, see Susan Haskins, *Mary Magdalen* (1993).

32 Cork Register of Penitents, 29 July and 6 August 1872.

33 *Ibid.*, 29 July 1872.

34 *Ibid.*

35 *Ibid.*

Dolours" when she became a consecrated penitent twelve years later. She was 20 when she entered, and "died happily" in the penitents' infirmary in 1896. Clearly her life in the institution was less joyous than her death. According to the Annals, in which she was referred to as "one of the six who came in on the day of opening":

> "For many years [she] struggled hard to accustom herself to the loss of her liberty. She happily, however, persevered in the paths of penance."[36]

It must be assumed either that Rev. Reed was deliberately misleading the Select Committee when he gave the impression that more than just four girls were being described - or that he had been mis-informed with regard to the evidence he presented under oath.

Eight days after the opening of the Refuge, a fifth prostitute, Ellen Manning aged 18, was registered. She too, was a patient from the Lock Hospital and had been sent by Rev. Reed. As was the case with so many girls entering Magdalen institutions in the period, both her parents were allegedly dead. She left the Home "in a bad disposition" a year later; and was found drowned in 1885.[37]

The Hospital Chaplain's referrals to the Cork Asylum were marginally more successful than those to the Order's other Houses - his access to local penitents doubtless prolonging their length of stay. Many of his New Ross and Waterford cases were not so easily pressured, and as we have seen, within days of their arrival they managed to leave voluntarily or get themselves "sent out".[38]

Yet in spite of his local influence at least nine of his prostitute-converts left "in a bad disposition" shortly after the Cork penitentiary opened; and two others, 18 year old Katie Fitzgibbon from Cork and 22 year old Bridget McCliffe from Fermoy, "escaped over the wall."[39] Some, on the other hand (no

---

36 Cork Register and Annals.
37 Cork Register.
38 This happened in the Limerick Home too. See for example, Mary McGuire, aged 40, sent to the Mother House by Rev. Reed in October 1876. Limerick Register of Penitents.
39 Cork Register of Penitents, 17 February 1874 and 13 August 1876.

doubt those he had in mind when he spoke of his "best cases") died early deaths in the Asylum soon after being consecrated. One such girl was Ellen Lynch, a nineteen year old orphan from Cork admitted "through his influence" in March 1873, and dying "a Consecrated penitent", less than three years later.[40] Ellen Daly, a 23 year old prostitute from Youghal was a similar case. Recommended by Rev. Reed in October 1872, she died "most happily" in March 1877. She too was a Consecrate.[41]

Though initially established for the reclamation of Government-registered prostitutes, the Cork Good Shepherd was soon receiving penitents from sources other than the hospital Certified under the Act. While Father Reed continued as a major influence - being listed as responsible for at least 30 of the 164 admissions recorded in the first 4 years - women were now sent from the female prison, the workhouse, applied "of their own accord" or, most frequently, were recommended by various other priests. The names of some of these prelates recur throughout the period, indicating that they worked in notorious parishes, or were fired with reforming zeal.

Notable amongst these was Rev. Shinkwin of South Parish, Cork, whose bizarre crusade against the prostitute community in his district in 1876, created a minor sensation. The Annals record:

"For more than a year, one of the curates, R. M. Shinkwin, had in contemplation the breaking up of 20 bad houses* where a great

---

40 *Ibid.*, 21 March 1873.
41 *Ibid.*, 1 October 1872.
*   Evidence from the two Government Enquires (1871 and 1882) suggests that these brothels might have been in Furze Alley, into which location, according to Rev. Maguire, all the city's common prostitutes had recently been herded. (See page 207). A sample four-year survey of admissions to Cork workhouse, however, indicates that in the period immediately preceding the crusade, Furze Alley could hardly have been as notorious as Culberts or Colberts Lane. Of approximately 750 prostitutes admitted to the workhouse between 1870 and 1874, the address of almost 100 was listed as Culberts Lane. Only 13 were recorded as living in Furze Alley. From Michael McCarthy's account, however, the place could have been North Street. Condemning Dublin's infamous Mecklenburgh Street area, he noted in 1902: "I remember when I was a boy there was a street of this description in the city of Cork known as North Street. It abutted Lavitt's Quay, close to Patrick's bridge, and I used to see the women of that street bare-headed and bare-breasted ... disporting themselves ... within sight of the most central part of the town. But I also remember that the priests of Cork at that time rose up and, with the co-operation of the landlords of the street, evicted the entire population of North Street.... There was a great deal of ostentatious formality, it is true, about the proceeding, such as religious processions through the street,

many Penitents [prostitutes], now inmates of our Asylum congregated. So one day in the month of June, as he was hearing confessions in the Church, he left the confessional suddenly and went to this ill-famed street draped in his soutane, biretta, and no weapon save his rosary and breviary. It was toward twilight. There the saintly priest knelt and in a loud voice commenced the rosary. All who passed, joined, and for the entire night never ceased praying. The poor penitents inside had their windows barricaded and doors locked. They made all the noise and clamour possible inside to try and drown the priest's voice, but as morning dawned grace touched their hearts. Our Blessed Lady triumphed over the Evil one. The poor creatures flung open their doors, joined in the rosary and told Rev. Shinkwin they would do as he pleased. After a little time he procured covered cars and had them sent up to us; that day we received 20. Nothing could equal the joy that rang through the Convent and Asylum ... "[42]

A quarter of a century later the incident, much embellished, was included in A. M. Clarke's biography of Mother Euphrasia. One "poor sinner" whom Rev. Shinkwin was striving to save:

"more hardened than the rest, openly mocked at them. She leaned out of the window, and taking a bottle of wine, said she would drink their health. The bottle broke between her fingers and seriously injured her hand. She regarded the accident as a judgement of God, and at once joined her companions in prayer and in expressions of earnest repentance. A procession of penitents was thus formed. They all declared that they would not leave the priest, to whom they owed so much, until he had placed them in safety within the walls of the Good Shepherd ... He took 20 to the Mother Superior of the Convent ... Day after day fresh penitents presented themselves, begging for admission. When four days had elapsed, their number amounted to fifty. The older penitents gladly gave up their own beds and best clothes to them ... The occurrence made quite a stir in the town, as it found its

blessing of the houses from which the women had been evicted, and so forth; but credit must be given for the fact that the street no longer exists." *Op. cit.*, p.287.
This, or a similar incident, was referred to by Rev. Reed giving evidence in 1881. He stated that about two years previously there had been "one street which contained probably 12 or 14 houses of ill-fame, and the priests were determined to clear out the whole nest; it was in a back lane or alley; we took public action; we called on the people attached to our confraternities to assist us; and by bringing public opinion to bear upon the question, all these houses were shut up." *Select Committee*, 27 June 1881.
42 Cork Annals, 1876.

way into the newspapers,* and was alluded to in the most flattering terms. The parish priests presented their indefatigable fellow-labourer with a handsome chalice, as an expression of their admiration for his heroic devotion."[43]

This dramatic conversion was possibly the result of alcohol rather than remorse; and if the figures quoted are correct, the effects of both had largely evaporated by the following day. Of the initial 20 converts allegedly brought by Rev. Shinkwin, only 11 are recorded - the remainder, so it would seem - in the sobering atmosphere of the Penitentiary regretting their impulsive action, and making a hasty retreat. As to the additional 30 women who supposedly presented themselves over the next few days, these are reduced to 4 in the Register - one of whom was admitted on June 28th, two on the following day, and one two weeks later.[44]

Even allowing for embellishment, it is clear that many of Rev. Shinkwin's women quitted the Home before being formally registered, while others, induced to remain, showed a marked reluctance to reform. Forty year old Mary Allan, for example, left after only two weeks "in a bad disposition"; to be followed a few days later by Ellen Brennan (aged 28) and Margaret Cooney (27) both in a similar frame of mind. The same description was applied to 19 year old Ann Donovan, who left in the following year.[45]

Of the remainder - 11 women - at least 7 were ill, which may account for their willingness to remain in the Home. Throughout this period various penitents were described in the Registers as "sent to hospital" - though to which one, and for what complaint, is not disclosed. Almost certainly, however, they were admitted to the Government Hospital for the treatment of venereal disease. Other disorders (even those that were fatal) were dealt with in the Penitents' Infirmary - where reform could continue uninterrupted and without danger of re-exposure to sin. The *Rules* suggest that even venereal patients were sometimes cared for by the Sisters:

---

*   The Annals reveal that far from "finding its way" into the newspapers, the story was deliberately released. In fact, an Appeal for funds to support the new inmates was placed in the local press.

43 A. M. Clarke, *op. cit.*, pp.306-7.
44 Cork Register and Annals, 1876.
45 Cork Register of Penitents, 27 June 1876.

"We should be very careful, in lingering illnesses, not to show any sign of being weary of nursing the patient, nor of repugnance for dressing sores. A sick child should never dread being a burden: to give her cause to do so, would be in direct opposition to the charity which should fill the heart of every Religious of the Good Shepherd."[46]

and there are indications that in the later period at least, penitents with "humiliating diseases" were cared for in the Asylum in Cork.

Nevertheless, part of Rev. Reed's testimony indicates that in Ireland in the eighteen-seventies and eighties, this was not the case. He stated that the Cork Lock Hospital often admitted prostitutes from Limerick. These were non-registered women who must have sought treatment voluntarily, since Limerick was outside the scope of the Acts. As well as these, a number of sick penitents from the Limerick Good Shepherd were also induced by the nuns to enter the new Hospital, since, according to his evidence, "when they are diseased they cannot be retained for treatment in the asylum". It is clear that a similar policy prevailed in Cork, though after 1886 when the Acts were Repealed and the hospital closed, the problem of venereal penitents must have recurred.

In 1882 James Curtis (visiting Surgeon to the Cork Lock Hospital under the Contagious Diseases Acts, and holder of various other appointments) and Rev. Thomas O'Reilly (Chaplain to the Good Shepherd in Cork) each gave evidence on this matter to the Select Committee. Both men reported that many women temporarily left the Cork Magdalen Asylum for treatment in the above institution - the priest producing a supporting statement from Sister Mary Coppinger, Mistress of Penitents, to this effect.[47] As was the case with prostitutes arriving from Limerick (an "unsubjected" district) these admissions to a "certified" C.D. Hospital were contrary to the law. This specified that once a woman's name had been removed from the Register (which automatically occurred when she left the activity or moved from the zone) she was no longer subject to the fortnightly examinations, and even if diseased, could not be admitted to a Government Hospital provided under the Acts.

---

46 *Rules for the Direction of the Classes, op. cit.*, p.163.
47 This would appear to be the only evidence of the Sisters' involvement in the controversy surrounding the legislation. Inevitably, it is supportive of the Acts.

In his evidence to the Royal Commission in 1871 Rev. Maguire had partially attributed the recent improvement in the state of Cork's streets to the fact that 46 prostitutes ("the worst of their type") were "constantly" in the Certified Hospital. This statement, referring not to the number of patients, but to the accommodation available, was incorrect. Considering the notoriety of the two subjected districts in Ireland and their reputation for venereal disease, hospital provision under the Acts for only 41 patients in The Curragh, and 46 patients in Cork, seems surprisingly low. Even more extraordinary is the fact that not all of the few beds provided were actually required. Only five weeks before Rev. Maguire's testimony, the 1871 Census had been carried out. Although the Enumerators' Notebooks have not survived, the Abstracts (containing numbers of persons in institutions) have information on the Government Lock Hospital, Infirmary Road, Cork. Having been opened less than two years earlier, it contained 25 patients, together with 5 female officers and a male Porter. At the following Census in 1881, the Lock Hospital, now described as in Anglesea-Place (off Infirmary Road) contained only 17 patients, together with 5 female staff. The Government Hospital in Cork was clearly larger than required, and for most of the time its wards were half empty.*

Possibly, as Rev. Maguire claimed, many Cork prostitutes moved from the district to escape registration, and others may have abandoned the activity altogether. It was alleged too, that the legislation resulted in an increased proportion of clandestine prostitutes or "privateers", who escaped detection and supervision under the law. Yet even allowing for these possibilities, it is evident that those responsible for the new legislation had overestimated both the ability of visiting surgeons

---

* Plans for the Government Hospital in Kildare too, over-estimated the anticipated number of patients. By 1872 the four-bed Segregation Ward had been converted to a Roman Catholic Chapel, reducing the number of beds available to only 37. As well as this, the proposed Future Extension indicated on the original Plan, was never built. Similar over-estimates were made in England. Accommodation at the Royal Albert Hospital, Devonport, for example, was particularly wide of the mark. Mr. Bulteel, Surgeon to the Hospital, and Secretary to the Plymouth Home for Fallen Women, stated in 1871: "I believe a good deal too much has been done at Devonport, and there is accommodation now which we shall never want. There are 150 beds and only 50 or 60 women. If the Government had provided hulks, as was the first suggestion, it would have saved an immense expense in building." *Royal Commission, op. cit.* (6230)

to detect the disease, and the extent, among prostitutes, of the contagion itself. By 1870, in fact, 12 out of every 13 women being examined were free from infection – a statistic used to bolster the arguments of both supporters and opponents of the Acts. Those in favour of the legislation claimed that frequent examination and treatment if required, had improved prostitutes' health, and had reduced the extent and virulence of disease. Repealers, on the other hand, argued that the low percentage of women needing treatment, proved the examinations to be unnecessary as well as obscene. They also claimed that prostitution in the subjected districts, being more concentrated in fewer women, inevitably led to individuals remaining longer in the activity, and being more seriously diseased.

Given the shortage of patients at the Lock Hospital in Cork, the evidence which its Surgeon Mr. James Curtis presented to the Select Committee in 1882, is not surprising. It was noted above that according to this and other witnesses, penitents from the Good Shepherd Mother House in Limerick, as well as from the Order's Cork Asylum, were admitted as patients to the Government Lock Hospital. This was regardless of the fact that whatever their previous history, as inmates of Magdalen Asylums, they were no longer registered women. He further stated that in 1881, in company with two local policemen, he had visited brothels in Limerick in an attempt to persuade the women (who were "like wild beasts", naked and cursing) to take advantage of treatment in Cork. The irregularity of this procedure – Limerick being an unsubjected district and its prostitutes outside the scope of the Acts – has already been discussed.

The under-used and over-staffed hospital in Cork was clearly an embarrassment to supporters of the allegedly vital, and bitterly contested scheme. This probably accounts for the unlawful admissions referred to above. They boosted patient numbers and helped justify the local application of the Acts. Such a policy, though improper, suited the Good Shepherd Sisters who were inevitably linked with the legislation in the city. It was also expedient from a general sanitary point of view. Accordingly, penitents (some of whom were not necessarily former prostitutes) unaware of their rights and ignorant of the law, were sent by the nuns to a highly controversial hospital, and held in illegal confinement until such time as they were cured.[48] The witnesses stated that when such patients were discharged every effort was made, usually successfully, to ensure their immediate return to the nuns.

Many of Rev. Shinkwin's converts were apparently of this category - the disease of some of them being at a hopelessly advanced stage. Catherine White, for example, aged 18, died only three months after entering the Home; and 16 year old Bridget Long left for the hospital and died in the workhouse infirmary.[49] Margaret Ward aged 16, Margaret Vaughan aged 30 and Margaret Connell aged 18, instead of being cared for in the penitents' infirmary, all "left for hospital" after remaining in the Home for approximately three months.[50] And in October the following year, Mary Flynn aged 20 and Ellen Cronin aged 21 were discharged in the same way - after which, following treatment, they returned to the Home. Presumably they left shortly afterwards, since no further reference to them occurs.[51] Another of the women, Mary Hayes, aged 29, left for the workhouse hospital in January 1877 - possibly to be confined. The medical condition of Rev. Shinkwin's three remaining converts is not documented; but one of these women, 32 year old Mary Donovan, stayed in the Home for four years.[52]

The above details are taken from the Cork Penitents' Register - a meticulous record of all inmates which was compiled for their own information by the nuns themselves. Such evidence puts the "mass conversion" into perspective, and demonstrates that then as later, the Order was not averse to misleading publicity. Further, it reveals how alarmingly ineffectual was the application of the Acts to Cork, and lends weight to the Repealers' argument that medically speaking, the legislation was worse than useless. Worse, since it held out an assurance (denied in reality) that prostitutes at large in Subjected Districts, must necessarily be free from disease. This was far from the case. On the forty-second day of the *Royal Commission of Enquiry* into the Acts (6 May 1871) Mr. Henry

48 Since there was no effective treatment for certain types of venereal disease in this period, women could not be detained for more than nine months, after which, they were released whatever their condition.
49 Cork Register of Penitents, 27 June 1876.
50 *Ibid.* For a History of Margaret Connell, see p. 221.
51 Cork Register of Penitents, 27 June 1876.
52 *Ibid.*

Richardson, Registrar of the Court of Probate at Cork was examined. This witness, a Protestant, was a member of what he described as a small association in Cork, formed for the purpose of repealing the legislation. In his opinion, the Acts had increased immorality in the city, since soldiers now felt that they could associate freely with prostitutes without fear of disease. He stated that one of the city's debating societies (composed of young men of the "better" class, such as sons of solicitors and professional men) had actually come to a resolution in favour of the legislation, on the grounds that it made immorality more safe. Outsiders visited Cork for the same reason, and he gave an example of a commercial traveller who, having recently indulged himself in what he knew to be a "protected" district, was now undergoing medical treatment in Dublin.[53]

Rev. Shinkwin's converts were described as particularly "degraded", inhabiting as they did, infamous brothels in the "lowest" part of the city. Their status as registered women is indisputable - their reputation and place of abode ensuring their appearance on the "Special" Police List. All such women were subject to compulsory examination every fortnight, and whatever their circumstances, suffered immediate detention for treatment if found to be diseased. Their presence in the notorious street on the night in question suggests that within the last fourteen days each had been given a clean bill of health. Yet soon after their admission to the Good Shepherd, most were in need of medical attention which was not provided in the Home.

Even more damning is the condition of other penitents, who, having entered the Good Shepherd direct from the Lock Hospital, were later required to return. Clearly, the disease of some venereal patients went undetected, while others, pronounced cured by the Government, were prematurely discharged.

Throughout the 1870s inmates continued to arrive from the Lock Hospital, the female prison (adjacent to the Good Shepherd) or on the recommendations of Rev. Shinkwin and various other priests. Some women, such as 22 year old Mary Collins who was admitted in August 1876, left in disgrace and died in the workhouse.[54] Others, such as Bridget McCliffe,

---

53 *Royal Commission*, 6 May 1871.
54 Cork Register of Penitents, 1 August 1876.

recommended by Rev. Reed a few days later; and 17 year old Bridget Hanley who arrived from the prison, escaped "over the wall".[55] Also admitted at this time were girls such as 26 year old Catherine Sullivan, 22 year old Margaret Downey and 18 year old Mary Dwyer, all of whom had to be sent shortly afterwards to the Lock or the "Queen's" Hospital*, as it was now being termed[56]. A few women entering the Home at this time, on the other hand, later left for America. Seventeen year old Rebecca Barry, for example (presumably from the Lock Hospital, since she was brought by Rev. Reed) actually married from the institution five years after her arrival, and then emigrated.[57] Others, such as Catherine Neville (who remained in the Home for six years) and Ellie Sullivan (whose history appears on pages 193-95) both aged 18 on admission and recommended by Rev. Reed, were found situations.[58] Another of his referrals, Eliza Stack, aged 16 when admitted in March 1877, was sent to London five years later, to work in a shop. She was described as having "got very well married".[59] Such cases were unusual, and as has already been noted, between 1872 and 1890, only 5 percent of the women went straight from the Penitentiary to regular employment.

Even a "placement" did not guarantee success. Minna Garden, for example, who entered the Home voluntarily in December 1872, was sent out as a servant to a Mrs. Lane in January 1878. She died shortly afterwards in the workhouse hospital.[60] Other cases were even more distressing. In May 1877, 22 year old Mary Byrne was brought to the Home by her mother. She left for hospital within a few weeks of her arrival, and died in the Workhouse "with terrible suffering".[61] In June the following year, seventeen year old Margaret Best, entered the Asylum "of her own accord". She left eight days later, "in a bad disposition", and hanged herself shortly afterwards. In the same year, Kate Curtis, a 17 year old girl from Macroom, Co. Cork was sent to the Home by a Rev. O'Flynn. She

55 *Ibid.*, 13 and 3 August 1876.
*   There is, of course, no doubt about these women's complaint. For a discussion of this term, see pp. 212-15.
56 Cork Register of Penitents, 4, 19 and 26 August, 1876.
57 *Ibid.*, 20 September 1876.
58 *Ibid.*, 18 May 1872 and 20 June 1873.
59 *Ibid.*, 1 March 1877.
60 *Ibid.*, 20 December 1872.
61 *Ibid.*, 7 May 1877.

left after eighteen months, and died in the Lock Hospital.[62] Twenty-five year old Ellen Kineally was admitted in June 1880. She left soon afterwards in a "bad disposition" but returned within a few days. Following her departure in 1885, she was found drowned. Finally Ellen Case, a 19 year old Limerick patient in the Cork Lock Hospital was recommended to the Good Shepherd by Fr. Reed in July 1880. Seven weeks later she was sent to the lunatic asylum.[63]

Though numbers of placements from English Refuges too, were disappointingly low, these formed a much higher proportion of "reasons for leaving" than was the case in the Irish Homes discussed in this study. As noted earlier, the greater variety and scale of domestic service in England was one reason for this; and there seems too, to have been less of that local prejudice - referred to by Rev. Maguire and discussed above - against employing women direct from Magdalen institutions. Fundamentally, however, as was noted in Chapter 3, the difference in results stemmed not from the Homes' inability to find situations for their penitents - but from their willingness to do so.

It was noted above that after leaving the Asylum, three former penitents died in the workhouse – the only acknowledged provision in the city, apart from the new Government Lock hospital, for those suffering from venereal disease. As we have seen, women hopelessly afflicted in this way were kept in segregated "foul" wards in the workhouse, where about one hundred of them languished until they died. Not all venereal patients, however, were prostitutes (though most undoubtedly were) and certainly not all prostitutes who entered the workhouse did so because of venereal disease.

A sample four-year analysis of admissions to Cork workhouse (1870-1873) reveals that approximately 700 prostitutes entered the institution in this period, some on more than one occasion. Twenty-six of these women died in the workhouse - three within a few days of being admitted, but some surviving for up to seven years. Thirty-one others were described, under the heading Physical Condition of Pauper, as "sick" or "bad" – though venereal disease was not specified. A further 49 were pregnant, 19 of whom

---

62 *Ibid.*, 9 June and 39 August 1878.
63 *Ibid.*, 12 June and 12 July 1880.

left before giving birth, while 30 remained for their confinements. Of the 30 infants born to prostitutes in the workhouse, 16 died – their mothers generally leaving almost immediately afterwards. The remainder took their babies with them when they left, though little William Ryan was sent out "to nurse" when he was three years old. He had been born in the workhouse in May 1870, his mother 23 year old Joanna Ryan, of "The Bush", having been admitted ten weeks before her confinement. She died in the Lock Division three years later.[64]

With "fair" condition being the most common description applied to prostitutes listed in the Cork Register of Paupers, it would seem that for the majority, destitution rather than ill health was the reason for their stay.

The following Table compares the age distribution of prostitutes on admission to the Cork workhouse in this sample four-year period, with that of penitents on admission to the Limerick, Waterford, New Ross and Cork Good Shepherd Homes.

Table 20
Age Distribution of Prostitutes on Admission to Cork Workhouse (1870-73) compared with that of Penitents on Admission to the Good Shepherd Asylums (during periods analysed).

Years	% of Total Cork Workhouse	% of Total Limerick G.S.	% of Total Waterford* G.S.	% of Total New Ross G.S.	% of Total Cork* G.S.
12-19	3	32	27	32	29
20-29	51	47	45	49	50.5
30-39	32	16	19	13	12.5
40-49	9	3	5	4.5	5
50 +	4	1	1.5	1.5	1

*For 2.5 percent of penitents in Waterford, and 2 percent in Cork, Age on Admission was not recorded.

It is clear from the above that while approximately 30 percent of

---

64 Cork Union Register of Paupers, Nos. 26276 and 28530.

all penitents admitted to the Good Shepherds were under 20 years of age, only 3 percent of prostitutes entering Cork workhouse in the sample survey were of that age group. Further, in contrast to the Magdalen Asylums, to which, even between 1870 and 1873 adolescents of 12 and 13 were being taken, the youngest prostitute seeking admission to the workhouse was aged 16, and only 2 were aged 17.[65]

In Cork, as this sample four-year period illustrates, most prostitutes preferred the workhouse to the city's penitentiaries, a preference which intensified as the century wore on. Eventually, the country's Poor Law system - a much detested episode in popular Irish history - was dismantled; leaving the destitute dependent on Homes run by religious orders, and recommended or insisted on, by priests. Recent exposures of cruelty, neglect and abuse in such places, suggest that by comparison, workhouses were innocuous institutions, inflicting far less damage on vulnerable unwanted women, and the children of the poor.

In spite of the reluctance of Cork prostitutes to enter the institution, and a high turnover of other inmates, the numbers at the Magdalen Asylum continued to be maintained. There was no question (as had been the case in the York Female Penitentiary in the 1880s, for example) of the laundry facing closure through lack of admissions and a dwindling workforce. This is illustrated in 1878, when the Duchess of Marlborough, wife of the Lord Lieutenant, visited the Foundation, inspecting first the Industrial School, and then the Penitents' "class":

> "... where they were all engaged in laundry work. When the Duchess got the first glimpse of our 164 poor sheep, she could not suppress her tears."[66]

This was the first of a succession of visits by highly-placed dignitaries, all of whom were "deeply affected", "touched" or "moved" by the sight of almost two hundred "lost sheep" washing away their lives. In 1880, H.R.H. the Duke of Edinburgh, Queen Victoria's second son visited the Magdalen Asylum, and was

---

65 Cork Union Minute Books and Registers of Paupers, 1870-73.
    Only 14 of the workhouse prostitutes admitted in this period were Protestants, 7 were married and 5 were widowed.
66 Cork Annals, 1878.

"much pleased" with the Penitents' House and the object of the order.[67] Three years later, members of the Royal Commission appointed to inspect prisons, also visited the Home:

> "Being anxious to understand the system employed with regard to the Penitents, many of whom had been frequent inmates of the adjoining prison, and there considered incorrigible. The Members were much affected seeing so many poor Penitents working happily both in the ironing room and class-room, and all expressed their astonishment at the striking contrast between them and the persons whom they had just left."[68]

More spectacular in April 1885, was the visit of the Prince and Princess of Wales, together with their 21 year old son, Prince Albert Victor, Duke of Clarence and heir-presumptive to the throne. The visitors went first to the Industrial School and then to the Chapel, which was much admired.

> "It had been arranged that the Royal party were to leave by the Penitents' Cloister, and in passing, the Princess asked our very honoured Mother if she could see the Penitents. They were all in the ironing room at the time, busily engaged at work. The Princess on entering was visibly affected, examined their work and spoke most kindly to several of them. She asked our dear Mother many questions about them and expressed the deepest interest and sympathy for them. The Prince of Wales asked for a sketch of the Order, the object of which both he and the Princess spoke of in terms of the highest admiration."[69]

Though gratifying, this visit could scarcely have been less appropriate. The Prince of Wales, whose first sexual adventure had occurred 35 years earlier at the Curragh Camp (the second of Ireland's "subjected" districts under the 1864 Act) was by now a practiced womaniser, whose unsavoury lapses were widely known, and the subject of coarse debate. His expressed admiration for a system that confined "fallen" women to a long-term Penitentiary, was remarkable in its hypocrisy, even for the Victorian age. Possibly more bizarre, was the fact that Prince Albert Victor accompanied his parents on their tour of the Home.

---

67 *Ibid.*, 1880.
68 *Ibid.*, 1883.
69 *Ibid.*, 1885.

At about this time he was stationed with the 10th Hussars in Dublin, and was soon known to be leading such a "dissipated life", that European Royalty buzzed with rumour - which was reported to his grandmother, the Queen.[70] His diverse activities were reputedly "sapping his already feeble physical strength", and his weakened constitution contributed to his untimely end in 1892. However unfounded were recent allegations regarding this young man,[71] enough is known of his private life to make his inspection of a Magdalen Home unseemly, to say the least.

Throughout this period (and culminating in the controversy surrounding the Contagious Diseases Acts) prostitution, along with sexuality in general, came under constant scrutiny and was the subject of "scientific" investigation, public pronouncement and general debate. Poverty, overcrowding and seduction were hailed as major factors in the women's downfall; but society was not exclusively at fault. It was felt that many of the fallen were the victims of their own shortcomings - of vanity in particular - and various forms of self-indulgence, pandered to from youth. Foremost amongst these, and curiously at odds with the elaborate fashions of the time, was always "love of dress". William Logan, William Acton and Arthur J. S. Maddison were among the many "experts" who saw this weakness as a major contributory factor; and as early as 1824, the London Female Penitentiary had pointed to "Dress-houses" (as well as visits to theatres and fairs) as powerful inducements to a life of sin. These were establishments:

> "From which the most miserable and forlorn of her sex, without a gown to her back, for a share of the wages of her iniquity may get handsomely attired from head to foot, and be thus helped on in her wretched career, until she sinks under disease and death, a victim to the avarice of others."[72]

A striking example from the Cork Annals demonstrates that the Sisters too, regarded "love of dress" as a preliminary to evil.

In 1899 a former penitent, Ellie Sullivan (given the name Alacoque in the Home) caused a stir of excitement when she

---

70 James Pope-Hennessy, *Queen Mary* (1959) pp.192-194.
71 The attempt made in the 1960s, to identify him as the Whitechapel murderer.
72 17th *Annual Report* of the London Female Penitentiary, 1824.

returned from America to visit the nuns. The Register lists her as one of Rev. Reed's early cases,[73] and she seems to have been a favourite with the Sisters, who treated her with more than usual indulgence. She was originally admitted in June 1873 when she was 18 years old, and, as noted above, after four years was one of the few women sent out from the Asylum to a situation. In 1879 she was re-admitted, and shortly afterwards the nuns sent her to America. Twenty years later the Annals provide the history of this woman (now apparently restored to society) who had once been a registered prostitute, and whose detention in a Government Hospital had been the means of her reform. She was the embodiment of Dr. Acton's theories on the social mobility of such cases, and represented the conclusive justification for the Acts.

> "Alacoque ran away from her home at the age of twelve years and came to her Aunt in Cork where she thought she could easily follow her own sweet will and indulge to her heart's content in her love for dress. She was not a bad child, but the passion for dress which was not checked in the beginning was, as we shall see, the first seeds of her destruction. Her Aunt lived in that part of the City where people were wont to pass an evening ramble. A certain class of well-dressed girls were in the habit of passing the house. The very loudness of their dress showed that they were not desirable companions, but the child's heart longed for such bright colours and she thought her cup of happiness would be full, if only she could dress like these and promenade as they did to be admired by everyone. She was not long in making their acquaintance and very soon our poor child lost her innocence. One of her gay companions took her to the Government Hospital,* from which she was brought here, where she remained for some years, wild and giddy at first but overcame herself a good deal, became a child of Mary and shortly afterwards we procured for her a good situation. Love of dress again showed itself, she left her place, went to Dublin and led a reckless life for some time."[74]

---

73 Cork Register of Penitents, 20 June 1873. See above, page 188.
*   If true, this is further evidence of the Act's faulty application in Cork. Having now been a prostitute for some time, she should have already been registered, and her fortnightly attendance at the Lock Hospital both automatic and compulsory.
74 Cork Annals, 1899.

A return to the Good Shepherd (where she could not settle after her "life of luxury") was followed by the nuns lending her money for her passage to America, after which they heard nothing of her for years. She now alleged that during this time she had married, been widowed, bought a hotel and "come into" shares in silver mines. She had then become paralysed and journeyed to England, determined to set up a Home for young Penitents. Mother Devereux who eventually talked to her, admired her fine ring:

> "She went into town, bought a lovely statue of Our Lady, got the ring melted down and made into a crown and sent up to Mother as a token of gratitude."[75]

The nuns were charmed; and completed her second entry in the Register as follows:

> "Getting on remarkably well since she left for America. Promises to leave in her will a sum towards a Preservation Class."[76]

There is no record of their having heard from her again.

This continued emphasis on the danger of working-class women indulging in "love of dress", highlights the social, as well as sexual double standards of the time. On the one hand, those struggling for respectability were required to cultivate a plain, neat appearance, and resist all "showiness" in dress. At the same time, the opposite was approved - even demanded - for those higher up the social scale. No matter how revealing were the elaborate costumes of the rich, these were modish rather than immodest; while gross displays of jewellry, far from being vulgar, indicated taste.

Nowhere was "love of dress" more apparent than in the English Royal Family, with the Princess of Wales (later Queen Alexandra) indulging this passion obsessively; and her son, Prince Albert Victor, so concerned with his appearance that he was known, scathingly, as "collars and cuffs". "Love of dress", it seems, was dangerous only in the lower orders, at the extremities of which were penitents and others of their kind. In Magdalen Homes, such vanities were easily remedied. Remorseless penance

---

75 *Ibid.*
76 Cork Register of Penitents, 4 April 1880.

was an efficient corrective; confinement and constant labour soon coarsened the most favoured of women; and garments that were shapeless and ugly, subdued the sexuality of all.

Passing through the Penitents' Cloister, the Royal party doubtless glimpsed the grim warnings, carved into each stone arch. Despite recent camouflage, one of these texts, deep-set, was still discernible in 1986 when it was pointed out to the author by a Good Shepherd nun. What seemed an apt title for this study, "Unless Ye Do Penance, Ye Shall All Perish", was, for the inmates at least, an unnecessary caution. Remorse and atonement – as the following schedule demonstrates – consumed their whole lives.

Magdalen Asylum Horarium

5.0	Rise
5.30	Morning Prayer
5.40	Work
6.30	Mass
7.45	Breakfast
8.15	Work
11.45	Dinner
12.15	Recreation
1.15	Work
3.30	Tea
4.0	Work
6.30	Supper
7.0	Recreation
8.0	Story Book
8.30	Night Prayers and Bed[77]

---

77 Good Shepherd British Provincial Archives, 13/4/10.
Quoted in Peter E. Hughes, "Cleanliness and Godliness", A sociological study of the Good Shepherd convent refuges for the social reformation and christian conversion of prostitutes and convicted women in nineteenth century Britain, p.471. Unpublished doctoral thesis (Brunel University, 1985).
See above, p.2.,ft.2.

7

The Good Shepherd Magdalen Asylum, Cork (part 2)

" If we follow the nun into her ... Magdalen Asylums, we shall find that it would be better for the public if she were dispensed with ... The Nuns' Magdalen Asylums do not decrease female immorality. They are devoted to lucrative laundry work, which must enhance the wealth of the religious. And they appear to draw only a sufficient supply of recruits from the immoral reservations to maintain their staffs!"[1]

In February 1883 the Good Shepherd Monastery in Sunday's Well lost its most generous benefactor when Richard Devereux, the Mother Superior's uncle died. As well as his initial contribution of £4,000 towards the cost of the Cork buildings - a factor which doubtless influenced the appointment of his nieces - he had, on many occasions, donated other sums; and was, as we have seen, a liberal patron of the Order's other Houses. Following her uncle's death, Mother Devereux's health began to fail, and soon caused such anxiety that the penitents resolved to "storm heaven". Accordingly, they assembled in the classroom, had candles lighted, and amidst fervent prayers:

"A great number had their hair cut off as a sacrifice to obtain the much asked for grace. The hair was afterwards sold and the proceeds spent on oil for the lamps which were kept continually burning for the same intention." [2]

In the wake of such devotion, Mother Devereux was soon "completely restored".

---

1 McCarthy, *op. cit.*, pp.437-8.
2 Cork Annals, February and November 1883.

198 *Do Penance or Perish*

Then in October 1886 the nuns mourned the death of Mr. James Hegarty who:

> "had worked for the Institution from the time he first formed the project of founding one of our Convents in Cork - in collecting for the buildings and subsequently getting the Annual Subscriptions - no evasions or rebuffs deterred him ... it was his greatest happiness to see so many poor penitents in the class and often when going to where they worked his face would beam as he said to the Sister present "Isn't it a grand sight to see so many of them safe".

Within a few days Bishop Dr. Delaney also died. He too, had been responsible for setting up the Home.[3]

Though not accountable to regular subscribers, and largely free (apart from the influence of the Bishop) from outside interference and control, the Good Shepherd Sisters relied, to some extent, on the support of the public. It was noted in Chapter 4 that the profits from a successful Magdalen Laundry not only supported the women, but contributed to the upkeep of the Congregation as a whole. Industrial Schools too, were highly profitable. Nevertheless, donations to the Convents were a vital source of income, and the loss of benefactors such as Richard Devereux and the two founders of the Home, was a severe blow.

A common feature of most English Refuge Societies throughout the period was their publication of brief Annual Reports for Committee Members, subscribers, outdoor missionaries, future employers and others who involved themselves in local Rescue Work. These records outline the year's progress, and give information on admissions, departures and those remaining in the Homes. Sometimes they include too, statistics of inmates' ages, lengths of stay and reasons for leaving. Continuous sets of these Annual Reports exist for a great many Refuges, and are to be found in numerous Archives throughout the country. They are, however, of limited value, since they provide no detailed information about the women themselves (who in any case, are never referred to by name) and are not necessarily an accurate guide to what was taking place. Only rarely (as is the case with the York Female Penitentiary, and the Lincoln Refuge, for example)

---

3 *Ibid.*, October and November 1886.

have complete complimentary records survived – material such as Ladies' Committee Books, Minutes, and the correspondence (including letters from former inmates) of a Home. Comparison of this less guarded evidence with that intended for public inspection reveals that the Annual Reports glossed over serious setbacks, and presented an optimistic, sentimental account of penitential Rescue Work. In view of the purpose of these publications, this is hardly surprising. Basically, the Annual Reports were financial statements, comparing Laundry receipts and subscriptions, with the Homes' outgoings and running costs. Since the two rarely balanced, the Refuges relied on public support; and to ensure the continuance of funds they presented their activities in an unrealistically favourable light.

The radically different structure and organisation of the Good Shepherd Institute ensured its Foundations certain advantages. They were not answerable to subscribers, who, donating perhaps one pound or ten shillings a year, required to be furnished with Annual Reports on progress, policy and funds.* And though less autonomous than independent Homes, they were spared the constant squabbles that took place between individual Committee Members; or worse still, the disastrous confrontations that were apt to occur when Ladies' and Gentlemen's Committees clashed over policy, or the day-to-day running of the Homes. Above all, they could rarely have encountered the endless staffing difficulties that beset lay Refuges. Instead, they drew on a team of zealously committed women, all of whom had undergone uniform training as nuns, were responsible to the Provincial Mother House, and were subject to their Order's object and rule. In such circumstances, and with the *Rules for the Direction of the Classes* to guide them, their conviction that the Homes were being run as the Foundress had instructed was secure.

In contrast, for smaller lay penitentiaries staffing was a nightmare. Onerous duties and low pay repelled many suitable applicants, and Homes were often dependent on those whose motives were suspect, and who, between the weekly visits of the Managers, ruled the establishments without restraint. Between 1849 and 1868 the Ladies' Committee of the York Refuge, for

---

* The above reference to Mr. James Hegarty "getting the Annual Subscriptions" suggests that part of the Sisters' income was, in fact, secured in this way – though to what extent this occurred is not clear.

example, dismissed a succession of Matrons and Laundresses who were unsatisfactory. Some were insubordinate or dishonest, while others, overwhelmed by the nature and the volume of the work, were simply unable to cope. More shocking, however, were those discovered to be drunkards, or whose conduct was hardly more virtuous than the females they controlled. Needless to say, such details were not made public, but are contained in the Minute Books and Committee records.[4]

Without this complimentary material the carefully worded Annual Reports are somewhat sterile - except, of course to those concerned with statistics rather than individuals. Isabella Corkhill's story, for example, detailed in Chapter 5, emerges from the correspondence and Committee Books of the York Refuge - together with the city's workhouse material. It is not to be found in the public portrayal of the Home. To a lesser extent this is the case with the Good Shepherd archives. The Penitents' Registers contain systematic and detailed information on each of the inmates in the Homes. They are an invaluable record of a particular group of women – otherwise largely unrecorded, and as such, are the major source on which this study is based. Nevertheless, these Registers, though fascinating, are of limited value unless combined with other sources. They lend themselves too readily to impersonal tabulation - which however calculated, tells us little of the individual women's lives. Sadly, this approach, characterised by an excessive use of statistics, formidable jargon and careful objectivity – has in many cases robbed history of its interest, its accessibility and its charm. Just as the Annual Reports of lay Refuges, therefore, are enhanced by supplementary material on the women themselves, so the Penitents' Registers are enormously enriched by the Annals.

The Annals contain information on both penitents and Sisters, recording incidents and events in the Homes with disarming candour and naivety. The Cork Annals in particular, reveal for example, the determination with which money for the Foundation was pursued; and indicate that the Order's early confidence in Mother Devereux was not misplaced.

Throughout the 1880s the reputation of the Cork Laundry soared (it was soon to be regarded as the finest in the city) with the result that there was a vast increase in the volume of work. In

4   Finnegan, *op. cit.*, pp.182-3.

1886 the Lord Lieutenant and his wife, together with a large party of visitors called at the Monastery at such short notice (the nuns were informed only the evening before) that the "usual decorations" were omitted. An account of the incident describes the different occupations carried out in the Home; but it is unlikely that many of the women were trained (as Lord and Lady Aberdeen were given to understand) in a variety of skills. More probably, as was the case in so many English Homes, the vast majority of inmates (and particularly the simple-minded) were restricted to heavy, routine labour in the Laundry. Only the most accomplished engaged in more delicate work. This was certainly the case in the Limerick Asylum, well-known in this period, for its lace. As noted in Chapter 3, for the purpose of the Census in 1901, inmates' occupations were listed. Seventy of the women were described as laundresses, 5 were seamstresses, 6 were domestic servants and only 3 made lace.

The visitors first inspected the Industrial School, then the Chapel, which was "greatly admired"; and "though Protestants" Lord and Lady Aberdeen knelt and prayed for some time in the Choir. They next proceeded to the Magdalen Asylum, where about 100 of the inmates were working in the Laundry:

> "It being an ironing day, [Lady Aberdeen] saw how the shirt-fronts were glazed, and spoke in the kindest and most encouraging manner to several of the penitents. The class-room was then visited, and the different kinds of lace, gold embroidery, plain work, book-making and knitting were examined.* Lord Aberdeen showed the greatest interest in the different kinds of work, and spoke of its variety as a wonderful means of interesting the penitents. He said that he had always imagined a Penitentiary to be a kind of prison, gloomy and cheerless, with nothing to vary the monotony of the life there, except scrubbing rooms or some such work, but that his visit had completely undeceived him, and that he was both surprised and delighted on being acquainted with the

---

* Three years earlier at the Cork Exhibition, the Penitents' work had received First Prize for gold embroidery, and a gold medal for crochet work. They had also submitted "beautifully bound" books. Cork Annals, July 1883.
According to the *Cork Examiner* (19 June 1902): "Vestment making and embroidery work of a superb character forms occupation for some of the inmates .... also lace work .... exquisite specimens of which can be seen at the Convent's stall at the Exhibition ..... [also] white silk Irish crochet collars ...... and a magnificent set of priest's vestments in white, worked with gold and jewels."

object of the order ... the cheerfulness of the Penitents and the many proofs of their industry and skill."[5]

They also visited the Penitents' Infirmary, and were moved to tears by one poor girl, only twenty-two and "very pretty" who was dying of consumption. She "suffered intensely" but "her penitence and sweetness of disposition were truly marvellous". She told them how happy her deathbed was, and how grateful she felt to the nuns. It was a scene that Lord Aberdeen said he would never forget.[6]

There were by now about 160 penitents generally engaged full-time in the Laundry; and since they were not paid wages and worked for longer hours than normal employees, it must be assumed that the enterprise was profitable.[*]

These women's subjection to long hours of unpaid labour, in conditions of humiliating restraint, continued with little change into the second half of the twentieth century.[+] By this time a powerful Trade Union Movement had evolved, compulsory education had been enforced and the position of women in general had dramatically improved. Such reforms had left the victims of the Female Penitentiary System, particularly in Ireland, virtually untouched. Yet ironically, "reformers" had established the Rescue Movement in the first place - founding and supporting individual institutions, and approving a system dangerously free from Government inspection or control.

Yet in spite of low running costs, many small Refuges struggled for survival - particularly those whose Laundries were ill equipped, badly managed, and (as penitent numbers fluctuated) inadequately or indifferently staffed. Nevertheless, their Managers were reluctant to undercut local competition; and certainly for the Good Shepherds, there is no evidence to suggest that free labour resulted in low-priced work. Clearly then, the latter institutions,

---

5   Cork Annals, 1886.
6   *Ibid.*
*   It certainly became so. According to the authors of *Suffer the Little Children, op. cit.,* "Accounts from the Good Shepherd Convent in Cork show an average profit on the laundry operation of the equivalent in today's money of £100,000 a year during the 1950s and 1960s. They illustrate that the nuns spent much of this on themselves, paying out enormous sums for instance to decorate their internal chapel. Money spent on the maintenance of their imprisoned and unpaid workforce was minimal." - p.290.
+   Such submission (and there are no indications of any organised protest or revolt - even on the part of women who had left, and might have helped their former companions) demonstrates why early manufacturers preferred a female or juvenile labour force.

operating on a vast commercial scale, were financially successful. Nevertheless, the Cork Foundation was reported to be constantly in debt - not merely because increasing volumes of work required extensions to the Laundry and investment in up-to-date machines.

Contributing to the Cork Asylum's pressing financial difficulties (and certainly regardless of them) were the costly improvements and decorations which continued to be carried out in the Chapel, for example, which had so recently been admired by the Prince and Princess of Wales and Lord and Lady Aberdeen.

In common with all Good Shepherd Monasteries and in compliance with the Order's Rules, each Section of the Cork Foundation was quite distinct. High above the city, and fronted by sloping terraces, the huge buildings "in the Venetian style of Gothic architecture" and designed by Mr. George Ashlin of Dublin, formed one continuous line. The Magdalen Asylum, however, containing the Penitentiary and Laundry section was separated from the Industrial School by the Convent itself. To prevent even the possibility of the children seeing penitents in the airing ground or elsewhere, the glass in the lower part of the windows was "artificially dulled". Behind the Convent was the Chapel, accessible to all in the enclosure, but reached by different corridors or cloisters. And although the entire Community worshiped together, "such measures have been taken for isolation that the one class cannot even be aware of the presence of the other".[7] The Penitents' cloister, for example (along which the Royal party had been taken) led direct from the Magdalen complex, to the left-hand isle of the Chapel. Here, ornately carved screens sectioned off the women from the choir, reserved for the nuns and with direct access to the Convent. The right-hand isle, again elaborately screened, was for the use of the Industrial Children, and linked directly to their quarters - the large building on the extreme right.

Where Foundations contained additional Classes, more complex segregation occurred. Thus in Waterford, as has already been noted, a room to the left of the altar ensured the complete seclusion of the Province's small Community of Magdalens. From

---

7   *Cork Examiner*, 18 July 1872.

204 Do Penance or Perish

this room they had direct access by a private covered way, to their own quarters.* And in New Ross an "exterior" wing was provided for the public, who entered this portion of the Chapel from the main street in Irishtown. Similarly, Limerick's exquisite domed Chapel, built in 1931,[8] allowed for the separation of the nuns, the penitents, and the Industrial and Reformatory girls.

In 1888 the Cork Convent acquired a new benefactor, a Mr. Brown, who donated £100 towards the decoration of the Chapel. When shown the completed work he regretted that the newly-fitted altars in the Children's' and Penitents' isles were without statues. This prompted Mother Devereux, "trusting as usual, to Providence", to immediately order four from Munich. For the Penitents' side, over St. Joseph's altar, she chose St. Peter holding keys, and, appropriately, a "very beautiful" Mary Magdalen. For that of the Industrial children, she ordered St. Aloysius[+] and - equally appropriate to her mind, perhaps - St. Agnes with a lamb.[9]

---

*   It has been impossible to obtain information about where the Order's "Magdalens" are buried; and the same question applies to those penitents who died in New Ross before 1878 when St. Stephen's Cemetery was opened. Presumably the "Consecrates", in spite of their elevated status, were interred in each of the Monastery's communal Penitents' plots.

8   The fact that the Community could afford this magnificent building in a period of such general distress gives some indication - if not of the wealth, then of the confidence of the Order at this time. Trusting not only to "Providence" but to public support from a society which was, by the 1930s, deeply reactionary, the Sisters were not disappointed. Apparently, a special appeal was made to the ladies of Limerick, many of whom donated their rings to help towards the cost. The white and gold Baroque-style chapel was stripped of much of its ornamentation for the public auction of the Convent's contents, in 1994. It remains, nevertheless, an extraordinarily beautiful building.

+   This extremely pious young man (1568-1591), who never committed a mortal sin, was canonised in 1726; and in 1926 declared patron of Catholic youth by Pope Pius XI.

9   A somewhat macabre role choice for the Industrial School girls, but one indicative of Mother Devereux's thinking; and entirely in keeping with the Order's attitude to virginity and sex.
     St. Agnes, whose name signifies "chaste" in Greek, is the special patroness of purity. According to the Rev. Alban Butler (1710-1773) - in an edition of *Lives of the Saints* which doubtless graced the Cork Convent shelves - in about 303 A.D., aged only 13, Agnes was sought in marriage by various sons of the Roman nobility - her riches and beauty exciting their desire. Having "consecrated her virginity to a heavenly spouse" however, the girl refused all honourable advances, and was condemned as a Christian. Far from betraying the least symptom of fear, she welcomed threats of death and torture, and offered herself to the rack. - "The governor seeing his measures ineffectual, said he would send her to a house of prostitution, where what she prized so highly should be exposed to the insults of the debauchees. Agnes answered that Jesus Christ was too jealous of the purity of his spouses to suffer it to be violated in such a manner, for he was their defender and protector. 'You may,' said she, 'stain your sword with my blood, but will never be able to profane my body, consecrated to Christ.' The governor

Mr. Brown was shown the statues on his next visit to the Convent, and asked to see the Bill. It was for £87, and the Annals record that he immediately presented Mother Devereux with the full amount.

Shortly after this event, some local disturbance so alarmed the Bishop and Reverend Mother that all new applicants to the penitentiary were refused admission. This extraordinary measure was possibly related to the recent closure of the "Certified" Hospital in the city, following the Contagious Diseases Acts' suspension and repeal. For an Asylum opened specifically for women recruited from this source, and set up in direct response to the new legislation, the situation was awkward. It was noted in the previous Chapter that there was early opposition to the Acts locally; and in April 1870, a Petition for their Total Repeal was presented to the House of Lords on behalf of the ladies of Cork. It contained 1,459 signatures, and the abolitionist journal *The Shield* noted that it was the second to be presented from the city.[10]

According to Rev. Maguire's evidence to the Royal Commission in the following year, there were a great many ladies in Cork who exerted themselves against the Acts, publishing placards and inviting support - which was not, however, forthcoming from the Catholic community, who were guided in this matter by their priests. Rev. Maguire's evidence indicates that opposition in Cork to the Contagious Diseases Acts stemmed largely from, and was led by, the non-Catholic section of the community - the Catholic clergy being strongly in favour of the legislation. He disapproved of

---

was so incensed at this that he ordered her to be immediately led to the public brothel, with liberty to all persons to abuse her person at pleasure. Many young profligates ran thither, full of the wicked desire of gratifying their lust, but were seized with such awe at the sight of the saint, that they durst not approach her - one only excepted, who, attempting to be rude to her, was that very instant, by a flash, as it were, of lightning from heaven, struck blind, and fell trembling to the ground." The governor then condemned her to be beheaded and Agnes "transported with joy on hearing the sentence, and still more at the sight of the executioner, 'went to the place of execution more cheerfully (says St. Ambrose) than others go to their wedding.'"

Rev. Butler continues with reflections which, hopefully, were not conveyed to the "Industrial" girls - though the choice of St. Agnes for their altar is ominous:

"Marriage is a holy state, instituted by God, and in the order of providence and nature the general or more ordinary state of those who live in the world. Those, therefore, who upon motives of virtue, and in a Christian and holy manner, engage in this state, do well. Those, nevertheless, who, for the sake of practising more perfect virtue, by a divine call, prefer a state of perpetual virginity, embrace that which is more perfect and more excellent ... The fathers ... are all profuse in extolling the excellency of holy virginity", which raises mortals "to the dignity of angels [producing] in the soul the nearest resemblance to God."

Butler's *Lives of the Saints*, Vol. 1, pp. 82-84.

10 *The Shield*, April 1870.

women "meddling" in such business, and was convinced that Catholics should be and were, content to leave these matters in the hands of the priests.* Questioned about the Abolitionists in Cork, he replied:

> "There are a great many ladies who exert themselves very much, and we do not approve of their putting placards before young females inviting them to read these Acts, of which women never heard before ... There is a certain portion of the community - of course I would not wish to give names, but they are composed chiefly of persons who are Nonconformists in religion - and they are very strongly opposed to this Act ... I feel it is a subject which ought not to appear before the public. I think it is a subject which any girl passing by can read, and unfortunately curiosity is more in women than in men, and whenever a woman sees a thing which she should not read she is almost sure to read it."

Nevertheless, he admitted that public opinion on the issue was divided, and that even some of the Catholic clergy were concerned that the new legislation might give too much power to the special police. The speeches and placards of the Acts' opponents had done "great mischief"; alarming some sections of the public, who now feared that respectable women - even nuns - might be molested by the police.[11]

Rev. Maguire who, except for a brief spell as army Chaplain in the Crimea, had spent his life in Cork, was arguably the most misogynistic of all witnesses giving evidence. Yet his attitude to prostitutes – "I would not care where they were so [long as] they

---

*   Mr. Henry Richardson, referred to above, noted that amongst respectable working men in the city there was some understanding of the Acts, and that a number of printers had signed a petition for their repeal. In his opinion the legislation had not improved the city's streets. Albert Quay, for example, was unsafe at night, open solicitation was tolerated by the police and abandoned women dogged passers by. His discussions with prostitutes had persuaded him that though they disliked them, the examinations would hardly deter a woman from entering the activity; and that in general the women approved of the Acts since they "removed the filth" from the profession. For this reason he objected to the legislation, which was designed, in his opinion, not so much to reclaim the prostitute as to "keep up a healthy supply of women for the gratification of the lusts of immoral men." *Royal Commission, op. cit.*, 6 May 1871.

11   Giving evidence to the Select Committee in 1882, Mr. Curtis, Surgeon to the Lock Hospital stated that there were 3 policemen (all married) entrusted with carrying out the Acts in Cork - Patrick Doyle, constable, and John Dooly and Timothy Louney, sub-constables. According to this witness these men were chosen for being advanced in age, sober, of good conduct, and of long standing. There was no truth in the allegations that they "dragged" women to the Lock Hospital or that they ever "put their hands upon a single female." *Op. cit.*, 20 June 1882.

were kept out of sight" - was unusual only in its harshness of expression. It was, after all, because of such views that the Penitentiary System endured into the late twentieth century. He informed the Commissioners that Cork priests had a particular method of dealing with such women. They sought to confine all prostitutes to a single "nest" and prevent their "swarming" all over the city. He regretted that the Corporation had recently been persuaded to close up Godsell's Lane - the terror of the community - since this had merely dispersed the evil. Acting promptly on their policy of hunting out both common prostitutes and privateers, however, the priests now had them all congregated in Furze Alley:

> "It is less injurious, inasmuch as it is not a temptation to a woman to go to Furze's Alley, and why? Because there is the worst infamy there, drunkenness, obscenity, fighting, rowing, robbing, everything, and a woman who falls into sin will for a long time be deterred from going there ... Each clergyman has a district under his charge, and we went and found them, and they gave us an immense deal of trouble. Whenever we find a woman of that stamp we always hunt her out; she may go to a place destined for them, and really while there, there is no temptation .... wherever we find a women of that class residing, and we do not know positively that she is bad, we always make inquiry, and if we find out that she is a woman of that class, we insist on the landlord or the person occupying the room to dismiss her. They generally obey us, because we come there often, and speak to them in a way that they must yield".

It was his opinion that such women should not be allowed in the streets at all, as most men would never dream of sinning but for their solicitations.[12]

With the much publicised Repeal of the legislation, in 1886, however, the situation changed. The stringent measures that had virtually criminalised, and certainly intimidated* prostitutes for

---

12 *Royal Commission, op. cit.*, 6 May 1871.
* A further criticism of the legislation was the fact that prostitutes submitting to the fortnightly examination suffered immediate detention if found to be diseased. Reference to the plan of the purpose-built Government hospital at Kildare, for example (Fig. 8) shows that women could be conveyed straight from the examination room to the hospital wards, with no opportunity to make provision for dependent children or otherwise put their affairs in order. Supporters of State Regulation played down such objections, but cases of this type were not infrequent, and one occurred in Cork in 1870. In March that year, nine year old John Doolan was admitted to the workhouse, destitute because "Mother in Lock Hospital." *Cork Union Register of Paupers*, 26 March 1870, No.27476.

the past two decades, were now abandoned as unworkable, immoral and unjust. The Abolitionists were vindicated and the Catholic clergy (who had vociferously supported the Acts) were forced to adopt a more moderate point of view.

We have seen that lay people, and particularly Catholic women, were discouraged by the priests from entering into the affair, with Rev. Maguire, in particular, objecting to women "meddling" in such matters. Nuns running Convent Magdalen Asylums, however, could hardly have been indifferent to the legislation, particularly if, as was the case with the Cork Good Shepherd Sisters, it affected both their own and the penitents' lives. Yet little is known of these women's response to what was probably the most controversial issue of the period - and one in which they were so intimately involved. Unlike the vast majority of women at the time, many members of Religious Orders, particularly Superiors, possessed enormous power. They were relatively independent, well educated, and commanded respect. Those involved in Rescue Work possessed unparalleled knowledge of numerous prostitutes undergoing reform. The Annals of the Cork Good Shepherd, however, are completely silent on the subject. In spite of the Convent's unique association with the Acts, and regardless of the detailed discussion of the new Magdalen Asylum at both Enquiries (to say nothing of the fact that the Home's Chaplain, Rev. Thomas O'Reilly, gave detailed evidence) no mention whatsoever appears in these records, of the much-debated legislation, its suspension or repeal. Further, the closure of the Hospital from which the Asylum's first cases were admitted, which had furnished the Refuge with so many inmates, and to which their diseased penitents had so frequently (but illegally) been sent - in effect, the closure of that institution responsible for the Order's presence in the city - was steadfastly ignored. Even the Annals' account of the urgent need for Probationary accommodation in 1889, though probably provoked by the event, makes no reference to the Hospital's closure.

The suggestion that nuns did not concern themselves with "worldly" or political matters is ruled out by their intense activity following the proposal to put Convent Laundries within the scope of the Factory and Workshop Act (see pages 223-24). On this occasion Mother Devereux wrote to Asquith and all the Irish M.P.s, and was extremely active and influential in what was far from a creditable cause. Unlike other incidents, which were studiously publicised to solicit funds, the Community's involvement in this particular matter did not "find its way into the newspapers". In view of the stance taken, and the apparent decline in the popularity of the Refuge, this was probably just as well.

Even had views on the Contagious Diseases controversy been expressed, however, they could hardly have differed from current orthodox thinking on the subject – particularly since the Bishop, in line with the rest of the Catholic Church, was known to approve of the Acts. It was, after all, in response to the reclamatory possibilities of the new legislation that he had invited the Order to Cork in the first place.[13] Superiors of large convents might have had more influence than most other women in the period, but ultimately their power was limited and could be resented – as Mother Pelletier, the Order's Foundress knew to her cost.* A display of intellectual or administrative brilliance, though viewed with distrust or even hostility could, if properly harnessed, be useful. Unorthodox opinions, however, particularly on matters which were not strictly the Convent's concern, were not tolerated, and could incur the lifelong resentment of a Bishop and his priests. An example nearer home is that of Sister Mary Francis Clare, the Nun of Kenmare. One of the most interesting women in Ireland in the period, a prolific writer, campaigner for women and defender of the poor, she was totally discredited for opposing her Bishop, and has only recently been regarded more favourably by the Church.

Nuns running Magdalen Asylums, then, though useful, and credited with almost supernatural grace were, when it came to issues such as these, merely women themselves. Their opinions on the legislation were unimportant – apparently neither valued, nor sought.

The single exception to this attitude occurs in the testimony of Rev. O'Reilly, who, as Chaplain to the Cork Good Shepherd Magdalen Asylum, gave evidence to the Select Committee in

---

13 The Roman Catholic Bishop Dr. Delaney, died in October 1886, just six months after the Acts were repealed. There is no doubt about his continued approval of the legislation. Mr. Curtis stated in his evidence to the Select Committee in June 1882, that the Bishop particularly wished him to pass on his opinion as to "the great benefit and good results of the Acts in Cork." *Op. cit.*, 20 June 1882.

* See the Biographies of the Foundress, *op. cit.*, all of which detail the appalling relationship between Mother Pelletier and her Bishop, Mgr. Angebault.

1882. As noted above, he produced a letter from Sister Mary Coppinger, First Mistress of Penitents - an important document since it is the only record of the Order's attitude to the legislation. Predictably, it was strongly in favour of the Acts.

Comparing inmates of the Cork Asylum (located in a subjected district) with "unsubjected" penitents in Limerick, Waterford, Belfast and New Ross, it was the opinion of this young nun and her colleagues that the Cork girls were "decidedly less vicious" than those in the Order's other Homes. They were "better disposed" and "more easily managed" from having been in the Lock Hospital; and their "character and deportment" had benefited from their stay. It was the Sisters' belief that the Lock Hospital:

> "has been the primary means of reforming a great number of girls, and has been productive thereby of much moral good. We have often sent girls from this asylum to that hospital, and have uniformly found the officials most obliging, coming for patients when requested to do so, and using their utmost endeavours to induce them to return to us as soon as they are discharged. Signed Sister Mary Coppinger."

The letter stated that in the ten years since the opening of the Home, approximately 100 penitents had been sent direct from the Lock Hospital to the Asylum, largely through the zealous exertion of the Chaplain, Rev. Reed. A further 150 women (not Lock Hospital patients) had been recommended to the Home by various other priests. According to Rev. O'Reilly, 80 percent of the Hospital Magdalens had "turned out well".

The Penitents' Register hardly supports this information, or the Sister's assertion that six penitents (not four) were received on the Home's first day. Cross examined by Mr. Hopwood, an opponent of the Regulation System, the Hospital Chaplain was reminded of the illegality of the proceedings he had just described:

> "Do you know that at the Lock Hospital the Government have no power to take in, and would refuse to take in, a person who was respectable?"

Rev. O'Reilly did not.[14]

---

14 *Select Committee, op. cit.*, 21 June 1882.

Many witnesses from the English Subjected Districts, and particularly opponents of the Acts, claimed that the behaviour of women going to and from the examinations was a public disgrace, with local inhabitants being subjected to scenes of gross indecency and misconduct, as troops of disorderly prostitutes converged on Examining Rooms. Some, anticipating detention, made their way in a drunken, morbid state, encouraged by companions; while others, more hopeful, shouted obscenities to scandalised passers-by. Released from the ordeal with a "clean bill of health" they were joined by rowdy male associates who had been lounging around in the neighbourhood till the women returned. Conduct of this kind was indignantly denied by Cork witnesses, most of whom claimed that few people knew about the legislation or even where the Hospital was. Rev. Maguire, for example, described the approach to the Hospital (which included the Examining Room) as in a back alley:

> "Where there are two entrances ... When I went first I could not tell where I was to go. I went to the wrong place first, and then finding a kind of secret door, I did not know how to enter it until I was directed, and it is by this door that the women enter ... I think there are certain days and hours for the various classes of women. The women of a better class generally drive up."

Even ten years later, according to Rev. Reed, few people other than those officially connected with the place, knew where it was; since the "great aim" of the Chaplain of such a Hospital was to "do the work as secretly as he can, without letting the public know much about it."[15]

It was also claimed that the public knew little of what took place in the police courts in Cork with regard to the new legislation, the whole business being kept "very secret", with cases being examined in private. Prostitutes brought before the bench were heard by the stipendiary magistrate only; after the ordinary magistrates and the reporters had left. And contrary to the practice in England, no cases appeared in the local press. It was said that the middle or "better" classes in the city (from

---

15 *Royal Commission, op. cit.*, 6 May 1871; and *Select Committee, op. cit.*, 27 June 1881. The lapse of a century made the former Hospital's location even more obscure; and I am grateful to Tim Cadogan, Executive Librarian, Cork County Library, for solving the mystery.

which group most nuns were drawn) were generally either apathetic and unwilling to direct their minds to the subject, or else in favour of the legislation.

Other witnesses touched on a matter which scandalised the public and dismayed even the staunchest supporters of the Acts. For some time, it had been widely alleged that in many subjected districts, prostitutes - regarding themselves as now under the protection of and working for the Government - boldly described themselves as "Queen's women". Originally, those discharged from examination had been issued with certificates stating their freedom from disease - a practice which had apparently increased their arrogance and earning power. Although this procedure was now discontinued, it was argued that the women were still regarded, both by themselves and the public, in an "official" light. Armed with a clean bill of health (which release after examination virtually gave them) they were apt to flaunt their enhanced status, and think themselves beyond the reach of all but the "special" police. The Acts' supporters denied these claims as malicious invention, designed to bring the legislation into disrepute.

Complaints of this behaviour in Ireland had first emerged about nine months after the legislation was fully enforced. A letter from a "Cork Lady", published in *The Shield* in March 1870, alleged:

> "My friend, Mrs. —, of —, Cork, has an old servant who was walking home lately at about 8 o'clock in the evening, when one of the town prostitutes pushed her off the flags, rudely saying, 'Make way for the Queen's woman'. [16]

Accounts of these and similar incidents in the city had reached the attention of the Commissioners in London, who pressed Mr. Henry Richardson, Registrar of the Court of Probate at Cork, on the point:

> Question 18642. "It has been stated at some of the meetings of the opponents of the Acts in Cork that the women call themselves "Queen's women" and "Government women"[17]

16 *The Shield*, 7 March 1870.
17 *Royal Commission, op. cit.*, 6 May 1871.

Mr. Richardson could confirm this only by hearsay; but from other sources it is clear that such reports were true. Prostitutes were, in fact, referred to and regarded themselves as "Queen's women", as is evident from the Penitents' Register of the Good Shepherd Asylum in Cork.

At the 1882 Enquiry there was further investigation into what was by now a major concern. In March 1882 Mr. John B. Kingston, a local Protestant Rescue worker and a gentleman of independent means, testified that since the application of the Acts to the city, prostitutes were inclined to shake off his ministrations, declaring that they were the "Queen's Women" and that the Queen "looked after" them. He stated that the Lock Hospital was commonly called the "Queen's Hospital" by Cork residents, and further remarked that he had actually received a letter from the establishment "dated" in that way.[18] Giving evidence a few weeks later, however, Rev. O'Reilly, the Good Shepherd Chaplain and a strenuous supporter of the Acts, categorically denied these claims, referring, as proof, to the testimony of the Good Shepherd nuns:

"Question 11403: I suppose you consider that you have a better means of forming an opinion on the subject than Mr. Kingston, who is not a priest? – Certainly.

Question 11405: Now did you ever hear these women speak of themselves as "Queen's women"? – Never; if they did I would know it.

Question 11406: Have you made inquiries of the nuns of the Good Shepherd Convent whether they have ever heard these women speaking of themselves as "Queen's women"? – I did, and they said, no, never.

Question 1407: Nor as "Government women"? – Nor "Government women", never."

Question 11408: I suppose if it were a common expression for them to call themselves "Queen's women", you would have heard the expression? – Without doubt."[19]

---

18 *Select Committee, op. cit.*, 31 March 1882.
19 *Ibid.*, 21 June 1882.

Yet the Sister recording Admissions to the Cork Good Shepherd had, over the past decade sometimes described the Certified Hospital in this way. While the Acts were in force, numerous prostitutes were sent direct to the Good Shepherds from the government hospitals at Cork and Kildare. Though usually recorded as "Recommended by Lock hospital, Kildare" or "Miss Farrell, Matron of Lock Hospital, Kildare", etc., from 1874 onwards, an inmate's origin (or destination) is occasionally listed as "Queen's Hospital", Cork. As no institution of that name existed in the city, this is clearly the "Certified" hospital - especially since entries of this type occur only during the limited period of the legislation. Further, the two female staff in the new institution - Nurse Riordan and the Matron Mrs. Walsh (or Welsh) are variously described in the Registers as recommending new penitents from the "Lock Hospital" and the "Queen's Hospital" - evidence that the names were interchangeable and the establishments the same.

Thus in June 1874, Mrs. Walsh (sic) of the "Queen's Hospital" Cork, recommended Anna Gamson, aged 25, to the Good Shepherd in Limerick. The woman had already been an inmate of the Asylum in Cork, and in less than a year was expelled from the Limerick Refuge for "bad conduct".[20] Three years previously in his evidence to the Royal Commission, Rev. Maguire had described Mrs. "Welch" as the Matron of the new Lock hospital - and "more instrumental" in bringing about these women's reform, than anyone he knew.[21] In August 1876 Catherine Sullivan, a 26 year old prostitute from Tralee, County Kerry was sent to the Cork Good Shepherd by Rev. O'Driscoll, the local prison chaplain. She was obviously diseased, as in the following year she "left for the Queen's hospital". After treatment she returned to the Home, and later went to her friends in America.[22] Twenty-one year old Mrs. Ellen Sheahan, from Macroom, County Cork, was another prostitute found to be diseased after entering the Home. Having been admitted to the Cork Good Shepherd in May 1879, she too, was sent to the "Queen's hospital" five months later. She did not return.[23]

Shortly afterwards, in December 1880, Kate Murry, a 22 year old prostitute from Queenstown was recommended to the Cork

---

20 Limerick Register of Penitents, 5 June 1874.
21 *Royal Commission, op. cit.*, 6 May 1871.
22 Cork Register of Penitents, 4 August 1876.
23 *Ibid.*, 19 May 1879.

Good Shepherd by Nurse Riordan at the "Queen's Hospital" in the City. She was later sent to the Good Shepherd in Bristol "on account of particular friendships".[24] Six years later, Julia Coughlan, aged 20, whose parents lived at Barrack Street, Cork, was also sent to the Refuge by Nurse Riordan, who was now, however, described as being at the "Lock Hospital" in the City. The girl was taken to London by her sister shortly afterwards.[25] These examples demonstrate not only that the prostitutes thought of themselves as "Queen's women", but that others did too. In recording a term used by the officers of the institution, or by the newly admitted penitents, the nuns were repeating what was clearly a common name.

Following the Enquiry, and the Cork Chaplain's emphatic denial that the term had ever been in use, reference in the Penitents' Register to the "Queen's Hospital" abruptly ceased. This was five years before the legislation was repealed.

In spite of the Repeal victory (or possibly because of it) the women themselves were probably resentful - particularly of those priests who had loudly upheld the legislation, and been most active in consigning "the scum", as Rev. Maguire described them, to the Magdalen Home. We have seen that many of these prostitutes, having undergone treatment for venereal disease, were conveyed direct from the hospital to the Good Shepherd Asylum - their "conversion" by Rev. Reed and his successors having taken place while they were confined, intimidated and sick. Indeed, it was his confidence that the women could be "worked on", while in this melancholy state, that had encouraged Bishop Delaney to press for the new Penitentiary in the first place.

With the Repeal of the legislation, the continued confinement of any such women in the Good Shepherd no longer seemed justified. More important - now that the hospital was closed and the Acts and their supporters fallen into disrepute - the women were less of an easy target. No longer harassed by the special C.D. Constables, and freed from the prison-like wards, they were less accessible, less docile and less amenable to the threats and cajolings of the priests. It is likely that from this period, the proportion of prostitutes entering the Good Shepherds sharply declined - and that other classes of "the fallen", such as

---

24 *Ibid.*, 8 December 1880.
25 *Ibid.*, 25 May 1886.

unmarried mothers, women of doubtful chastity and bold, "simple" or abused girls, were increasingly targeted for reform.

Yet, though of long-term significance for Irish society - the effects of such attitudes and practice were to reach far into the twentieth century and claim alternative victims for rescue - the changing composition of those entering the Homes was not the most immediate outcome of the Certified Hospital's closure. More important initially, was the fact that in Cork, the Good Shepherd Monastery itself felt under threat. It was clearly feared that attempts might be made to rescue the rescued - to restore to society those women who were "saved". Encouraged, perhaps, by the Abolitionists, emboldened by their new status, and embittered by the conduct of the priests, it seems evident that some prostitutes urged the release of those still in the Asylum, and they were not without support.

Fears that the Home would be infiltrated, undermined by bogus penitents, who, once admitted, would persuade others to abscond, were perhaps excessive. Few prostitutes, after all, would have relished the prospect of entering, however briefly, such an appalling institution, which had swallowed up so many of their kind. Yet such alarms, however exaggerated, were not entirely groundless. Similar schemes had shaken other Refuges, and at some time during their history, each of the Irish Good Shepherds was to expel new admissions for "enticing others to leave". The Limerick Register for 1876, for example, records that Mary Hennesy, who had been in the Home for only five months, "escaped over the wall with two young penitents";[26] and in the following year Sarah Russell aged 30, after 5 weeks in the Home:

> "was sent out for making a plan to go over the wall with some young penitents. Had been in our Asylum before."[27]

Something of the kind occurred in Cork, in 1888. The Register of Penitents records that in April 1882, nineteen year old Margaret Hartigan, originally from Limerick, was admitted, for the second time, to the Cork Home. Six years later, (July 1888) the following comment was added in red ink:

---

26 Limerick Register of Penitents, 8 July 1876.
27 *Ibid.*, 7 March 1877. Sarah Russell had been admitted to the Home in April in the previous year, but had left "after a short time."

"Expelled for trying to induce children to run away from the Asylum".[28]

The Annals for 1889 provide further information - unfortunately, lacking in detail:

"We have long felt the want of a separate house to receive our penitents on their entrance, and as our holy rule expressly desires it we were most anxious for it. From circumstances that occurred in the City, our [new] Bishop was deeply interested in having some place provided where penitents on their entrance could be cut off from communication with those within, knowing that means would be taken to procure the departure of some among them at the time. Having no place of this kind, we were obliged to refuse applicants for admission, and this made our dear Mother more and more anxious to provide for the future."[29]

Probationary Wards, limiting the unsettling influence of new arrivals and testing their fitness for reform, were by now a common feature of many English Refuges; and Mother St. Euphrasia had recommended their use years earlier, to prevent "the wolf entering the fold". The prospect of admitting women whose sole intention was to induce others to leave was now so alarming, that in future all newcomers were to be isolated from the rest of the class.

Shortly afterwards, the Cork Convent's latest benefactor, Mr. Brown, made another timely visit to the Home, and donated £400 for the new scheme. Although the estimates turned out to be £540, Mother Devereux "trusting to Divine Providence" to make up the difference, authorised the work.[30] The Probationary Unit - a chilling dormitory containing washing facilities, a nun's cell and what appears to be a "solitary" room - was built at first-floor level. Situated at the back of the penitents' building, it was linked to a staircase in the main block:

28 Cork Register of Penitents, 18 April 1882.
29 Cork Annals, 1889. It is quite possible that the alarm was due to some other cause. External factors such as Race Week, for example (which the Managers of the York Penitentiary dreaded) were capable of depleting a Refuge; and according to Mr. Curtis, who as well as being Surgeon to the Government Lock Hospital, was visiting physician to the Protestant Refuge in Cork, "I remember the time when, if a ship or a regiment came into Queenstown, and a letter was thrown over the wall of that refuge, they would all be out of it in 24 hours." *Select Committee, op. cit.*, 20 June 1882.
30 Cork Annals, 1889.

"by means of a [covered] bridge so that if serious illness at any time came on or that any other cause made a separation of the Penitents desirable, the object could be easily attained."[31]

At the time of the Home's closure in the early nineteen-nineties, when only a few elderly women inhabited the vast penitentiary buildings, this part of the Magdalen Asylum had been unused for years.

Within a few months of his latest donation, Mr. Brown was on his deathbed and was visited by Father Sheehy, Chaplain to the Home:

"He asked, almost in a whisper, 'How much does Rev. Mother want for the new House?' and on Father Sheehy's replying £140, he told him to go to his desk and bring him his pocket book ... and with trembling fingers the poor old man took out £140 which it contained."[32]

A further glimpse of Mother Devereux's character appears in the Annals for 1892, by which time she had been Superior of the Foundation for almost sixteen years. The irony of a notorious brothel-keeper providing the Convent with funds, possibly accounts for the odd behaviour of the Superior of the Home.

"Three letters came which caused no little excitement. Our dear Mother seemed delighted when showing a cheque which came in one, and the Sisters present were pleased, but could not account for the great pleasure it caused. She threw it aside then and said with contempt 'Ten pounds. See this.' - Then showed an Attorney's letter announcing that a Miss Lack (?) of Fermoy, of whom we had never heard, had died 14 years ago, and desired that at her sister's death, which now took place, a portion of her property should come to us. This was to realise over £300. All were really glad and attributed the good news to St. Joseph, to our Lady of Perpetual Succour, etc., but our dear Mother cut them short by treating the letter with disdain, saying 'Three hundred pounds. What is three hundred pounds, only fit to be thrown over the House.' All looked at her in amazement and then, taking up another letter she said, 'Read this.' It was from

---

31 *Ibid.*
32 *Ibid.*

Rev. Fr. O'Flynn, saying that Miss Preston, whose death had been long expected, had died leaving us the "inconsiderable" sum of £2,400. Were those not three remarkable letters by the same post. Miss Preston had formerly led an evil life and been the cause of leading many astray by keeping a house for evil purposes. Grace touched her heart and she became truly penitent. Having consulted Fr. O'Flynn as to the disposal of her means, he told her that in reparation for the past, she was to bequeath her ill-gotten money to our Magdelene Asylum, for the benefit of similar cases to those she had once injured."[33]

It has been noted that penitents who left English Refuges "unsatisfactorily" and before their training was complete, were rarely re-admitted. A further entry for 1892 indicates that the new Probationary Unit - "The Home of the Sacred Heart" was run on much less rigid lines. Together with evidence from the Registers, of women returning again and again, this quotation demonstrates the extraordinary tolerance of the Good Shepherd Sisters in this respect:

"One penitent died this year. She had been frequently admitted and was always most restless, idle and unsatisfactory. She was found to be only making a convenience of the House when-ever she required a few days rest, and was given to understand that she would not be again received, having refused to leave "The Home of the Sacred Heart" to enter the class. Everything that could be said and done to retain her was resorted to, but in vain - she had had her few days rest in the Home of the Sacred Heart and wanted nothing more, so departed. Some months afterwards as our Chaplain was hearing confessions about 9 o'clock, Julia knocked at the door of his Confessional in the North Cathedral and asked for a note which would obtain her re-admission, as she said that otherwise, she had no chance of being received. He tore a leaf from his pocket book and wrote, 'Dear Sister, please admit bearer, T.D.' She was allowed to enter the Home of the Sacred Heart, but little hope was entertained that she would be willing to go to class, or sincerely think of forsaking the path of evil in which she had wandered for many years. However, after a few days a cough commenced, which increased to such a degree that she was glad to go to the infirmary, and very soon it was found that consumption was setting in. Grace at length touched her heart, and her

33 *Ibid.*, April 1892.

repentance, though at the eleventh hour, was a truly sincere one ... she had been brought up in an orphanage under the care of Nuns, and in her last illness it was strange how vividly the teachings and impressions of her early days returned and seemed completely to efface from her memory the dark days of her sin. Her patience, humility and gratitude were extreme ... when the Infirmarian was wiping the sweat of death from her brow, she said, 'Leave it. Our Lord sweat blood for me and how I have offended Him.' She died in agony, while singing hymns."[34]

Deathbed scenes abound in Victorian opera and fiction - their creators lingering shamelessly round the dying and deceased. In the diaries, correspondence and biographies of the period too, a similar absorption is apparent, the reader being relentlessly exposed to painful details of illness and death. It is in Rescue literature, however, that the art is most developed, with tragic sinkings and paroxysms of remorse as death approaches, being fulsomely portrayed. Even the brief Annual Reports wallow in such pathos, but the fact that cases are anonymous, and designed to bring in funds, reduces their appeal. Material not intended for publication is generally more convincing, and, conventions of the period apart, it is clear from these sources, that many penitents, like "Julia", ended their lives in an agony of suffering and guilt.

But was there an end to this atonement? Having once been rescued from a life of sin, how much penance was the reclaimed prostitute, the unmarried mother, or the victim of incest, love or rape, required to perform? Was it, in fact, a sentence which, far from rehabilitating the sinner, condemned her to a lifetime of remorse? The histories of many of the women in this study indicate that for them, the latter was the case.

The Annals record that in May 1884, for example, "Vincent", a Consecrated penitent, died in the Home. Ten years earlier, "whilst in the midst of her career of sin, and in a half intoxicated state" she had thrown herself into the river. She was dragged out by the Watchman and some passers by, who took her almost lifeless body to the City's North Infirmary. Eventually, the doctors revived her and she allowed herself to be taken to the Good Shepherd, "for a few days", without any idea of remaining. She spent the rest of her life in the institution, tending the sick in the Infirmary, until she herself fell ill, and "suffered much" for

---

34 *Ibid.*, 1892.

many months.[35] The Register shows that before her conversion and new identity this unhappy woman was 26 year old Ellen Forde, of Cork. After three years in the Home she became a Consecrate, and when she was dying in 1883, she "got the Silver Cross"[36]

Occasionally, even Consecrated penitents, and hopeful cases like the "Children of Mary" (awarded a medal for good conduct) were repelled by such a prospect, and left the institution. If, chastened and defeated, they sought re-admission, they seldom recovered their former privileged state. A girl given the name "Clotilde", for example, who died in 1888, had spent some years in the House. Although she became a Child of Mary, she left the Asylum, returned to her "evil life", and became "steeped" in crime - without, however, relinquishing her medal, which she "many times smuggled into prison". Though not very penitent, she eventually re-entered the Home, and "yielding to an impulse of grace" made a confession. Two days later, a sudden illness caused her death.[37]

The Register shows that this young woman was Margaret Connell, one of Rev. Shinkwin's celebrated band of converts, who had required hospital treatment in 1876, only three months after entering the Home. Since that date, she had been in and out of the Refuge at least five times. At the time of her death in 1888, she was about 30 years old.[38]

Another such penitent was "Velagi of the Dolours", who died in 1905. She had been admitted:

> "about 27 years ago. After some time she became a Child of Mary and was going on very well until induced by some friends to go out again. Soon she fell away into the greatest disorders and was put into prison. Against her will she was brought back to us, and for a long time struggled hard against pressing temptations. At last grace triumphed".

She worked until a week before her death in hospital. Her remains were brought back to the Asylum, and buried in the communal penitents' plot.[39]

---

35 *Ibid.*, May 1884.
36 Cork Register of Penitents, 20 April 1875.
37 Cork Annals, 1888.
38 Cork Register of Penitents, 26 June 1876.
39 Cork Annals, 1905.

Another Consecrate, "Liguri of the Dolours", had formerly been one of that debased band of prostitutes who, like the "wrens" of The Curragh and the tramping women of Aldershot, slept rough on the outskirts of a military camp. At the time of her death in July 1913, the Annals recorded:

> "She was brought to us from the jail in 1877. She lived in the bush [Queenstown] for thirteen years and during that time never slept under the roof of a house except the jail. She was called the Queen of the Bush. One day she saw a companion of hers fall over a cliff she ran at once for the priest and met him coming to say mass for the nuns and told him what had happened and asked him to come with her to the place. He said he was going to say Mass for the Nuns. "What nuns" she said. "The nuns can do without a Mass, but come with me to a damned soul." He did so and got the girl removed to the hospital. When she recovered she came to us and became one of the best penitents we ever had. Liguri would often say to the Mistress of Penitents when speaking of that child "Mother, you watched her well but I did more. I saved her damned soul for you." She became a consecrated penitent and worked hard for years until her health declined and she was confined to the Infirmary, though wheeled into Mass."[40]

This woman was probably Margaret Twoomey, who at the age of forty, in July 1877, was referred to the Cork Asylum by Rev. O'Driscoll, the prison chaplain.[41]

Unlike the smaller Refuges and Homes, whose laundries were modest affairs, the establishment at Cork became a model of its kind. At this time, however, before the introduction of new machinery, and pending extensions and alterations to the building itself, an increasing volume of work was overwhelming even those penitents most anxious to atone. The tedium of the work and the

---

40 *Ibid.*, 1913.
41 Cork Register of Penitents, 22 July 1877.
    During the 4 year period 1870-1873, seven prostitutes whose residence was "The Bush, Queenstown" were admitted to the workhouse in Cork. One of these, 40 year old Mary Donovan, who entered in December 1871, remained for almost ten years.
    In his evidence to the Select Committee in 1882, Mr. Curtis stated that before the application of the Acts, some thirty women lived in the "Bush" - a place in Queenstown "where there are trees and furze, a wild space, overhanging the shore." According to this witness, had it not been for the compulsory examinations and "civilising" influences of the Contagious Diseases legislation, these women would have remained "like animals" hidden in the dens in which they lived and died. *Op. cit.*, 20 June 1882.

long hours of labour, aggravated by the women's total confinement to the institution and lack of stimulation or change, remained constant. But investment in equipment eventually led to improved capacity, making the success of the laundry reasonably secure. Starching and ironing were particularly labour-intensive and exhausting, and in 1889 Mother Devereux bought a machine "which irons and glazes most beautifully the fronts of thirty dozen shirts per day". This was followed by two smaller machines, a collar ironer and a washer, all worked and heated by gas. The laundry on working days was said to be quite a "curiosity", and the work so beautifully accomplished that a further increase in orders was continually going on.

Soon afterwards, considerable improvements were made to the laundry itself – to allow for the huge increase in the supply of work, and a new system of starching. The whole place was tiled with stable brick "so dry and comfortable underfoot which is a great advantage to our poor Penitents".

Expansion continued, and in 1892 an extension was built to house a new packing room - "now absolutely necessary", and above this, additional cells for nuns. The ironing room, too, was enlarged. In spite of the good will of the penitents, however, who laboured relentlessly and were "always praying for an increase of work", these expensive improvements built up a heavy debt.[42]

Early in 1895 the nuns were appalled to hear that the Home Secretary, Mr. Asquith, had introduced a Bill to put Convent Laundries within the provisions of the recent Factory and Workshop Act. The proposed legislation (intended to regulate not just Convent laundries but "any laundry carried out by way of trade, or for the purpose of gain") would not only regulate the hours of work, recreation and meal times of the penitents, but would ensure safety and sanitary provisions, and allow Government Officials to inspect the premises and interview the women (not in the presence of the nuns) whenever they chose. Even worse, was the rumour that:

"All inmates of Laundries were to have a free day every week to go out and enjoy themselves. What a pleasant prospect for the Sisters in charge of the Penitents!!"

---

42 Cork Annals, 1889-92.

As the Bill had already passed its Second Reading, Mother Devereux lost no time in writing to Asquith, pointing out the dangers involved in exposing the penitents to such "unnecessary intrusions". She stressed that the laundries were established, not for the gain of the nuns, but for the support of the inmates undergoing reform; and wrote letters to all the Irish M.Ps. (including Mr. Sexton, the Leader of the Irish Party), asking them to oppose the Act. Similar pressure from other institutions led to an adjournment for further enquiry, together with the suggestion that the investigations might be more acceptable, if carried out by a Committee of Ladies appointed by the Government. Far from mollifying the Act's opponents, this proposal increased their dismay, with one Bishop declaring - and being quoted with approval in the Annals - that it would be bad enough to subject the nuns to the investigations of Government Officials, but not so evil as sending a "bevy of women to pry into their affairs".[43] Such comment reveals how removed from their own sex these nuns were - particularly in the eyes of the Church. Apprehensions concerning Government interference in discipline and control, however, were the most alarming, since reduced surveillance and increased freedom for the penitents, endangered the very essence of Rescue Work. These fears mobilised diverse resistance; and in the flurry of letters, pamphlets and petitions that ensued, old rivalries and distinctions were, for once, ignored.*

In the event such laundries were exempted from the Act - opposition proving so successful that an amendment to the Bill excluded all "inmates of an Institution conducted in good faith for religious or charitable purposes." The Bill became law in July 1895 - a shameful decision which, for over half a century left inmates of Convent Magdalen Asylums unprotected, laundry conditions unregulated, and hours of work subject to no restraint. But the threat of Government intervention continued, and was not without effect. In the Cork Refuge further improvements were rapidly made to the laundry equipment and buildings –

---

43 *Ibid.*, 1895.

* This solidarity did not last for long. Four years later (when the threat of Government Inspection re-emerged) it was lamented at the English Reformatory and Refuge Union Annual Conference of Managers: "When the question was fought before, we had amongst our supporters the Roman Catholics. They objected *in toto* to anybody going into their places, and the result was they fought this tooth and nail."

some of which (particularly safety precautions) being alarmingly overdue. For example, it was not until a fire broke out in the ironing room, early in 1896, that fire hoses were installed; and only after a second, potentially disastrous fire a few weeks later (in rooms under the Industrial School dormitories!) was it considered necessary to build a fire escape. A short time later (1897) both the ironing room and the washhouse were enlarged and refurbished, and a small wing was added to house the new gas engine and boilers. These improvements, belatedly carried out, were designed not so much to enhance penitents' lives (as the Bill itself would clearly have done); but to ward off Government intervention, and to cope with increasing flows of work. This was particularly the case with the new arrangements for the drying room. For years conditions in this workplace must have been intolerable, but now, new equipment dispersed steam – moistening and cooling the atmosphere.[44]

These extensive alterations were financed in part (though a large debt remained) by a Grand Bazaar, the preparations for which took several months. Religious intolerance limited the outcome. Cork's Lord Mayor, having attended the Installation of the Protestant Bishop, was denounced from the pulpits. So offended were many of the city's Protestants, that they refused to assist in the Gala, and only £1,600 was raised. The Bazaar occasioned a curious incident which lent some excitement to the inmates' dreary lives. On the last morning of the Fete, it was discovered that intruders had broken into the new packing room the night before and stolen some of the laundry awaiting delivery.

> "The robbers had left in the middle of the packing room their very soiled linen and socks, which they had replaced by the fine underwear and silken hose of some very stylish officers, whose parcels had been carefully arranged on the previous evening. One of the penitents indignantly took a sweeping brush and swept the clothes away for burning, exclaiming, 'tis many a day indeed since you made acquaintance with a wash tub.'"

More ominous, in view of the two near-disastrous fires which had so recently occurred, "matches were strewn about in all directions", clothes were displaced and the outer bars of the

---

44 Cork Annals, 1895-97.

window were bent. The Industrial School kitchen too, had been robbed of pieces of bacon. Several of the missing articles were later found in a pawn shop, and on the evidence of two penitents who identified the stolen goods, two men (one a soldier and one a returned convict) were imprisoned respectively, for one and a half and for two years.[45]

Opposition to the proposed Factory and Workshops Act had not been limited to the Good Shepherd or any other Convent Asylums, though the scale of their operations and the fact that they admitted inmates for life, made them particularly sensitive to change. The prospect of Government regulation (and in particular, the notion of inmates' rights) had alarmed too, the hundreds of Protestant Penitentiaries in England, many of whose laundries were well below envisaged standards, and whose finances ruled out the possibility of major reform. It was recognised that the proposed legislation spelt the closure of many of the smaller, vulnerable Homes; and that even those surviving, would lose much of their former autonomy. The Reformatory and Refuge Union summed up the bitter feelings of betrayal provoked by the new proposals:

"... The great work of reformation - of reclaiming the moral and spiritual wastes, and changing the characters of those who belong to the "dangerous" elements in society into useful, law-abiding, respectable citizens - this work has been done voluntarily by Christian and Philanthropic men and women. The State and the community at large have reaped all the advantages resulting from these voluntary labours, and it has not cost them one penny ... many tens of thousands have been reclaimed. The gain to society is incalculable; for every vicious person thus saved would have continued to prey upon society, and many would eventually have been a charge upon the nation for support in prisons or workhouses ... And what does the State now propose to do? Because certain commercial and speculative undertakings have been brought under the inspection of the "Factory and Workshop Act", it is now proposed that all Christian and Philanthropic Institutions, where a like industry is being carried on as part of the discipline and training of the inmates shall be also placed under similar inspection ... The State may now show its appreciation of the past voluntary services of these Institutions (1) by recognising

---

45 *Ibid.*, 1897.

that [they] are altogether distinct and separate from purely trade enterprises. (2) By legislation, outside of the Factory and Workshop Act; so as to ensure that Inmates, while being industrially reclaimed, are safeguarded from insanitation and other abuses, but without in any way interfering with the needful facilities for promoting their moral and religious welfare."[46]

The success with which the proposed Bill had been resisted was undoubtedly a triumph for the Homes; but many of them, in common with the Good Shepherd in Cork, were jolted into improving working conditions. The Albion Hill Home in Brighton, for example (established in 1854 as the Brighton Home for Penitents) noted in its *Annual Report* for 1896:

> "The Committee are indebted to the active and successful efforts of the Reformatory and Refuge Union in petitioning the Government to free charitable institutions from the restrictions of the new Factory Bill, but recognise the importance of conforming, as much as possible to its requirements. Every endeavour is being made not to overtax the energies of the girls, and it is noticeable that the girls generally complain after leaving the Home, of the much heavier work in domestic service."[47]

Though some had been established earlier, the vast majority of Magdalen Asylums were set up in the heyday of Rescue Work - the middle decades of the nineteenth century when conditions for the poor were at their worst. Indeed, they were so appalling, that the short-comings of Refuges were regarded by comparison (and mindful of that class of women for whom they were intended) as of little account. In the 1830s the new Poor Law legislation, devised to deter all but the destitute from applying for relief, had designedly made conditions in workhouses "less eligible" or more repellent, than those outside. Refuges, of course, wished to attract, rather than deter admissions, but a similar attitude prevailed. To indulge these sinners' comfort would, it was feared, not so much ensure their repentance, as reward their vice. At the very beginning of the Rescue Movement, the London Female Penitentiary, for example (established in 1807) had found it necessary to reassure subscribers that prostitution was not encouraged by the establishment of Magdalen Asylums. It was pointed out that no

---

46 *Notes on Work Amongst the Fallen*, No. 76., November, 1905.
47 Forty-first *Annual Report* of the Albion Hill Home, 1896.

sane female would plunge into such infamy on the mere prospect of admission to a penitentiary - where she would be confined to constant labour, for a limited time. Further, once dismissed, she would never be re-admitted.[48]

A number of Homes such as the New Ross Good Shepherd - where, as we have seen, early conditions were appalling - were founded irresponsibly, with a callous disregard for the unfortunate women in their care. They sprang up without funds, neglectful even of those who ran them, and with inmates being overworked, under-fed and inadequately housed.*

In spite of improved conditions in many Refuges following the Factory Bill debate, some Homes continued as they started - overcrowded and unhealthy, with an unprotected workforce, laundries that were primitive and practices unsafe. And no matter how updated their machinery, many of the institutions clung to the harsh, outdated rules of their founders, stubbornly resisting any calls for change.

It was suggested in an earlier Chapter that strong, docile women, useful in the laundries, were most under pressure to remain - becoming, as their penance lengthened, and their chances of leaving grew dim, dull drudges, conditioned to their lot. While critical, Maddison, (referring chiefly to short-term Refuges in which the tendency had less impact) clearly regarded the policy as short-sighted, rather than wrong:

"A very strong prejudice exists, especially among the younger girls, against going to a Home. For the most part this prejudice is unfounded, girls who have entered Homes with no real intention to reform have proved failures, and after leaving the Homes, have circulated an evil report concerning them - they have blackened the homes to whiten themselves ... On the other hand, instances are on record of unwise and inconsiderate treatment of girls ... and those mistakes have been magnified by bad women ... The girls know well that in many instances the Homes are dependent upon them for their very existence - the girls are wanted and sometimes

---

48 Fifth *Annual Report of the London Female Penitentiary*, 1812.
* This had apparently been the case in the Mother House itself, where, "the hardships of the Novitiate may be gathered from a letter written by a novice, in no spirit of complaint, but rather of rejoicing, not long after she had received the habit. 'In the refectory the only dish provided for us was cabbage, moistened with a little vinegar, and at midday some very indifferent soup. We never had a fire in the Novitiate; we used to go out in the snow, and stamp our feet to get a little warmth into them.'" A. M. Clarke, *op. cit.*, p.161.

sought with a view to making two ends meet. Strong girls who can do laundry work are readily admitted, and given plenty of work to do - perhaps more than is desirable; while poor, weakly girls, who require rest, nourishment, and a lengthened period of careful treatment before they can do hard work, are rejected."[49]

This increasing proportion of strong, but often simple-minded cases retained in the Homes, reflects the failure of the Female Penitentiary Movement as a whole. It supports too, Michael McCarthy's contention, quoted at the beginning of this Chapter, that inmates were admitted and discouraged from leaving, not so much to reduce immorality as to maintain the nuns' laundries. These women were rarely common prostitutes (the avowed object of concern) nor were they capable of profiting from the training they received. They may have worked well in the laundries, but freed from the discipline of the Homes, they were frequently unable to cope. This problem haunted Rescue Workers in the later part of the period, since, as noted earlier, it was estimated by the turn of the century, that 30 per cent of those applying to Penitentiaries were of the feeble-minded class. Some institutions were prepared to admit only one in five women of this type, while others refused to admit them at all, believing that as such large numbers were now of this category, they should be rounded up and placed in specially designated Homes.[50] Above all, Refuges were daunted by the prospect of "placing" such girls. They feared sending them to situations which, though tempting, were beyond their limited grasp. All too frequently such cases ended in disaster, with a loss of public confidence, and a reluctance to take on women from the Homes. There is no doubt too, that many of this category who were found employment, were shamelessly exploited by the families for whom they worked.

The Good Shepherd Sisters had fewer reservations about such women, who, it was hoped, were destined not for outside

---

49 Maddison, *op. cit.*, pp. 104-5.
50 For example, the Lady Superintendent of the Southfield Long Home, Westbury-on-Trym, noted in 1914, that in the Laundry:
"A special difficulty of the past year has been that many of the senior girls are of weak character and limited mental power. As a consequence, the new comers .... instead of being restrained by the elders, they have followed a bad lead, and many troubles have arisen accordingly. The passing of the 'Mental Deficiency Act' should prevent such things from occurring in the future; as we do not propose to receive any girls who come under the Act." *Bristol Female Penitentiary Report for 1914*, p.5.
See also, *York Female Penitentiary Annual Report, 1905*; and *Notes on Work Amongst the Fallen* pamphlets in this period.

occupation, but for life within the Homes. Much of the heavy, unskilled labour was increasingly performed by them; while continuity was provided by those who, trained and closely supervised, could get through vast amounts of work. Even for the Good Shepherds, however, an increased proportion of the feeble-minded had its drawbacks. Standards must have suffered, and nuns in charge of laundries (where high quality work was demanded) were subject to additional strains. In the absence of classification the increasing numbers of those with weak intellects had further repercussions. Their growing presence must have adversely affected more hopeful cases - who, for their part, were doubtless deterred from entering or remaining in Homes containing high proportions of this type.

By 1911 the financial difficulties of the Cork Foundation (there was now a debt of at least £10,000, with large interest repayments) led to a Public Appeal. Commentary in the local press indicates that even with the passing of the Victorian era, there was little change in Irish society's attitude to the "social evil". The diminishing source of income from the Industrial School - built to accommodate 170 children and now containing less than half that number - together with the fact that other laundries in Cork were proving "sadly" competitive, raised the spectre of the Convent's closure:

> "Can anyone contemplate the possibility of such a Refuge being closed, with no door open to the wretched and homeless, with no hope of rescuing them from the temptations of their lot and the thraldom of their passions, with no-one to care for them, to watch them, to tend them, to wean them away from themselves, to provide them with work which would save them from the curse of idleness, to hold up before them the mirror of self-sacrificing lives and spotless chastity, but on the contrary to allow them to roam the dark streets, pollute the moral atmosphere and pass their lives in the haunts of vice until the prison portals or the dark grave closes over them? Would any Corkman wish this to take place?"

Apparently not - but Cork's enthusiasm was clearly on the wane. It was noted with regret, that the Appeal's Public Meeting had raised only £1,000; and that a previous generation of Corkmen had, for the setting up of the Home, subscribed ten times that sum in a single day.[51] It would seem in fact, that by the end of the

---

51 Newspaper cutting fixed in the Cork Annals.

period, the Cork Asylum could no longer rely on the generosity of the general public. The following inscription appears on a small building set between the Community's Industrial School and the Sisters' Burial Ground:

> "This bakehouse was erected through the generosity of Countess Murphy to help this Institution at a period of great need. A.D. 1911." *

After hours of fatiguing labour and dreary silence, recreation might have cheered the inmates and afforded some relief. The chapter devoted to this topic in the Foundress' Rules, however, suggests that even in their lighter moments, this was not the case. For again, the detection and prevention of evil was uppermost in the mind of the Foundress, who stressed that it was in the recreations that the Demon lay in wait for the children, to "tempt them to do wrong":

> "The hours of recreation are those which require most watchfulness on the part of the Mistresses. It is generally during recreation that evil projects are formed, bad friendships commenced, that the children lead each other astray by conversations contrary to morals and against authority, by words equally fatal to those who pronounce them and those who hear them. Who can tell the ravages produced in souls by bad conversations? The worst is that these disorders are sometimes caused by those we watch least, because they have gained our confidence."[52]

Accordingly, Mistresses should not allow themselves to be "surrounded" during recreation, nor prevented by one group that claimed their attention, from watching another. In particular, "children" seeking each other out, or keeping apart from their companions so that their conversations might not be heard, must be closely observed. These, rather than the boisterous ones, were those who committed sin.

Mistresses performing surveillance duty were not to converse together, but to disperse - "so that the children be, and feel they

---

* This bakehouse (which provided bread for the whole community of approximately 400 women and children at this time) did not employ the penitents, but some of the Monastery's older Industrial School children. For an account of work in this unit in the mid-twentieth century, see Matley, *op. cit.*, p.117. According to this source, 220 loaves were made daily, 6 days a week.

52 *Rules for the Direction of the Classes, op. cit.*, p.132.

are, watched". And if rain confined them indoors, penitents were to be employed during recreation at some household work. Even then, normal conversations were forbidden. Each "child" was to remain in her place and "turned towards the Mistress who should not tolerate whispering".[53]

No woman, then, was to have a moment's privacy or relaxation. For every minute of every day - perhaps for the rest of her life - her conduct was regulated and her every movement watched. It is, of course, impossible to know how closely the instructions of the Foundress were followed; but in a highly authoritarian structure like the Good Shepherd, it is unlikely that individual Convents were allowed to relax the Rules. Evidence from the Annals, together with the chilling testimonies of women detained in this Order's Magdalen Asylums and Industrial Schools during the 1940s, 50s and 60s suggests that the contrary was the case, and that if anything, the Irish Sisters grew harsher in their treatment of the inmates, than even the Institute required.

It was recommended in the Rules that during recreation, attempts should be made to divert the "sad thoughts" of the penitents. Innocent amusements such as organised games and rounds, were acceptable pastimes, though Mistresses were warned that even songs, unless carefully selected, could be more dangerous than conversations. "Pious canticles" were considered most effective in bringing the children back to a "holy joy". Running and dominoes, and scenes from Sacred History, arranged as dramatic pieces, were also approved entertainments. Feast days such as New Year's Day, should be marked by a partial suspension of work, and extraordinary amusements, such as a Magic Lantern and playing shop, should, on special occasions, be allowed. It is easy to forget that it is women, not juveniles, who are here being discussed.

The Annals of the Irish Houses contain few references to recreation - though one occurs in 1891, when, to mark the visit of the Mother Prioress of Belfast, the Bishop together with a number of priests said Mass at the Cork Convent, and afterwards visited the classes. He approved the plays and other innocent amusements for the penitents. A further reference to their pastimes occurs in a detailed case history from 1907. The account

---

53 *Ibid.*, p.38.

indicates, incidentally, that by that time (the "Government" Hospital having now been closed for almost twenty years) venereal disease was being treated in the Home:

In May that year "Mary Anastasia", a consecrated penitent died:

"She came to us from the jail at 16 years of age in 1878 - a bright talented girl but very impertinent - so much so that we were obliged to send her away to her Aunt. She came back next day and persevered for years, until she became a Child of Mary. She was then sent to Canada, where after a short time she became very delicate and came home to us again - she was received with open arms. In about a year she recovered her health and gave her life to God - begged permission to join the Consecrated and look on this House as her home and became a most useful child in the Laundry, lace-work, and embroidery, which she learned easily and taught to others. She was very clever at painting, illuminating and decorating, specimens of which can be seen through the House. She used to recite beautifully and always took the principal parts in plays, till her health broke down. It was a great trial for her to be no longer able to work for the House. She was attacked with a most painful and humiliating disease, which she bore with heroic patience ... scarcely able to speak toward the end."[54]

The Register reveals that she was Maria Carroll, who had been recommended to the Home by the prison Chaplain 30 years before. In 1880 she had been sent to Montreal.[55]

It was noted in the previous Chapter that the Cork Convent was fronted by sloping lawns and stone terraces. These gardens were for the use of the nuns, the penitents being restricted in their recreation to a special enclosure at the side of the House. In 1902, a farm of eight acres, adjoining and overlooking the penitents' ground came up for auction - and the nuns, anxious that it might fall into undesirable hands, felt compelled to buy. The Sisters now used this area for their recreation, leaving the Terrace quite deserted.

As for the new grounds:

"On great feasts the Penitents and Industrial children in turn are taken there."[56]

---

54 Cork Annals, May 1907.
55 Cork Register of Penitents, 19 June 1877.
56 Cork Annals, 1902.

This was as close as they got to the outside world.

As has been noted, to ensure the continuance of long established practice it was precisely at this time that the Foundress' *Rules For the Direction of the Classes* were distributed for the guidance of each of the Order's nuns. Further English editions (one in 1943, for example) were brought out, and until the 1960s each Sister was required to read a Chapter of the book every day of her life. This hardly indicated change. From this source alone, it is clear that until the middle years of the twentieth century - and probably later - the penitent's life was all but intolerable.

Even more disturbing is the fact that the methods urged above were still in force beyond the mid-twentieth century, when basic attitudes remained the same. The following passage from an M.A. Education thesis, was written by a Good Shepherd Sister in 1961, and describes current practice in the Homes. By this time the women (no longer referred to as penitents, but as "emotionally disturbed") had progressed from being "children" to "girls". And the Good Shepherd Sister was no longer the First Mistress of Penitents or Dormitory Mistress, but the "Mother" of the Group. It is clear that these were cosmetic changes only. The Order's main concern - the detection and suppression of a specific "sin" - far from having diminished in the modern world was, if anything, more developed. The process was now, however, referred to as "mental hygiene".

"The following are the principles on which the rules for the supervision of the dormitories are based: silence to maintain order, and silence to prepare the girls for a good sleep. While in the dormitory, the Group Mother should stand where she can observe everything. She waits until all are asleep before she retires. Her room is off the dormitory and is locked. However, she has a slide in her door allowing her to observe the dormitory during the night. Now mechanical devices are also used, magnifying even the slightest noise ... In extremely difficult classes the Group Mothers train themselves to awaken two or three times during a night to check the dormitories ... A dim light must be kept burning at all times and it must always be possible to observe the washroom facilities ... During the day the dormitories are locked and no one may go to them without special permission ... because of certain types of disturbances, this area is one of the gravest concern."[57]

57 Dorothy J. Thompson, "The Psychology of the Good Shepherd Nuns in the Re-Education of the Emotionally Disturbed". (M.A. Thesis, University of St. Marys, Halifax, Canada, 1961), pp.44-45.

As late as the 1960s, then, the Order betrayed a morbid obsession with the sexuality of others - a disturbing preoccupation of the "virtuous", with vice.

Between 1872 and 1890 a total of 1,215 women and girls became inmates of the Cork Magdalen Asylum, some of them being admitted to the institution on more than one occasion. Table 20 shows the age at which these women were registered over the period - the youngest being 12 (two girls) and the oldest 60 (one woman). Eighty percent of admissions were under 30 years of age.

Table 21
Age on Admission: Cork Good Shepherd 1872-1890

Years	Total 1,215	Percent
12-19	353	29
20-29	615	51
30-39	153	13
40-49	57	5
50-59	16	1
60	1	.08
Not Given	20	2

For 108 women in the Cork Asylum (9 percent of the total) place of birth was not listed. Compared with the Order's other Homes (Limerick 48 percent, New Ross 50 percent and Waterford 40 per cent) an unusually large proportion of those for whom this information was recorded came from the city and county in which the Institution was built. 74 percent of inmates over the period could be classed as local. Non-Irish inmates were from England (11), Scotland (8) and Wales (5). One woman had been born in Malta.

Table 22
Birthplace of Cork Penitents: 1872-1890

	Total 1,107	Percent
Cork City	520	47
County Cork	294	27
Nearby Counties*	118	11
Other	150	14
Non-Irish	25	2

*Limerick, Tipperary and Waterford.

Table 22 shows how Cork penitents were admitted to the Magdalen Asylum over the period. The unusually high number of Prison and Lock Hospital referrals is a reflection of the Asylum's links with the Contagious Diseases Acts. Father Reed's personal "batch" (52 additional admissions of this category) are included in the recommendations made by Priests. Rev. Shinkwin was responsible for at least 22 of these referrals, and Rev. McCarthy, the Good Shepherd Chaplain, for at least 31. Unless closely connected with the Convents, priests are not necessarily recorded by name in the Registers.

Table 23
By Whom Recommended: Cork Good Shepherd
1872–1890

	Total 1,215	Percent
Own Accord	573	47
Priests	358	29
Prison	90	7
Other Nuns	44	4
Female Relatives	30	2
Miss Farrell (Lock H.)	25	2
Former Inmates	21	2
Good Shepherd Nuns	18	1
Ladies	11	0.9
Other	45	4

For 48 of the penitents in the Cork Asylum over the period, Reason for Leaving was not recorded. Of the remaining 1,167, practically half were described as leaving the Home of their own accord - almost the same proportion of inmates who had arrived in this way. Only 18 percent of penitents, however, both entered and left the Institution voluntarily.

Table 24
Reasons for Leaving: Cork Good Shepherd
1872–1890

	Total 1,167	Percent
Own Accord	564	48
Family/Friends	116	10
Hospital	91	8
Expelled	66	6
Left for Situation	60	5
Left for America	57	5
Died	51	4
Workhouse	36	3
Escaped	22	2
Lock Hospital	21	2
Other Mag. Asylums	20	2
Insane or Lunatic	10	1
Other	53	5

The above Table contains additional categories for penitents leaving. Five percent went to America, for example, 2 percent were admitted to the Lock Hospital, and a few of the women were sent to the Lunatic Asylum. Included in the category "Other Magdalen Asylums", are 5 referrals to Good Shepherd Homes in England, and 9 to Homes run by other Orders.

Two young inmates were allowed to leave the Asylum as they were discovered to be "not fit subjects for a Magdalen Home" - but whether this resulted from their extreme purity or depravity, is not disclosed.

For only approximately half the admissions in the period (653 women) was it possible to calculate length of stay in the Cork Asylum.* The average time spent in the Home by inmates for whom this information is available was 3.1 years. Fifty percent of the women, however, remained for less than one year.

---

* Date of admission and departure has to be recorded for this calculation. The latter information is frequently omitted in this source.

Table 25
Length of Stay in Cork Good Shepherd from 1872

	Total 653	Percent
Under 1 week	26	4.0
1 - 2 weeks	18	2.8
2 - 4 weeks	54	8.3
1 - 2 months	54	8.3
2 - 6 months	108	16.5
6 - 12 months	62	9.5
1 - 2 years	118	18.1
2 - 5 years	103	15.8
5 - 10 years	84	12.9
10 - 15 years	11	1.7
15 - 20 years	3	0.5
20 - 30 years	3	0.5
30 - 40 years	0	0
40 - 50 years	1	0.2
50 years +	8	1.2

Only 7 admissions over the period were Protestants, and two of these converted to Catholicism. Of those for whom the information was recorded (973 inmates) 44 percent were orphans and 35 percent had only one parent living. Thirty-five of the women (3 percent) were married and 4 others were widows.

For comparative purposes Table 26 gives the overall statistics for each of the Homes. It is apparent that girls admitted to the New Ross Asylum (over fifty percent of whom were "brought" or recommended by priests) were more likely to die in the Home or be detained for longer than those entering the other Irish Houses. Further, they were significantly less likely to have entered of their own free will. Rev. Maguire's confidence that girls would be sent to America or otherwise "procured situations" was clearly either misleading or misplaced. For three of the Homes only five percent of inmates departed in this way (and even then not necessarily through the efforts of the Sisters) while in the Waterford Asylum only one woman in a hundred left to take up a job.

Table 26
Overall Statistics

	Limerick 1848-78	Waterford 1842-1900	New Ross 1860-1900	Cork 1872-1890
Died in Home	7 %	8%	10%	4%
Average Stay	3.0 years	4.6 years	6.7 years	3.1 years
Ent. Vol.	43%	49%	22%	47%
Left Vol.	34%	63%	39%	48%
Rec. by Priest	41%	27%	51%	29%
Escaped	5%	1%	4%	2%
Situation	5%	1%	5%	5%
Age 12-19 on Admission	32%	27%	32%	29%

By the turn of the century the strict rules and close confinement that had always dominated the Penitentiary system were being relaxed in most English Refuges, few of which, in any case, had been as austere as the Good Shepherds and other Magdalen Asylums run by nuns. Small Protestant Homes had invariably made use of neighbouring churches for Sunday worship, so that penitents, even in the early years, were rarely completely withdrawn from the world.[58] Now, annual outings became a regular feature; with inmates from the York Female Penitentiary, for example, going to the seaside at Whitby, Scarborough or Filey; enjoying picnics and flower-picking expeditions on local farms; and having tea at Rowntree's Cocoa Works, or in the Bishopthorpe Palace grounds. Girls at a Home in Eastbourne were taken to the local picture house on special occasions, or on trips to Beachy Head; and the younger inmates of many Homes were encouraged to join the Girl Guides. In anticipation of their departure, inmates nearing the end of their stay were sent out

58 As early as 1814, for example, the First *Annual Report* of the Dublin Female Penitentiary, noted that Sunday worship was "private", while the Home was based in its temporary, Eccles Street accommodation. By the following year, however, the new premises were occupied, and arrangements were already being made for the women to attend public Sunday Services.

alone on errands; and in general there was a move towards a more normal, less institutionalised way of life.[59]

Such changes, apparent in most Homes and welcomed by contributors to Rescue literature in general, were highlighted in a brief history of the Movement, published by the London Female Preventive and Reformatory Institution in 1907. In contrast to the much more liberal, current practice, the harsh regime and discipline in earlier Homes was now criticised as being:

> "often very rigid, if not punitive. In [some] cases hair of the inmates was cut off, and a distinguishing garb had to be worn. Such Institutions were often known as 'Penitentiaries', and the inmates were almost invariably designated 'penitents'. In some of these Institutions the buildings were designedly rendered gloomy by the windows being obscured, so that the inmates were severed from the outside world almost as effectively as if they were in prison ... It is, however, only right to say that nearly all these Institutions have long since been modernised and are now well abreast of the times."[60]

This was not the case with the Good Shepherd Asylums, where the above conditions still overwhelmingly prevailed and were to continue to do so for the next half century.*

It was not until 1922 that two Cork penitents were allowed outside the enclosure. Release was only for one day, and since the circumstances were extraordinary, the privilege did not herald a relaxation of the rules. Both women were then in their seventies, and had each been in the Home for half a century:

---

59 See for example, the York Penitentiary Society's *Annual Reports* for 1901 and 1903; and the *Report of the London Conference of Managers and Superintendents of Preventive and Reformatory Institutions*, 1921 - in particular its Session devoted to "Games, Entertainments and Recreations in Homes for Girls and Women"
60   Taylor, *op. cit.*, pp.30-31.
*   From the testimony of former inmates, as well as the author's own familiarity with the buildings themselves, it would appear that by the nineteen-sixties the Irish Good Shepherds were lagging behind the Order's updated standards elsewhere. Not only were "mechanical listening devices" still something of the future, but the swimming pools, gymnasiums and tennis courts that "many of the good Shepherd Institutes are now equipped with" were still lamentably absent. Nor was there any evidence of the "Commercial, Home Economics, and Beauty Culture Departments [that] are practically universal in the educational setup of the Good Shepherd." Thompson, *op. cit.*, p.40.

"On 29th July two of our oldest consecrated penitents - Magdalen and Mary of the Dolours had the happiness of celebrating the Golden Jubilee of their entrance to our House just 50 years ago, having come to us July 29th, 1872. They were allowed the privilege of a visit to our House in Clifton Cork, having been invited by the Mother Prioress, and returned that evening laden with presents and greatly refreshed and gratified with their visit."[61]

The Mother Prioress of the recently established Clifton House was none other than Mother Mary of St. Magdalen Devereux, now almost ninety years of age and who, within five weeks of the visit, would be dead.

The second of the penitents (if she remembered her name after fifty years) was Mary McMahon, already described as one of Rev. Reed's initial "batch" of prostitutes admitted from the Government Hospital on the Home's first day. She was then 19 years old. The other woman was Catherine Ahern, who had been admitted, not on 29th July, but almost three weeks later. She was the seventh inmate to be registered at the Home, and the first of many prostitutes to be sent up by the young zealot, Rev. Shinkwin. She was then aged 27.[62]

Having each spent 56 years in the Penitentiary, and one day outside, the two women, now aged 75 and 83, died within four days of one another, in 1928. The hopes of Mother Euphrasia, Father Reed and Canon Hegarty were realised. They were secure of these "children" to the last.

Rev. Shinkwin's labours too, were fruitful. The successors of his early converts - the last remnants of the Magdalen Movement - are now housed in the Order's premises in Clifton. And they are still in the care of the nuns.

---

61 Cork Annals, 1922.
62 Cork Register, 29 July and 15 August 1872.
    The curate's public role as a Magdalinist, curious though it was, cannot be said to have damaged his career - as the following inscription shows:
    "This Foundation Stone of St. Joseph's Convalescent Home, Clifton, Cork, was laid by the Rt. Rev. Monsignor Michael Shinkwin PP. VG. Dean of Cork, December 8th, 1908".

Epilogue

In 1933 Mother St. Euphrasia Pelletier, the Foundress and first Superior-General of the Congregation of Our Lady of Charity of the Good Shepherd of Angers, was beatified. Within a quarter of a century the fruits of this blessed woman's work could be found in almost every non-Communist country in the world – particularly Ceylon where 68 of the Order's Houses were now established. By then a total of 9,556 Good Shepherd Sisters were involving themselves in the "spiritual direction" of 2,600 "Sisters Magdalens", 1,300 "Auxiliaries" and 47,692 "pupils and children" – many of whom were elderly women.[1] In Ireland, where they were still referred to by the public as "Magdalens", penitents continued in confinement until the domestic washing machine made the vast laundries no longer profitable; but it was not until the nineteen-nineties that the last of the Convent Magdalen Asylums were eventually closed.

Hundreds of survivors of the system are still alive, and thousands more are dead, their history unrecorded. Many of these women's lives were damaged, sometimes destroyed, in a warped attempt to wipe out female "sin". Confinement, forced labour and senseless atonement, obsessively urged was but part of their penance. Often, the separation from a child was an added torment, and some, without hope and resigned to that unnatural existence, remained in the Homes until they died. The incarceration of such women says little for their families or society; but without the Convent penitentiaries and an Order of

---

1   These statistics and terms are contained in the 1958 revised Appendix to Bernoville, *op. cit.* (1963).

custodians prepared to profit from such practice, these detentions could not have taken place.

This obsession with repentance, this unwholesome pre-occupation with the sexuality of others is an aspect of the system curiously ignored by its apologists, who recommend that Magdalen Asylums be judged not from the present viewpoint, but "in the context of their time". Such apologists seem unaware of the fact that even in the mid-nineteenth century when these Homes were established, the imposition of enforced celibacy and confinement with hard labour were punishments normally reserved for felons - convicted and sentenced by the State to a fixed rather than undefined term of imprisonment. Even then, when attitudes to female sexuality were far removed from present standards, such was not the general consequence of casual, extra-marital, or even involuntary sex.

Equally glossed over is the fact that the Magdalen System endured for generations. "Its time" was any point in its existence - including the 1970s, when admissions to these institutions were still taking place. By clinging to outdated notions of sexual morality, it was surely the perpetuators of the system rather than its critics who ignored the context of their time. The fact that men were never punished for their part in these women's "downfall" is a major cause for condemnation. Even more iniquitous is the fact that any woman held in such a place against her will (whether for a week or for the rest of her life) was unlawfully and immorally detained.[2] Whatever the circumstances of her admission, an adult not made aware of her absolute freedom to leave, was effectively denied her civil and constitutional rights.[3]

Attempts have also been made to class the nuns as victims - to portray them as powerless instruments of a patriarchal rule. Pushed into the Church by their families, desexualised themselves, and expected by society to be both jailors and "carers", they performed an unenviable task with reluctance, and as best they could. All this is unconvincing. Their own fanatical commitment, the distasteful relish with which they carried out

---

2 Unless committed by the courts - and only a fraction of the total fell within this category.
3 Minors could, of course, be placed in Magdalen Asylums by their parents or guardians; but their involuntary detention should not have continued once they had reached adulthood.

their activities, their determination to inflict their rule on others and their refusal to change until forced to do so, counter such excuses, which, in any case, fail to account for the harsh treatment highlighted in recent exposures of the system.

For feminists, the knowledge that many penitents were victims, helplessly submitting to their situation, is unappealing - a factor which perhaps explains the lack of sympathy the subject has aroused. More shocking to most people is the role of women in this work. Yet for those determined to acquit women of responsibility, another option presents itself. Having purged themselves of sexuality, the Sisters should, perhaps, be freed from gender-label altogether. They had, after all, embraced "perpetual virginity" - a state which, according to one authority on the subject, raises mortals "to the dignity of angels".[4] In the eyes of the Church, then - without sex, and without sin - they were no longer ordinary beings, and perhaps this is how such women should be viewed. Regrettably, however, it would appear to be the case that in striving after sanctity, they lost something of humanity too.

---

4   Butler, *op. cit.*, p.84.

Bibliography

Acton, W., *Prostitution* (edited by P. Fryer, London, 1968, first published 1857)

Aikenhead Mary; Her Life, Her Work and Her Friends, by "S. A." (Dublin, 1879)

Albion Hill Home, Brighton. Forty-first Annual Report (1896)

Arnold, M. and Laskey, H. *Children of the Poor Clares, the Story of an Irish Orphanage* (Belfast, 1985)

Beeton, Mrs. I. *The Book of Household Management* (London, 1901, revised edition)

Bernoville, G. *Saint Mary Euphrasia Pelletier, Foundress of the Good Shepherd Sisters* (Dublin & London, 1963, reprint – first published 1959)

Blessed Mary of Saint Euphrasia Pelletier, First Superior-General of the Congregation of Our Lady of Charity of the Good Shepherd of Angers. Written by A Religious of the Congregation of the Good Shepherd (London, 1933)

Bristol Female Penitentiary Report (1914)

Butler, Rev. A. *The Lives of the Fathers, Martyrs and Other Principal Saints.* Vol. I. (London and Dublin, late nineteenth century edition)

245

Butler, J. E. *Personal Reminiscences of a Great Crusade* (London, 1896)

Clarke, A. M. *Life of Reverend Mother Mary of St. Euphrasia Pelletier, First Superior-General of the Congregation of Our Lady of Charity of the Good Shepherd of Angers* (London, 1895)

Classified List of Child-Saving Institutions, Including those Certified by Government or Connected with the Reformatory and Refuge Union or Children's Aid Society, to which are Added Complete Lists of Homes and Institutions for Women and Inebriate Retreats. (Reformatory and Refuge Union, London, 1935)

Clear, C. *Nuns in nineteenth-Century Ireland* (Dublin, 1987)

Conferences and Instructions of the Venerable Mother Mary of Saint Euphrasia Pelletier, Foundress of the Generalate of the Congregation of Our Lady of Charity of the Good Shepherd of Angers (London, 1907, first published 1885)

Deacon, R. *The Private Life of Mr. Gladstone* (London, 1965)

Dear Daughter (RTE Documentary, 1996)

Donovan, P. *The Christian Brothers in New Ross, First Century, 1849-1949* (Wexford, 1952)

Downey, E. *Illustrated Guide to Waterford* (1915)

Doyle, P. *The God Squad* (Dublin, 1988)

Drennan. P. *You May Talk Now* (Blarney, 1994)

Dublin Female Penitentiary Annual Reports (1814-18)

Englishwoman's Year Book (1900)

Epiphany Laundry Home Leaflet (no date)

Fawcett, M. G. and Turner, E. M. *Josephine Butler, Her Work and Principles and their Meaning for the Twentieth Century* (London, 1927)

Female Aid Society: Eighty-sixth Report (Sixty-fourth Annual Report of the Female Mission to the Fallen), 1922

Female Mission to the Fallen Reports (1867-76)

Finnegan, F. *Poverty and Prostitution, a Study of Victorian Prostitutes in York* (Cambridge, 1979)

Glynn, J. "The Catholic Church in Wexford Town, 1800-1858", in *The Past*, No.15 (1984)

Guardian Society Annual Report (1815-23)

Guy, F. *County and City of Cork Directory* (1886)

Haskins, S. *Mary Magdalen* (London, 1993)

Holy Rosary Parish Golden Jubilee Souvenir, 1898-1948

Irish Independent Eucharistic Congress Souvenir Number (1932)

Irish Sisters of Charity Souvenir Book, 1843-1943 (Dublin, 1943)

Kerr, Rev. *The Fold of the Good Shepherd Limerick, 1848-1931* (Limerick, 1931)

Les Blanchisseuses de Magdalen (France 3/Sunset Presse Documentary, 1998)

Letter to the Public on an Important Subject, Establishing a Magdalen Asylum in Dublin (1767)

Lincoln Asylum for Female Penitents, *Annual Reports* and Ladies' Minute Books (1849-1910)

List of Preventative and Rescue Homes, Associations and Workers in the Diocese of Canterbury; and Report (1914)

Logan, W. *The Great Social Evil; its Causes, Extent, Results and Remedies* (London, 1871)

London Female Penitentiary Society Annual Reports (1808-87)

London Female Guardian Society, Annual Reports (1815-88)

London Female Penitentiary and Guardian Society Annual Reports (1888-1907)

Longfield, A. K. *Guide to the Collection of Lace* (National Museum of Ireland, 1982)

Luddy, M. *Women and Philanthropy in Nineteenth-Century Ireland* (Cambridge, 1995)

Maddison, A. J. S. *Hints on Rescue Work, A Handbook for Missionaries, Superintendents of Homes, Committees, Clergy, and Others* (London, 1898)

Magnus, P. *Gladstone, a Biography* (Ninth Edition, London, 1978)

Mahood, L. *The Magdalenes, Prostitution in the Nineteenth Century* (London, 1990)

Matley, M. *Always in the Convent Shadow* (Guernsey, 1991)

McCarthy, M. J. F. *Priests and People in Ireland* (Dublin and London, 1902)

McHugh, P. *Prostitution and Victorian Social Reform* (London, 1980)

Midnight Meeting Movement for the Recovery of Fallen Women (Twelfth Annual Report, 1873)

Notes on Work Amongst the Fallen (No. 76, November 1905)

Pope-Hennessy, J. *Queen Mary* (London, 1959)

Power, Rev. P. *History of Waterford and Lismore* (1937)

Practical Rules for the Use of the Religious of the Good Shepherd for the Direction of the Classes (Angers, 1898)

Prayers for Homes for Women and Rescue Associations (Religious Tract Society, London, late nineteenth century)

Raftery, M. & O'Sullivan, E. *Suffer the Little Children: the Inside Story of Ireland's Industrial Schools* (Dublin, 1999)

Record of Proceedings of Conferences of Managers & Superintendents of Reformatory and Industrial Institutions (Reformatory and Refuge Union, London, 1896 and 1911)

Reformatory and Industrial Schools Systems Report, 1970 (Dublin, 1970)

Reformatory and Refuge Union Red Book, Being a List of Workers in Reformatory, Preventive, and Child-Saving Institutions, in Connection with the Reformatory and Refuge Union and Children's Aid Society (First Edition, London, 1890 & Fifth Edition, 1907)

Reformatory and Refuge Union Reports (1856-1906)

Report from the Royal Commission on the Administration and Operation of the Contagious Diseases Acts, 1866-9 (House of Commons, 1871)

Report from the Select Committee on the Contagious Diseases Acts; together with the Proceedings of the Committee, Minutes of Evidence, and Appendix (House of Commons, 1879)

Report of the London Conference of Managers and Superintendents of Preventive and Reformatory Institutions (1921)

Rescue Work (pamphlet, 1920)

Rescue Work; an Inquiry and Criticism (pamphlet, 1919)

Robins, J. *Fools & Mad, a History of the Insane in Ireland* (Dublin, 1986)

Sell, Rev. Dr. *Alice Grand Duchess of Hesse, Biographical Sketch and Letters* (London, 1884)

Sex in a Cold Climate (Testimony Films Documentary for Channel Four, 1998)

'St. Faiths' Home, Lostwithiel, Cornwall, Article, Cornwall County Council Library.

Tait, Dr. W. *Magdalenism, an Inquiry into the Extent, Causes and Consequences of Prostitution in Edinburgh* (Edinburgh, 1841, later edition 1852)

Taylor, W. J. *The Story of the Homes, their Origin, Development and Work for Fifty Years* (London, 1907)

Thompson, D. J. *The Psychology of the Good Shepherd Nuns in the Re-Education of the Emotionally Disturbed* (M.A. Thesis, University of St. Mary's, Halifax, Canada, 1961)

Tierney, P. *The Moon on my Back* (Dublin, 1993)

Touher, P. *Fear of the Collar: Artane Industrial School* (Dublin 1991)

Wake, H. *Princess Louise, Queen Victoria's Unconventional Daughter* (London, 1988)

Walkowitz, J. R. *Prostitution and Victorian Society; Women, Class and the State* (Cambridge, 1980)

Waterford's Presentation Community, a Bicentenary Record, 1798-1998 (1998)

York Penitentiary Society *Annual Reports,* (1822-1919)

York Penitentiary Society Ladies' Committee Books (1845-87)

York Penitentiary Society Ladies' Visitor Books and Miscellaneous Correspondence

York Penitentiary *General Regulations* (from 1822)

GOOD SHEPHERD RECORDS:

Annals of the Monastery of the Good Shepherd, Sunday's Well, Cork, 1870-1971

Annals of the Convent of the Good Shepherd, Limerick (typescript summary) 1826-1909

Annals of the Convent of the Good Shepherd, New Ross, 1860-1913

Typescript History taken from the Annals of the Convent of the Good Shepherd, Waterford, 1858-1900

Register of Penitents of the Asylum of the Good Shepherd, Cork, 1872-1890

Register of the Names of Penitents who were in the [Limerick] Magdalen Asylum Before the Sisters of the Good Shepherd Took up the Charge (1828-48)

Register of the Names of Penitents Received since the Foundation of the Monastery of the Good Shepherd, Limerick, 1848-1888

Register of Penitents of the Asylum of the Good Shepherd, New Ross, 1860-1900

Register of Penitents of the Asylum of the Good Shepherd, Waterford, 1842-1900 (List of the Names of Penitents Admitted into this Asylum and their Discharge)

Statistics of the Province of Ireland, from 1848 to November 1887

NEWSPAPERS:

Cork Examiner (1872, 1902)

Chronicle and Munster Advertiser (1848)

Daily Mail (1862)

Daily News (1869)

Kerry Chronicle (1856)

The Shield (1870-86)

The Waterford Chronicle (1858, 1895)

The Waterford News (1892-1928)

WORKHOUSE RECORDS:

Cork Union Minute Book, 1874

Cork Union Register of Paupers, 1870-73

York Board of Guardians Register of Deaths, 1877

CENSUS MATERIAL

Census Enumerator's Notebooks, 1901

Index

Of the penitents referred to in the text, only those thought to be of particular interest have been included in the index. Their names are printed in italics.